THE SHADOW OF KEYNES

THE SHADOW
OF
KEYNES

Understanding Keynes, Cambridge
and Keynesian Economics

Elizabeth S. Johnson
Harry G. Johnson

The University of Chicago Press

The University of Chicago Press, Chicago 60637
Basil Blackwell, Oxford

Library of Congress Cataloging in Publication Data

Johnson, Elizabeth S.
   The shadow of Keynes.

   1.   Keynes, John Maynard, 1883–1946.
   2.   Keynesian economics.   I.   Johnson, Harry Gordon,
1923–1977.   II. Title.
HB99.7.J64   1978   330.15′6   78-56338
ISBN 0-226-40148-0

To

Robert H. Johnson, M.D., F.R.C.P. (C)
Physician and Friend

In appreciation of a life spent caring for others

Contents

Preface

During the past few years there has been a marked resurgence of interest in the personality and economic theory of John Maynard Keynes and of the impact of his thought on modern economic ideas. The interest in the personality of Keynes has been stimulated by the commencement of publication of the output of an immense scholarly enterprise sponsored by the Royal Economic Society, *The Collected Writings of John Maynard Keynes*, by the volumes produced by the annual Keynes Seminar held at the University of Canterbury, by the *Essays on John Maynard Keynes* collected and edited with loving care by Keynes's nephew Milo Keynes, and by the appearance of a number of memoirs and biographies concerning other members of the Bloomsbury circle who were Keynes's intimate friends. Interest in Keynes's economic theories had already been given a new impetus by Axel Leijonhufvud's book *On Keynesian Economics and the Economics of Keynes*, which drew a sharp distinction between what Keynes actually wrote and what modern Keynesians had made of his ideas in constructing 'Keynesian' models of the operation of the economy and of the instruments the government could use to control and stabilize these operations. This distinction has been taken up and developed most explicitly by 'radical' writers, both economists and non-economists, who have sought to forge Keynes's name to their own critiques of capitalism and revolutionary manifestos.

Interest in the influence of 'Keynesianism'—defined broadly as a set of economic ideas loosely derived from Keynesian theory —on modern economic and political thought has been largely confined to the intellectual circles and communications media of

Keynes's own country. This is partly a result of the fact that modern British economics has been so largely identified with the name, teaching and discipleship of Keynes, but is also explained by the discussion in Britain arising from the apparent loss of control by the government and its economic civil service of the country's economic management—a loss of control blamed on the deficiencies of economics in general and Keynesian economics in particular, rather than on the political and social characteristics of British society that have brought it about.

The essays presented in this book claim to be neither contributions to scholarship and documentation in the history of economic thought (or monetary thought, or Keynes's own thought), nor essays in the interpretation of Keynes's writings and the reconstruction of what he 'really' meant (or should have meant, or could conveniently be construed to have meant) that is of lasting scientific value and direct current relevance. Neither of the authors is a professional historian of economic thought, let alone a professional scholar of the history of ideas. In any case, the character of Keynes, together with the largely 'oral tradition' style of British economics of his time—a style which relies heavily on allusion to and caricaturization of the work of a few eminent contemporaries and predecessors rather than on a meticulous documentation of sources—would make such an endeavour a lifetime scholarly exercise.

These are, instead, essays written largely in the process of trying to understand Keynes, as a historical personality and as an economist whose work remains influential in both academic economics and popular economic ideas, and particularly to understand him in relation to his habitat of Cambridge and the post-Victorian British society in which he lived. They have been grouped in five sections, focussing respectively on Keynes the man, his academic milieu of Cambridge before and after the first world war, his little-known early work on Indian currency and war finance, the Cambridge environment of his disciples in the 1950s, and analyses of the 'Keynesian revolution' and of 'Keynesian economics' as it has evolved. Most of the essays have appeared before, but in widely diverse places, not always easily accessible; three of them are being introduced in print for the first time.

We stress the problem of understanding, because we are not English, or British, at least in the narrower concept of the term now employed in Britain, but Canadian—brought up to think of ourselves as British, but in British estimation colonials and —much worse—almost indistinguishable from those revolting Americans. We have no first-hand knowledge of Keynes and his world, nor even the English up-bringing that would have conditioned us to the acceptance of English standards in assessing them. Our view is from outside both the United Kingdom and the historical epoch to which Keynes belonged.

We arrived in Cambridge, an environment alien to anything in our own experience, as young adults and very quickly were confronted by the need to understand the life and work of a great man who was only recently deceased. After we had left Cambridge for Manchester and then Manchester for Chicago, and had later returned to England to live part of the year in London, we became increasingly concerned about understanding the nature of British society and of British economics in particular, as it had been in Keynes's time, as a key to understanding the rapid changes that had been and were currently taking place, both in British society and in its dominant economic ideas. This collection of our individual and joint essays represents the fruits, such as they are, of that endeavour.

Keynes was a forceful, brilliant and quirky individual, and English society has a repellent fascination, especially for North Americans. We are conscious of the fact that our writing is occasionally personal and passionate on those accounts, and we are only too aware that some of the subjects we discuss and observations we make would, in England, be classified as matters that everyone on the inside knows, but also knows should not be revealed to those outside, especially not in print for all to read. Yet what is unspoken or taken for granted, peculiar to a special segment of English society at a particular place and time, is not only relevant but necessary to know for a proper understanding of Keynes and his world. In such a spirit we offer our observations, and though they may be biased, our bias is declared.

In conclusion, we wish to thank Robert Nobay and Jim Feather for encouraging us to publish this book, and Arnold Collery, Jacob Frenkel, Robert Nobay, Don Patinkin and Edward Shils for

encouraging us to write about subjects peripheral to our main
activities as, respectively, an editor and an economic theorist.
Finally we wish to thank the editors of the various journals and
conference volumes, the names of which are recorded, for their
kindness in permitting republication of items from their pages,
and Polly Steele for invaluable help with the manuscript.

The Graduate Institute of   Elizabeth S. Johnson
International Studies   Harry G. Johnson
Geneva, Switzerland
January 1977

Acknowledgements

Ch. 1. Michael Parkin and A. R. Nobay (eds.), *Essays in Modern Economics* (London: Longman, 1973), pp. 216–27.

Ch. 2. *Journal of Political Economy*, Vol. 82, No. 1 (January/February 1974), pp. 99–111, and in Joan Robinson (ed.), *After Keynes* (Oxford: Basil Blackwell, 1973), pp. 12–25.

Ch. 3. Don Patinkin and J. Clark Leith (eds.), *Keynes, Cambridge, and the General Theory* (London: Macmillan, 1977), pp. 90–7.

Ch. 4. *Economic Journal*, Vol. LXX, No. 277 (March 1960), pp. 160–5.

Ch. 6. *History of Political Economy*, Vol. 6, No. 3 (Fall 1974), pp. 261–77.

Ch. 7. Don Patinkin and J. Clark Leith (eds.), *Keynes, Cambridge, and the General Theory* (London: Macmillan, 1977), pp. 98–114, and *Encounter*, Vol. XLVII, No. 2 (August 1976), pp. 82–91.

Ch. 8. *Osaka Economic Papers*, Vol. XX (2), No. 36 (March 1972), pp. 9–22.

Ch. 10. *Encounter*, Vol. XLII, No. 1 (January 1974), pp. 28–39.

Ch. 11. *Minerva*, Vol. XV, No. 2 (Summer 1977), pp. 201–13.

Ch. 13. *Canadian Journal of Economics and Political Science*, Vol. 26 (February 1960), pp. 150–5.

Ch. 14. *American Economic Review*, Vol. 61, No. 2 (May 1971), pp. 91–106.

Ch. 15. Milo Keynes (ed.), *Essays on John Maynard Keynes* (Cambridge: Cambridge University Press, 1975), pp. 108–22.

Ch. 16. *The Banker*, Vol. 125, No. 596 (October 1975), pp. 1159–61.

Ch. 17. *Spectator*, Vol. 237, No. 7741 (6 November 1976), pp. 14–15; reprinted in Robert Skidelsky (ed.), *The End of the Keynesian Era* (London: Macmillan, 1977), pp. 88–94.

Ch. 18. *Canadian Journal of Economics*, Vol. 9, No. 4 (November 1976), pp. 580–94.

Part I
Keynes the Man

1
Keynes from His Papers

Economists are a special breed who, more than other men, live, eat and breathe their subject—which, for all the formidable language, is rooted in the real world. John Maynard Keynes was a book collector and a friend and patron of writers and artists, but these were incidental activities; life presented itself to him as a progression of economic problems to be solved and theoretically formulated. As he was also an active publicist of his own solutions and intensely involved with them, his professional papers reveal his private personality in all its live contrariness to a high degree.

It was my good luck, as one of the editors of Keynes's collected writings, to read my way through a large part of these papers. I was not an economist, I was not English and I came from a different education and background. The England of Keynes's youth and of his prime was fast vanishing, but these pages called back shapes out of the dispersing mist. Most vividly they evoked the presence of Keynes himself. He was a charming, irritating—and unmistakably great man.

I never met Keynes. When my husband and I arrived in Cambridge in January 1969, he had already been dead for over two years. And yet his memory was very present and alive in the place—a sense of a sort of aura still hovering over everything he had touched. People spoke affectionately of 'Maynard' as if he had just been gone away for a little while, in that manner in which one speaks the dead friend's name to conjure him back to life again, if only for an instant. People still wondered aloud, 'What would Maynard think?'—which was the habitual reaction of his circle to any new idea or proposal. These people, most of them twenty years or so younger than Keynes, mourned him as a contemporary.

You may imagine then my feeling of excitement when I first saw Keynes's papers and held some of them in my hands. After his death they had been sorted out into two lots in the top of the house at 46 Gordon Square. Those having to do with economics and public life were bequeathed to Richard Kahn, and those that were purely personal were to be deposited in the library at King's College, Cambridge, with the stipulation that they were not to be available until all the protagonists were dead. Before the papers left Gordon Square they were used by Roy Harrod in writing his *Life of John Maynard Keynes*.[1] They were then divided into the two categories, public and private, put into tea chests and taken by van to Cambridge. The economics papers were literally jammed, one stack on top of another, into a big cupboard without any shelves, in the old Marshall Library in Downing Street. That was the way I first saw them, heaped together in bundles and boxes and old-fashioned wicker files that crumbled to the touch. Many of them were coated with that greasy library grime that comes away on the hands and is so hard to wash off; some of the typed outside copies seemed to be vanishing faintly before one's eyes, with yellowed fraying edges, ridged with the rust of decaying paper clips. On the other hand, the inside papers, protected, were fresh and white and authoritative-looking, with the high-quality embossed writing paper of those palmier days; the signatures of the famous stood out boldly inked as if newly inscribed.

Bundle after bundle turned up from the various periods of his life. There were schoolboy essays from Eton, papers written for the Cambridge Apostles, a sheaf of encouraging letters from Alfred Marshall to his most promising student, the first memoranda of a fledgling civil servant, the lecture notes of the aspiring young don—these last complete with pasted-in paragraphs from the current newspaper columns, to be used as bad examples of the conventional wisdom of City men and bankers who should know better. There were the scissored and cannibalized drafts and redrafts for the Report of the Commission on Indian Finance and Currency, a bewildering load of miscellaneous Treasury memoranda from World War I, notes for political speeches and talks to groups at the House of Commons, cheque-stubs and pocket diaries elastic-banded together, jotted figures that look like records of winnings at bridge, passages copied out of books for remembering. Then there were the thirty-four-odd bulky scrapbooks into which his mother pasted the thousands of newspaper cuttings mentioning his name—in varying tones of admiration and vituperation—from English, European and American newspapers and magazines. A lifetime on paper.

Part of the fun of editing papers is the pleasure of legitimate eaves-dropping—voyeurism made respectable. But much depends on the subject. Keynes's father kept a diary, but it was very dull—he would say 'Florence was very upset', but he would not say what she was upset about. As an adult, Maynard Keynes did not keep a diary or any kind of daily journal, but his letters and memoranda, though businesslike, could also be chatty and deliciously or maliciously catty. He lived a busy and varied life; he was involved in so many undertakings and knew so many people, that the papers are full of encounters with famous names—General Smuts, Shaw, the Webbs, Wittgenstein, T. E. Lawrence, Frank Harris, Stanley Baldwin, to mention an assorted few.

At first glance, certain things leapt out—Keynes's suggestion as junior clerk of two years' service that the Indian Government's conception of the requirements for a Director of Statistics was hopelessly outdated; the small green notebook in which he recorded his first earnings from his writings (in September 1908 the sum of 7s 6d from the *Economic Journal* for a note on 'Rents, prices and wages'); his declaration of conscientious objection to conscription; a list of invitations and sampling of acceptances to a party at 46 Gordon Square studded with the now well-known names of Bloomsbury; his farewell letters on leaving the Paris Peace Conference; a bet with Winston Churchill on the outcome of the 1929 election; a few amusingly libellous memoranda that flowed from his desk during the years of World War II. There were intriguing bits like scraps of paper with notes exchanged with—whom?—comments passed during boring meetings, and the odd phrase or paragraph noted down for future literary use. Most provoking to the curiosity are the echoes of something he

had written in an earlier letter in a correspondent's reply. Sir
Ernest Cable's remark when he and Keynes were grappling over
the Indian Finance and Currency Report with Austen Chamberlain ('Your description of chairman's brain makes me shriek with
laughter') makes one long to see that description. From the days
before typists and carbons were in general use there are precious
few of Keynes's own letters, except those he considered important enough to make a copy or a draft in his own writing.

Then there were the few fascinating bits that got into the
economics papers by mistake—an erotic sketch of Leda and the
swan, deftly pencilled by a gifted Bloomsbury hand; a letter from
a friend recounting the delights of a homosexual pick-up in a
pub. These had got into the wrong box—but generally speaking
things had been well sorted.

The papers had already been sorted according to time and
subject as a result of Harrod's work. This must have been an easy
and natural division because of Keynes's own habit of sticking
anything he was doing onto a spike; and as he tended to be
intensively involved in one subject at a particular time the
material on the spikes was automatically sorted. When a spike
became full he dumped its contents into a wooden box or chest.
(In fact he liked to visit country sales in search of old chests for his
papers, and had quite a few of them.)

What is it that makes a man consciously save his papers,
including the inconsequential scraps of scribbled conversation
exchanged at committee meetings? What are the intimations of
immortality? Part of the answer, I am sure, lies in simple inertia,
but beyond that people had the habit of keeping things in the
rambling houses and capacious attics of those more spacious
days when nothing lost its value or ever wore out. However,
there assuredly was a great deal more to it than the accident of
time and space. Keynes *knew* that he was a great man. Nurtured
from the start as the brilliant boy, the eldest pride and joy of a
cultivated, intellectual Cambridge family—his father a logician
and registrar of the university, his mother one of the earliest
graduates of Newnham College—he knew from the beginning
that *Keynes* rhymed with *brains*. And very early on, first among
his Cambridge and Bloomsbury friends and then, by the time he
was thirty, out in the wide world, he must have learned that with

his witty, charming talent of reason he could persuade others to go along with him—if not all the way in his direction, at least considerably far along the path. So he saved the record, because he was proud of it, because he had a sense of family and a sense of history, and because he knew it was a valuable one.

There is so much—lists of books read, lists of books bought, a list of 'Papers to be Written', followed 'Monographs', 'Treatises', and 'Textbooks', the whole scheme dated 30 January 1909. There are plans with chapter headings for whole books, including 'An Introduction to Economic Principles', which was to run to three volumes with the note that these might be sold as Penguins at sixpence each, with a de luxe edition at three guineas. For a book to be called 'An Examination of Capitalism' he had already started the first chapter on 'The Babylonian economy'.

But there are big gaps. The files he had removed from the Treasury turned out to be only a few drops from a vast ocean of memoranda contained within the bounds of the Public Record Office. Here and there are questions left hanging. Did he ever write that anonymous article that so-and-so asked him for? Why did he treat a certain person in such-and-such a way? And for such a busy man, many of the pages of his diaries, expectantly scanned for clues, turned out to be disappointingly blank.

Nevertheless a strong sense emerges of a personality—delightfully impetuous when young, charming with its wit, admirable in its quick intelligence and generous sympathy, impressive in its capacity for intense hard work—and insulting in its arrogance born of absolute self-assurance. One gets echoes from the letters of his correspondents: some people pitch their letters to the tone of the person whom they are addressing, or at least the tone as they conceive it, and this can vividly conjure up a sense of Keynes's personality, or of the part of his personality to which the writer is attempting to appeal. In addition, Keynes seems to have been the kind of person to whom some people address their mental conversations. In the thirty-four years between 1911 and 1945, a French financial journalist named Marcel Labordère wrote him a long series of letters on the money market and his own ideas of economics. Margot Asquith, as a widowed old woman unable to sleep at night, poured out her diatribes against her husband's former adversary Lloyd George to Keynes (regardless of the fact that he had re-espoused Lloyd George's cause in the meantime).

The papers also demonstrate very clearly the speed and energy with which Keynes worked. He seems to have been a non-stop worker, even on holidays. He claimed himself to write 1000 words a day, a good professional average, but the volume of paper shows that on many days he exceeded this, even assuming that he was not counting dictated letters. Throughout the 1920s and 1930s he must have averaged close to an article a week for the press—and this on top of lectures, journal articles, books, memoranda for various bodies, editing the *Economic Journal* and other projects. While he was in the Treasury during both world wars the volume was certainly as great, if not even greater.

He started his working day with breakfast in bed. (When Duncan Grant and Vanessa Bell decorated some cupboard doors for him by depicting the contrasting breakfasts eaten in London and Rome, the doors were the doors of a *bedroom* cupboard.) He accomplished a great deal of routine work, much of it financial, in the mornings while still in bed. He kept track of all his dealings very methodically, preserving cheque-stubs and broker's statements in the manner, one imagines, of his thrifty and orderly parents and ancestors. When he was young he of course wrote his own letters out by hand, as did, at that time, practically all of his famous correspondents. After World War I he used a typist and kept carbon copies, so that the volume of what was preserved became automatically swollen after 1919. He seems to have dictated many of his letters—some of his last secretary's shorthand notes still exist—but lecture notes, articles, memoranda and still many other letters were written out by hand.

One form of communication that Keynes did *not* like was the telephone. He admitted that it was useful for calling up intimate friends and must have used it for keeping in touch with his brokers, but in 1922 he was complaining in a letter to the *New Statesman* of the nuisance of having to leave his study on the third floor and to be interrupted by

any unconcentrated person who finds it easier to ring up than write a postcard, any hostess making up her party, any American tourist to these shores who thinks he would like a few words with me, is entitled by the existing conventions, *and is able*, suddenly and at any hour to interrupt my business and make me attend to theirs. . . .

This overdemocratic habit of intrusion so exasperated him when he was negotiating in Washington that he concluded that the only way to get an uninterrupted interview with an important person was to shelve the appointment and achieve the conversation by calling the person up on the phone himself.

Keynes started off his career in the military department of the India Office, not very enthusiastically, whiling away his time between memoranda on the dating of lieutenants' commissions and the despatch of pedigree Ayrshire bulls to Bombay, by working on his own dissertation on probability with which he hoped to gain a King's College fellowship. But the situation changed when he was moved to the Department of Revenue, Statistics and Commerce, where in the brief two years he spent there he began to lay down a sound knowledge of the special peculiarities of the Indian financial and currency situation. This interest persisted when he went back to join the faculty at Cambridge, and although his lectures there were on money and the stock exchange, he kept up his contacts at the India Office, in 1911 producing a long paper on 'Recent developments of the Indian currency question' for the Royal Economic Society, which became the nucleus of his book on *Indian Currency and Finance*.

The Indian currency system was an extremely complicated one, grown up over the years. One is impressed by Keynes's seemingly effortless mastery of its detail—every tree in the wood is there and standing in its right place. The research for the book resulted in his appointment to the Royal Commission on Indian Finance and Currency of 1913–14. When one reads through the evidence and the various drafts of the Commission's Report, it almost seems that Keynes, the youngest member (he was thirty) amongst all those bankers and businessmen and titled individuals who had spent their working lives in India, was the only person involved in the hearings who really understood the system. (The one exception was Lionel Abrahams, the India Office civil servant who had invented much of it and who was Keynes's mentor.) Nor had Keynes ever set foot in India.

This mastery of detail enabled him to complete a 60-page plan for a state bank for India in a little over a month. Marshall, who had had his own experience with the Indian system, said that he was 'entranced by it as a prodigy of constructive work. Verily we old men will have to hang ourselves', he wrote, 'if young people can cut their way so straight and with such apparent ease through such great difficulties.' Finally, Keynes became deeply involved in the redrafting of the main report. Here his complete grasp of the whole field enabled him to rescue his confused colleagues from perpetrating a logical mistake and to win their consent to a major change in principle by a small change of wording in two crucial phrases.

This command over detail stood him in good stead when he entered the Treasury in 1915. The Treasury was a small body in those days; often it was necessary for him to master the facts and write the needed memoranda on some totally new subject within twenty-four hours. During two weeks in September 1916, he reported to his father, he had 'written three major memoranda, one of which has been circulated to the Cabinet, and about a dozen minor ones on all kinds of subjects, as well as helping . . . with the Vote of Credit and the Budget, and keeping going with routine, and the *Economic Journal* in the evenings'.

My fellow-editors who had worked for the Treasury during World War II, where they were accustomed to the redrafting of their thoughts by many hands, were surprised to find the department so small in World War I that Keynes's minutes and memoranda went via the Joint Permanent Secretary straight to the Chancellor of the Exchequer, with usually only the slightest of verbal changes on the way. More often than not, if the Americans were concerned, the change would be designed to make the memorandum more cautious and tactful. Keynes's memoranda thus became official documents; his handwriting exists beside the printed Cabinet Papers in the Public Record Office. He was in charge of all foreign lending and borrowing, an astonishing position of influence for a man hardly turned thiry-five.

Keynes's resignation from the Paris Peace Conference—where he was the chief Treasury representative—changed the manner of his work again, and took him from being a member of the establishment to being its informed outside critic, a sort of official-unofficial position he was to occupy for many years. He wrote *The Economic Consequences of the Peace* during August and September 1919; the book was published 12 December 1919, and became a runaway bestseller. It is a book written in great passion and yet with much solid information in it. Keynes was able to turn it out so quickly not only because of the vehemence of his feelings, but also because he had so much material at his finger tips. He not only incorporated his plan for the cancellation of inter-allied debts and the financing of the reconstruction of Europe into his chapter on 'Remedies' (this plan had been adopted as official policy by Lloyd George, but was rejected by President Wilson), but he also simply lifted informative sections on Germany's capacity to pay reparations from the Treasury memorandum that he had produced on the subject. And, to the fury of the Poles, who discovered it, he made use of large chunks of information from the German representatives' replies to the allies when they were pleading their case. Nevertheless, he gave away no official secrets, and he sent out seventy-three free copies of his book to former colleagues, friends and acquaintances in a list that reads like a top-stratum sample of *Who's Who*.

The Economic Consequences of the Peace was a turning point in Keynes's life: although he never once stopped being an economist, for the next twenty years he was also conspicuously and devotedly a journalist and propagandist, trying to persuade the world to follow a path of reasonableness in article after article. He himself saw to the syndication of these articles over the world press—with a very clear idea of just how much money each kind of article in each particular paper should bring in. The success of *Economic Consequences* gave him a wide and partisan audience—he was venerated in Germany and vilified in France. There is plenty of evidence from the clippings in the scrapbooks and his exchange of correspondence with former Treasury colleagues that these writings exerted a strong influence on the side of moderation in the long and rather tedious series of international meetings and confrontations that attempted to accomplish all the mopping-up needed after the Treaty of Versailles.

Because of the speed and apparent ease with which Keynes

worked, one is tempted to imagine him as dashing into print. 'Fling pamphlets to the winds', he said. But the details of one of the projects which he undertook at this time illustrates very well not only his seriousness, but his great capacity for taking pains with things in order to get them right, and his resourcefulness when confronted with obstacles over a long haul. This was his editorship in 1922 of the series of twelve *Manchester Guardian Commercial* supplements on 'Reconstruction in Europe'. The idea was to present the problems and their possible solutions in articles by the foremost authentic experts of the time; the result was a 782-page volume of bound issues. It was published in French, German, Italian and Spanish, as well as being distributed in England and the United States.

Keynes was anxious to get the very best, and not only those whom he described as the 'flash' contributors. Carl Melchior, head of the German financial delegation to the peace conference, was only one of many acquaintances from his wartime and Paris experience whom he was able to call upon for help. For example, he was able to ask for assistance from the Premier of Belgium, and in England he could go to Asquith and Lord David Cecil among many others. He was persistent in tracking down contributors—when he could not get Lenin, he settled for Gorky; when Bergson declined, he went for Croce. He was particular to get a balance of shades of opinion, and careful, particularly with Russia and the new countries, to get material from the inside, to balance what was put out by the embassies.

He took an enthusiastic interest in every detail—from the quality of the paper to the design of a special decorative heading, from the printing of facsimiles of the bank notes of the new European countries to the assembling of dignified photographs of the bearded captains of the world mercantile marine, and the collection of a wonderful series of cartoons on the high cost of living in Victorian England and nineteenth century France, as well as in the England, United States and Germany of the early 1920s. He kept up to a twenty-one-day production schedule over twelve issues. He wrote fourteen articles himself, four of which reappeared as part of *A Tract on Monetary Reform*. He interested himself in arrangements for distribution of the supplements, and took fifty copies with him to the international meeting at Genoa to give to key people—he was attending the conference as the special correspondent of the *Manchester Guardian*. The British financial delegation, headed by the Chancellor of the Exchequer, held a special meeting to hear him discuss his article on a plan for the stabilization of the European exchanges. They thought this too radical to endorse officially, but they held a second meeting to discuss his article on 'The forward market in foreign exchanges' and brought these suggestions into the British draft proposals.

But while Keynes produced weekly articles and investment columns for the *Nation* and letters to the newspapers and pamphlets to persuade, he was also working away at the basic economics that finally emerged as *A Treatise on Money* and *The General Theory of Employment, Interest and Money*. Here one finds him working in a different way, not rushing his words into print, hot off the griddle, but teaching through his material over a period of years, discussing it with and testing it on colleagues. *A Treatise on Money* had a long gestation period, from 1924 to 1930. Keynes was not completely satisfied with it, but got it out quickly in the end. Then Piero Sraffa, Richard Kahn, James Meade, Joan Robinson and Austin Robinson (who nicknamed themselves 'the Circus') devoted a whole term to discussing it with Keynes. Their discussions had an important influence on the transition to the ideas of *The General Theory*, on which Keynes had begun to work. By 1934 he was lecturing from early proof sheets, and in January 1935 he sent proofs to Dennis Robertson for comment. But Robertson was not in sympathy with what Keynes had written, and the second proofs were read and commented on and adapted from discussions with Richard Kahn, Joan Robinson, Roy Harrod and Ralph Hawtrey. Some extensive revision took place in light of these discussions—but this fascinating story is the subject of *The General Theory and After*, edited by D. E. Moggridge, volumes XIII and XIV of *The Collected Writings of John Maynard Keynes*.

Working, relaxing, endlessly devising, the personality that emerges from Keynes's papers is very strong. Often as I read them, I asked myself, 'If I had actually met him, would I have liked him?' In spite of some doubts, the answer would almost certainly have been 'yes'—I would have been charmed.

Evident from the earliest times are a great deal of youthful impulsiveness, and a great generosity of spirit. Keynes was always for the underdog—lashing out against a proposal to fix a quota system for Indian students at Cambridge, vigorously championing the rights of women in the university and in the outside world. He courageously stood up for his conscientious objector friends in their struggles with their local tribunals and courted trouble by putting himself on record, as a conscientious objector, in his own terms, 'to surrendering my liberty of judgement on so vital a question as undertaking military service'.

He never surrendered his liberty of judgement. It was not cold judgement. His dramatic and idealistic resignation from the Paris Peace Conference came at the end of five months of attempt after attempt to achieve a just settlement. While the statesmen of Europe haggled over the milliards of will-o'-the-wisp reparations with which they confidently hoped to solve all their financial problems, he tried to fight against the lack of imagination that insisted on the delivery of milch cows as a partial payment from a starving Austria. (According to the British Director of Relief in Austria, it was only through Keynes's initiative in the Supreme Economic Council that famine was averted there in 1919.)

During the long months in Paris Keynes arranged to have the German financial representatives brought to stay near by so that some real discussion could take place; some of the story is told in the memoir 'Dr Melchior: a Defeated Enemy'. At these meetings Keynes gave the Germans the impression of trying very hard to understand their difficulties and to arrive at the truth. He was so much a proper Englishman, very alert for the main chance whenever the interests of the Treasury or his country were at stake—yet he treated the ex-enemy as human beings and they divined his sympathy.

Quick and generous sympathy, the free giving of his time and himself—this is the impression one receives from the letters and replies to letters, from the clippings and contemporary reports. The periodical *Time and Tide*, in a character sketch of Keynes written in 1921, described him as 'endowed in a high degree with the power of making half an hour's conversation an event that lives in the memory and feeds the mind'.

With so much goodness, gaiety and charm evident, what is there in his papers to dislike? With deeper reading certain doubts set in. In the beginning he seems to have been rather a social snob, regaling his parents with the names of the great and near-great with whom he had been hobnobbing. At the same time he was very quick to make use of any of these acquaintances, even while sometimes seeming contemptuous of their political need to compromise—in spite of the respectful care with which he wrote to them. One of these was Austen Chamberlain, another was Asquith (here Keynes defended the relationship by saying 'My real friend is Margot'); both these men were considered by some to have been under Keynes's thumb, although this is not borne out by the papers. His influence was not of the *éminence grise* kind; his advice was sought at certain specific points. In turn he could ask for help, and did, when he needed it. His real influence was more general and cumulative—he influenced public opinion and that influenced the politicians.

He was an opportunist, ready to step into action the first chance he got, purposefully inserting himself into the Treasury by reminders of his presence in the shape of helpful memos. He was pushing, at first for his own advancement, but later to get things done as he saw right; he was absolutely confident of his own ability to solve his own country's—and other countries'—problems.

This self-confidence—and his early success—made him very arrogant. He was quick, he was resourceful, he was proud of his power to see straight through to what he thought was the heart of the matter. He was impatient and intolerant of slower human beings, and this is the way he generally regarded Americans. When he first went to the United States on a special financial mission with Lord Reading in 1917, he earned Reading's admiration and gratitude for his quick grasp of all the complex details of negotiation—but also, among the Americans, he earned a reputation for intolerable rudeness. Later he mellowed and managed to work amicably and profitably with those individual Americans whom he found sympathetic. He had the Englishman's habit of regarding ordinary Americans as uncultured and naïve—and crass, to boot, in wanting to be paid back their war debts. While he also did not like most Frenchmen and had many tiresome controversies with them, it seems to me that he took more trouble to

butter them up, as representatives of an older, polished civilization, than he took with the unsophisticated Americans. But he
did make exceptions for kindred spirits.

Part and parcel of this intellectual and social arrogance was his
insularity. This took a number of forms. His Cambridge–London–Sussex axis was his universe. As a youngster in the India
Office he refused the small advancement of a resident clerkship
(which would have involved being on call in London) because it
would have meant disrupting this rhythm. While he was prepared to be abroad for long periods on Treasury business and
near the end of his life spent many months in the United States,
travel did not seem to be something that he appreciated as a
learning experience. Although like any privileged Englishman of
his class he took holidays on the continent and even ventured to
Morocco and Egypt, these were holidays; and it did not seem
important to him, as an expert on Indian finance, to go to India to
acquire information at first hand. He was appointed to a Royal
Commission on tariff policy that was supposed to travel and take
evidence there in 1921–22, but when he had to choose between
taking the time to travel to India and fulfilling his responsibilities
in England, he resigned from the Commission. I think he automatically assumed that as an Englishman he had nothing particularly valuable to learn by travel.

Another aspect of his insularity was that of class. He had no
sort of imagination about what life might be like for the working
class, although he was very concerned with making their life
richer and safer, and to extend to them the delights of leisure and
culture enjoyed by his own kind of people. His sympathies were
with the underdogs, but his experience gave him no idea of their
problems. He knew them only as servants. His advice was
middle-class advice. When prices were rising he suggested that
housewives should transfer their purchases from articles that had
increased more in price to those that had increased less—not very
useful counsel to the working-class woman who had no money to
juggle around anyway. In 1939 his plan for compulsory savings
held little attraction for people who had never been accustomed
to the idea of having anything to save. The unescapable fact is
that Keynes was not the common man—and this not only
because of his intellectual and personal gifts but because of the

advantages of his time and place and especially of his individual upbringing.

My husband and I were invited to tea by Keynes's parents at their house in Harvey Road in the spring of 1949. To two young Canadians this was a revelation of another world. One received the impression of a highly ordered and highly organized life, tea at a certain time, dinner at a certain time, a day blocked out to accommodate the duties of the servants. Then there was the rather daunting conversation: one felt that these cultivated elderly people, established over the years in their comfortable Cambridge home, were confident to express an opinion on any subject in the world whatsoever, absolutely certain in the rightness of their views and of their right of authority to assert them.

There is a passage in Chapter 2 of *The Economic Consequences of the Peace* in which Keynes describes the expectations of the pre-1914 world, which is interesting for what it takes for granted:

The greater part of the population, it is true, worked hard and lived at a low standard of comfort, yet were, to all appearances, reasonably content with this lot. But escape was possible, for any man of capacity or character at all exceeding the average, into the middle and upper classes, for whom life offered, at a low cost and with the least trouble, conveniences, comforts, and amenities beyond the compass of the richest and most powerful monarchs of other ages. The inhabitant of London could order by telephone, sipping his morning tea in bed, the various products of the whole earth, in such quantity as he might see fit, and reasonably expect their early delivery upon his doorstep; he could at the same moment and by the same means adventure his wealth in the natural resources and new enterprises of any quarter of the world. . . . He could secure forthwith, if he wished it, cheap and comfortable means of transit to any country or climate without passport or other formality, could despatch his servants to the neighbouring office of a bank for such supply of the precious metals as might seem convenient, and could then proceed abroad to foreign quarters, without knowledge of their religion, language, or customs, bearing coined wealth upon his person, and would consider himself greatly aggrieved and much surprised at the least interference. But, most important of all, he regarded this state of affairs as normal, certain, and permanent.

Here Keynes is describing his own experience, and extending it to a generalization: that success was possible *for any man of capacity or character at all exceeding the average.* What he leaves out is the fact of his extraordinary background—the inestimable advantages of Harvey Road, of Eton and King's and Bloomsbury—advantages not shared by every man of capacity and character, be he English working man or American tourist. Keynes was very proud of his family background, but seemed to be a little myopic about what a head start it had given him in the world.

I met Keynes through his papers, and I was both charmed and exasperated. Harvey Road may have given him what to my eyes were weaknesses, but it also gave him his tremendous strengths—faith in his own good sense and faith in his ability to bring about the ultimate triumph of human reason. 'I still suffer incurably from attributing an unreal rationality to other people's feelings and behaviours (and doubtless to my own, too)', he wrote in 1938 in 'My Early Beliefs'. He also spoke of 'the impulse to protest'. He protested against suffering, poverty, and ignorance, and he had a vision of better times when the main economic problems of the world would be solved.

It is difficult to resent a man who strove to go so far ahead of his time. He never stopped trying for better solutions. 'I do not hope to be right. I hope to make progress,' he jotted down on a piece of paper which somehow managed to be kept.

This is so modest—did he really believe it? He could strike an attitude and might have charmed himself. Yet, I think that he saw himself in history and meant what he wrote.

2
Scientist or Politician?

John Maynard Keynes—scientist or politician? The reader of the popular press of a generation ago would have had no doubt of the answer: that Keynes, a swinging weather vane of a man, was the most unscientific of individuals—a cartoonist's dream. He was Keynes the india-rubber man: the *Daily News and Chronicle* of 16 March 1931, carried an article headed 'Economic Acrobatics of Mr. Keynes' and illustrated it by a sketch of 'A Remarkable Performance. Mr. John Maynard Keynes as the "boneless man" turns his back on himself and swallows a draught'—the draught, a glass marked '15 per cent Protection.' After years of preaching the virtues of free trade, he had first announced the end of laissez faire and now urged a revenue tariff on the country. As an exasperated political opponent remarked on another occasion—complaining of the man who in 1925 said wage costs were too high and in 1929 wanted higher prices: 'It is difficult to reconcile Mr. Keynes the politician with Professor Keynes the economist. He seems to be both right and wrong!'*

Keynes himself had no such difficulty. In his own opinion, he was always right. He had a clear idea of his own role in the world; he was the economist—at first Cassandra, croaking prophecies of doom about the economic consequences of reparations and the gold standard, prophecies which came all too true—and then as he gathered stature, the chief economic adviser to the world, to

*The remark was made by Sir Laming Worthington-Evans, Conservative secretary of state for war, in a letter to the *Evening Standard*, 6 May 1929, part of a published exchange with Keynes at the time of the 1929 election campaign. During this election Keynes not only supported but took the lead in originating the Lloyd George program to remedy unemployment.

the Chancellor of the Exchequer of the day, to the French minister
of finance whoever he was, to the president of the United States.
Keynes the economist initially thought of himself as the educator,
the persuader, the man who would assemble all the relevant
information and thereby start the reverberation of public opinion
that would echo back to the politicians who 'have ears but no
eyes', as he once said. Then, as he became established as an
expert, he came to think of himself more as the economic scientist, the technician, the mechanic who is called in to fix the
machine when the self-starter is broken. He hailed President
Roosevelt as the first head of state to take theoretical advice as the
basis for large-scale action.

'For the next 25 years, in my belief,' he wrote in 1932, 'economists, at present the most incompetent, will be nevertheless the
most important, group of scientists in the world. And it is to be
hoped—if they are successful—that after that they will never be
important again.'[1]

Keynes had a generally low opinion of politicians as charlatans
who manipulated the public with their propaganda and obsti-
nately clung to the accepted shibboleths until the winds of
change forced them to tack. He knew himself to be an intellectual
and a scientist, but he was a very *political* economist, addressing
himself to the big problems of his time. As the high tide of the
nineteenth century ebbed away and the waves of the twentieth
came rolling in, as the world struggled out from the aftermath of
the 1914–18 war with its old antagonisms and old sovereignties,
the new hopes of peace and progress were bogged down by old
debts and old habits. Poverty stood in the midst of what should
have been plenty, and in Britain, less hard hit than Germany or
the United States, one quarter of the working population was
unemployed. How was the world to get out of this mess? In
Britain, what could be left to the individual and what must be
done by the state? No longer, as Keynes wrote in 1927, would
'private ambition and compound interest . . . between them
carry us to paradise'[2]—the system could no longer be trusted
to correct itself. The problems were political problems, and for
Keynes they were intellectual ones.

For all that, he was a natural politician. He inherited the Liberal
politics of his parents and at Cambridge was a Liberal president of

the Union. During the early part of his life, he often appeared on the platform to speak for Liberal candidates. He was asked to stand for election himself many times—by all three parties—but he preferred the more powerful background role of expert counsellor and adviser. Yet he had, in fact, so many of the traits of the politician that it is hard to think that they could not have influenced his advice.

His opportunism meant that he reacted to events immediately and directly. He would produce an answer, write a memorandum, publish at once, whatever the issue—be it the German mark or the French franc, birth control, the Lancashire cotton trade, buying British, economic sanctions, or compulsory savings for a joyful hereafter. In the World War II Treasury, he nearly drove some of his colleagues crazy with his propensity to keep a finger in every pie. 'Don't just stand there, do something,' would have been his present-day motto. In a broadcast discussion with Sir Josiah Stamp on unemployment in 1930, he said: 'If we just sit tight there will be still more than a million men unemployed six months or a year hence. That is why I feel that a radical policy of some kind is worth trying, even if there are risks about it.' Both Conservative and Labour governments—in the 'fatalistic belief that there never can be more employment than there is,' as Keynes had expressed it in 1929—sat tight during the twenties and thirties, instructed by the civil servants of the Treasury school whom he later characterized as 'trained by tradition and experience and native skill to every form of intelligent obstruction'.[3]

Keynes instead was ready with ideas—ideas of his own, and the current ideas of others that he made his own—and ready with recipes for trying them. They were practical, inventive solutions—such as his proposal to use legislation originally framed to permit the government to stockpile war materials for the additional purpose of minimizing price fluctuations. Characteristically, the proposal might be presented as a three-, four-, five-, or more point agenda. He explored alternatives, giving what he considered the preferred order of adoption. Often he tied up a package deal; he was always happy if he could pick off two birds with one stone and get in a little social benefit while solving an economic problem. He was always ready to commit himself to definite figures—unkind persons said that he made them up.

Other people say that he was very good at making them up, and that he had a sense, a feel, for what the right figure ought to be. In any case, he cannot be blamed entirely for making up figures, for well into the 1920s there was a great scarcity of economically relevant statistics; it was Keynes who laid the foundations for providing this branch of economic information in Britain. For example, in editing his 'Reconstruction in Europe' supplements in 1922, he devoted several pages in each issue to following current trade fluctuations, making use of the London School of Economics and Harvard 'Business Barometer'. The establishment of the Department of Applied Economics at Cambridge in the 1940s owed much to his influence.

In doling out his economic prescriptions Keynes's style was to make a direct appeal to action—to governments, to heads of state (as in his 'Agenda for President Roosevelt') or to individual citizens. Often it was an appeal for internationally concerted action. At the planning stage of the World Economic Conference of 1933, he urged all governments *simultaneously* to adopt programmes of public spending, supported by gold certificates issued by the Bank for International Settlements, to restore world prosperity. 'What is the charm to awaken the Sleeping Beauty, to scale the mountain of glass without slipping? If every Treasury were to discover in its vaults a large *cache* of gold . . . would that not work the charm? Why should not that *cache* be devised? We have long printed gold nationally. Why should we not print it internationally? No reason in the world, unless our hands are palsied and our wits dull.'[4]

This call to action is typically phrased. As Keynes himself said: 'Words ought to be a little wild—for they are the assault of thoughts upon the unthinking.'[5] Talking on the radio about unemployment in 1931, he hazarded the guess that whenever you saved five shillings you put a man out of work for a day; on the other hand whenever you bought goods you increased employment. 'Therefore, oh patriotic housewives,' he urged,

sally out tomorrow early into the streets and go to the wonderful sales which are everywhere advertised. You will do yourselves good—for never were things so cheap, cheap beyond your dreams. Lay in a stock of household linen, of sheets and blankets to satisfy your needs. And have the added joy that you are increasing employment, adding to the wealth of the country because you are setting on foot useful activities, bringing a chance and a hope to Lancashire, Yorkshire, and Belfast.[6]

I have not consulted the contemporary newspapers to learn whether this appeal showed up in the department stores' takings in the January sales, but one result *is* recorded—the cartoonists had a field day depicting the middle-class 'little woman' sallying forth on a spending spree, loading up hubby with parcels and saddling it all on Mr. Keynes. Were these words a little too wild? In a later radio discussion Keynes was careful to explain the difference between hoarding and *useful* saving.

One should note that he finished what he wrote about 'wild' words by adding,

When the seats of power and authority have been attained, there should be no more poetic license.

He liked to call for timely action—*now is the time* to buy sheets, to appoint a board, to settle the world's currency system—and he had his favourite words. He was fond of using the phrases 'the prospects for' and 'the progress of' and the word 'consequences' in his titles, all implying a logical sequence or plan for development. He was ever ready to present his 'drastic remedy' or his 'radical plan' or to approve a 'bold measure'—fancying himself as the *enfant terrible*—although he always saw his changes working within the established system.

He was optimistic—where others saw the beginning of a long industrial decline, he felt the country was 'in the middle of a painful adjustment'. Addressing international delegates to a meeting of the National Council of Women (his mother was president) in June 1930, he explained that England was suffering 'from a sort of *malaise* of wealth'—saving money faster than she was spending it, economizing on the use of labour faster than finding outlets for it, raising the standard of living a little too fast— and he described these phenomena as 'the growing pains of progress, not the rheumatism of old age'.

On this occasion, he talked of England's social achievements, in which he took pride. He had a strong vein of patriotism, in

spite of his internationalism during the twenties. He was per-
petually fussing about the possibility that British lending abroad
was diverting funds from investment in home industry,
(perhaps, subconsciously, like the mad general in the film 'Dr.
Strangelove,' worrying about the sapping of 'precious bodily
fluids'). He did not want to see his country become a rentier
nation and miss out on the action, he had his own ideas about
how Britain should honour her debts before devaluation, and he
looked to her to take the initiative and leadership in all his
international proposals.

He enthusiastically supported any leader whom he thought
could carry out a policy of which he approved. After the terrible
things he had said about Lloyd George, that goat-footed Welsh
Witch, in connection with the Treaty of Versailles, he supported
him vigorously in the election of 1929 and wrote (with Hubert
Henderson) *Can Lloyd George Do It?* the pamphlet that became the
textbook of the Liberal campaign. When taxed with what he had
said about Lloyd George's conduct of the coupon election, he
replied: 'I oppose Mr. Lloyd George when he is wrong; I support
him when he is right.' It was the same with Winston Churchill.
And in 1930 Keynes commended the enterprising spirit of Sir
Oswald Mosley in putting forward a national economic plan,[7] but
he did not write about Mosley after that.

He was flexible. Having, in 1931, after much thought, publicly
deserted free trade to recommend a revenue tariff with all his
might, the moment that England left the gold standard and made
such a tariff economically unnecessary, he dashed off a letter to
The Times calling attention to the now primary importance of
devising a sound international currency system; the discussion of
domestic protection should wait until later, he said.[8] And, in
1937, as the rest of the country breathed a half-sigh of relief after
painfully climbing out of the slump, he looked ahead in two *Times*
articles to ask how to avoid a future occurrence of such a situation.

Flexibility—or inconsistency? He was branded as 'inconsistent.' When he was attacked for coming over from free trade to a
revenue tariff, he lampooned his critics:

I seem to see the elder parrots sitting around and saying: 'You
can *rely* upon us. Every day for 30 years, regardless of the

weather, we have said, "What a lovely morning!" But this is a bad bird. He says one thing one day and something else the next.'[9]

Even Keynes's critics had to admit that he never tried to pretend when he changed his mind. And he usually explained just why he had done so. But he was not always so flexible. When he was still in his thirties, he was youthfully uncompromising, insisting that the Treaty of Versailles must be revised, unwilling to live with it and accept it as a political necessity. As time went on, he became more amenable to compromise: 'My own view is that I want as much as I can get,' he wrote of a League of Nations proposal in 1930; 'but I do not want to wreck the whole project by asking for more than I can get'. In the course of time, he even came to tone down—publicly, that is—some of his caustic language. Writing to the literary editor of the *Daily Mail* in 1932 about some small alterations that he wished to make in an article on England's war debts to America, 'chiefly with the object of avoiding strong language,' he replaced the phrase, 'when one reads the rubbish reported from Congressmen, much of it altogether beneath the intelligence and dignity of human nature,' by the much milder observation, 'when one reads what Congressmen say to reporters.'

Between the two wars he was very energetic, vigorous and visible on the surface of English political life. Articles, pamphlets, and books appeared perfectly timed for the opening of a conference, the preparation of the Budget—or perhaps for the preparation of the public for the inevitable economic consequences of some past decision or event. The political pamphlets were priced at 6d. and 1/–; *The General Theory* sold for 5/–. Margot Asquith objected to the publication of the article on the American debts in the *Daily Mail*: 'You sd. have sent it to the *Times*, as those who read the *Daily Mail* are mostly in the Servants Hall (I never take it in).' He was careful to send his articles, punctiliously presented, to *The Times*, the *Manchester Guardian*, the *Nation*, and the *New Statesman*; at the same time, he never missed an opportunity to publish the same material in more swashbuckling form in the *Daily Mail*, the *Daily Express*, and the *Evening Standard*.

But as with every real politician, nine-tenths of the Keynes iceberg was invisible. Only the small group of those in the know could have been aware of his leadership in 1920 in organizing an appeal to the League of Nations for an international loan and also the first international conference of economic experts in Brussels—civil servants, not politicians; his part in the thinking and research which went into the Yellow Book that reviewed and restated the objects and aspirations of the ailing Liberal party; the questioning that led to his adoption of the revenue tariff policy in the behind-doors Economic Advisory Committee, months before he expressed this change of heart in public; his crucial dominance of the Macmillan Committee of Inquiry into Finance and Industry. And just like every practising politician, he maintained contact with an extensive network of influential friends and acquaintances to whom he could go for help if necessary, because they would do the same with him. His correspondence files are almost a *Who's Who* for an era— not only in the fields of economics and politics, but also in society, literature, and art. The day that he surfaced and was observed lunching alone with Ramsay Mac-Donald, the stock market rose.

Yet Keynes insisted that politics was not his role, that he was more valuable in his chosen capacity as adviser. It was a case of emotion versus intellect; some of his contemporaries thought of him as an emotionless, coldly logical machine. Writing of Lloyd George's political craft with introspection into his own personality clearly in mind, he remarked: 'A preference for truth or for sincerity *as a method* may be a prejudice based on some aesthetic or personal standard, inconsistent, in politics, with practical good' (*A Revision of the Treaty*). His radical approach seemed to destine him for the Labour rather than the Liberal camp, but he shied away from Labour dogmatism and anti-intellectualism. To proclaim any dogma as infallible and applicable in all cases, he said, debating the merits of the two parties at a Liberal summer school, was 'voluntarily to shut oneself out from any scientific approach to economic problems by means of experiment and investigation'. Also, the Labour party was a class party, Keynes said, 'and the class is not my class. . . . the *class* war will find me on the side of the educated *bourgeoisie*' ('Am I a Liberal?').

In considering Keynes one can never forget his social background. There were his cultivated, thrifty, donnish parents—

non-conformist in outlook, if not overtly religious—comfortably settled in middle-class Cambridge. To this heritage was added the polish of Eton and King's and the sophistication of Bloomsbury and of the high-ranking civil service. He had the know-how and the aplomb to make and lose a small fortune and to re-establish himself again before he was forty. His confidence sprang partly from his parents' accepted place in Cambridge society but it was rooted even more powerfully in the consciousness of his own superior intellect, reinforced by a superior education and its consequent career in the outside world.

As the son of his philosopher father and socially conscious mother, he sought in politics a party that in the changing conditions of the time would create a society both economically just and economically efficient, while still preserving individual liberty. He stayed with the Liberals, the party of his parents, by standing intellectually outside of it, despite his campaigning and committee work and participation in summer schools. From his parents he inherited the late Victorian nonconformist belief in the necessity and possibility to the improvement of society by the application of reason and the sense of obligation to one's social inferiors that went with it. (The same attitudes appear in the Fabianism of the Webbs, but Keynes seems to have regarded the Webbs as a little naïve.)

Large-scale unemployment was the basic problem that Keynes came to focus on. His received view of the world was of a society in which each man had his appointed place, and it was an injustice for him not to be allowed to feed his family and retain his self-respect in fulfilling the task ordained for him. Economic theory then taught that if there were not enough jobs, the labouring force would divide up the supply of work, driving down wages in the process—a hardship to the worker and no challenge to the employer to make himself more efficient, Keynes said. His solution, when he wrote 'The Question of High Wages' in 1930 was to increase the workers' real wages by providing social services.[10] In a letter to the *Manchester Guardian* he told a story about the little girl who, when asked if the poor should be made like the rich, replied, 'No, it would spoil their characters'. The story was offered tongue-in-cheek, but does one detect the social worker's instincts of his mother?

An achievement that gave Keynes great satisfaction was his wartime scheme for compulsory savings or, as he later chose to call it, 'd⌐ferred pay.' He told the Cambridge Fabian Society that he had made it 'outrageously attractive' to the working class, although the working class seems to have been singularly unenthusiastic about it. He regarded it, characteristically, not just as an expedient for financing the war, but as an opportunity to demonstrate the difference between the totalitarian and the free economy.

> For if the community's aggregate rate of spending can be regulated, the way in which personal incomes are spent and the means by which demand is satisfied can be safely left free and individual . . . the only way to avoid the destruction of choice and initiative, whether by consumers or by producers, through the complex tyranny of all-round rationing. . . . This is the one kind of compulsion of which the effect is to enlarge liberty. Those who, entangled in the old unserviceable maxims, fail to see this further-reaching objective have not grasped, to speak American, the big idea.[11]

Toward the end of *How to Pay for the War*, he sums up the scheme as 'the perfect opportunity for social action where everyone can be protected by making a certain rule of behaviour universal'. It is economically just, it is economically efficient— and the smell is undeniably paternalistic. Keynes grappled with the problems of the twentieth century, but he never really extricated himself from the view of society, and his own position therein, in which his parents had reared him.

Unemployment was a problem that according to orthodox theory should not exist, but it was the problem that would not go away. He grappled with it with a moral indignation and persistency that conjures up the spirit of another great grappler, John Bunyan, the subject of a biography by Keynes's maternal grandfather, the nonconformist minister John Brown. 'Is not the mere existence of general unemployment for any length of time an absurdity, a confession of failure, and a hopeless and inexcusable breakdown of the economic machine?' Keynes demanded in his 1930 radio dialogue with Stamp. Stamp, so addressed, observed: 'Your language is rather violent. You would not expect to put an earthquake tidy in a few minutes, would you?'

It took the years from 1923 to 1936 for Keynes to tidy up the theory of the earthquake. In an address on the occasion of the centenary of the death of Malthus, Keynes quoted Malthus himself on the relation of experience to theory, distinguishing between that partial or confined experience that a man gains 'from the management of his own little farm, or the details of the workhouse in his neighbourhood'—which is 'no foundation whatever for a just theory'—and 'that general experience, on which alone a just theory can be founded.' Keynes claimed for Malthus 'an unusual combination of keeping an open mind to the shifting picture of experience and of constantly applying to its interpretation the principles of formal thought.' Here, in his emphasis on adaptation to change and constant referral back to the facts, he stated his own ideal of how a social scientist ought to work.

As I have documented earlier, Keynes behaved from day to day in public like a working politician. In private, he was deeply and seriously concerned with the science of economics. He kept coming back to the central problem that the existing theory would not explain. At first, he was content to dazzle by demonstrating that a fuller knowledge of economic theory and statistics than his professional colleagues possessed would support conclusions different from those prompted by their understanding of the economic orthodoxy. But eventually, his intellectual honesty and his concern for economic science brought him to believe that it was not the incompetence of the orthodox economists but the received theory itself, that was at fault. Modifications within the framework of orthodox economics were not enough; a frontal attack on the framework itself was required.

So Keynes produced *The General Theory* as a proof—by the standards of the prevailing economic orthodoxy itself—that, contrary to orthodox beliefs, the normal state of economic society was not full employment, but general unemployment. As a corollary, government policies aimed at raising the level of employment were not mistaken and arbitrary interferences with a well-functioning and efficient economic machine; instead, government interference was absolutely necessary in order for the machine to work at all. Thus, Keynes behaved as a scientist in the crucial sense: having found the existing body of scientific know-

ledge in economics increasingly unsatisfactory as a tool for solving the problems that he considered important, he produced a
new and rival theory that would explain the discrepancies between the orthodoxy and the observed facts—discrepancies
which formerly had to be explained as special cases.

Recalling Malthus on partial and general experience, how
much did Keynes's enthusiasms, his inventiveness, blind his
science? One of his early reactions to unemployment in the *Manchester Guardian* supplements was to put it down to overpopula-
tion; a critic accused him of letting his advocacy of birth control
affect his conclusions. If he had been less a patriot would he
perhaps have been so troubled by the idea of foreign lending? If
his upbringing had not inclined him to think of foreign food as
less wholesome than home grown, or if he had not bought a
Sussex farm for himself and invested a lot of his college's money
in a large farm estate in Lincolnshire, would he, after he reverted
from his 1931 recommendation of a revenue tariff to his lifelong
belief in free trade, have made an exception for tariff protection to
agriculture? If his father had been a docker, and not a well-to-do
academic philosopher, how would he have dealt with unemployment?

In the world as it was then, security and independence were
the lot of a few; the housewives whom Keynes urged to go out
and buy sheets were middle-class housewives with money in the
bank to provide for the future. Yet, in his ideal society, he desired
security and independence for everybody. However, he could
conceive of it only in terms of his own experience: social happiness was employment for every one, each in his appointed place,
his own niche.

Keynes believed unquestioningly that anyone in England with
enough ambition could rise to his proper position in society. Nor
did he have any question as to whether it was just for a man who
had risen as rapidly as he had to be able to rely so implicitly on the
full-time dutiful service of others who did not have those advantages. (What were the thoughts of the servant, who earned
perhaps £1 a week, when he was sent to the bank to fetch £10 or
£50? Keynes was fortunate if the servant, like himself, did not
bother his head about it.) Social injustice existed only in there not
being enough jobs to go around. If there were servants with

talents or character above their appointed stations, they deserved help, financial or advisory, from their betters; it was the obligation of the employer and ultimately the state to make it up to them in welfare benefits and other social transfers.

So that, although Keynes thought of himself as a radical, one can see that he took a conservative, even an archaic view of society. His 'radical' solution of government maternalism has now become the received orthodoxy. Even so, his social philosophy made a great leap forward: he said that it is wrong for a government to expect people to study, work hard, be honest and responsible, in order to fit themselves for a place in a society presumed to be anxious to employ and make good use of them, when in fact the economic policy of that government precludes a large number of its citizens from having an opportunity for employment and a decent career; government has a responsibility to society to follow an economic policy that will satisfy these expectations.

We are left with two problems that did not trouble Keynes. We still have not solved the problem of equal opportunity, which Keynes took as a matter of course. We do not yet know how to reconcile the boring nature of many jobs with freedom for the human spirit; Keynes, who thought about it in terms that reflected his own social background, looked forward to more automation, less work, and the enrichment of leisure time by cultural activities provided by the state.

In summary, in my judgement, Keynes was a politician, but a politician whose constituency was not electoral but intellectual—he had to be a scientist to be a politician. And he was a good enough scientist, with a strong enough sense of scientific integrity, and a strong enough aesthetic preference for truth, to recognize eventually that the social science he knew was not good enough to solve the problems he recognized as politically important and that he had to reform the science to make it politically relevant and useful. He was a scientific political economist. One can emphasize either the 'scientific' or the 'political'—and which adjective one emphasizes depends of whether one is writing a political biography of the man himself or a history of economic thought. Both adjectives are appropriate and both are necessary to characterize what the man was and what he contributed to British society and British social history.

3
Keynes as a Literary Craftsman

It might seem to an economist that discussing Keynes as a literary practitioner is beside the point—like trying to dissect Shakespeare as an actor. The style, however, reveals the man; and Keynes's unmistakable literary style illuminates fundamental attitudes, characteristics, and habits of the economist.

Economics as a discipline has at least its share of unclear, inelegant and pedestrian writers. I doubt that there are many other economists whose works can be read as literature in their own right. Not all of Keynes can be read this way—*The General Theory* is not what one settles down to in anticipation of a good read in bed—but *The Economic Consequences of the Peace* is compelling at even half a century's distance, *A Tract on Monetary Reform* serves as a model for its kind, and *Essays in Persuasion* and *Essays in Biography* are pure enjoyment.

The *Essays* and the posthumous *Two Memoirs* are literary Keynes at his very best. They also represent Keynes's own selection from the large body of his writing that was directed towards the generally educated, intelligent lay reading public. With the passage of time many economists are unaware of the number—300 or so—and the scope of the articles that he wrote for both the quality and the popular press. They may be more aware of the existence of the scores of memoranda and reports that he wrote officially and unofficially for the advisers and would-be advisers of the British government.

The point is that Keynes was a professional journalist as well as an economist, and regarded himself as such. He acted like a professional propagandist for whatever was his personal cause of the moment. He wrote regularly, and for money; during his earlier career, at least, he regarded the money part of it as important enough to bargain about.* One could argue indeed that in a certain sense all his writing was journalism of one order or another—from his plan for a state bank for India, quickly put together for a Royal Commission's report, to *A Treatise on Money* and *The General Theory* which, though presented as academic works, sought to produce instant cures for pressing economic ills. He wrote for the present moment, to the best of his ability at that moment, and, with his notorious predilection for changing his mind in adaptation to changing circumstances, nothing was ever intended as his last word. He wrote in 1927 ('Clissold,' *Essays in Persuasion*):

> . . . this is not a good age for pure artists; nor is it a good one for classical perfections. Our most pregnant writers today are full of imperfections; they expose themselves to judgment; they do not look to be immortal.

Human beings are often most discerning of the qualities in others that they themselves possess. In praising the willingness of H. G. Wells to expose himself to judgement, he showed a fine appreciation of J. M. Keynes. He was not the man to be chagrined in the slightest to find his yesterday's winged words wrapping today's fish and chips.

Keynes wrote quickly in a rather crabbed handwriting, usually with little changing or crossing out, except perhaps when expressing an emotional piece of personal vituperation. One has the impression that he worked hard and intensely, but also that the performance came to him easily and would have appeared easy to the onlooker. From his early days in the Treasury in World War I, and even earlier, he was able to draft quickly and clearly and to get something down on paper in response to a demand and a deadline. As an editor—and I am not thinking so much of the *Economic Journal* as his tour de force for the *Manchester Guardian* of the twelve 'Reconstruction in Europe' supplements put together over 1921–23—he was full of resource and endlessly adaptable.

* Keynes's attitude later, when he had given up writing as a means of income, was the subject of an exchange of letters between himself and the editor of the *Listener*. 'A Delicate Question of Payment', *Encounter*, Vol. 43, No. 5 (November 1974), pp. 24–8. To Keynes it was a matter of principle.

Economic Consequences made him first comparatively and enjoy-ably rich, and then when he lost in speculating in the German mark, it paid his losses. Before this best-seller his earnings from writing were the usual academic chicken-feed, but after he had become a household name he regarded his writings as a regu-lar source of income and bargained with the Government of India, who wanted him for another Royal Commission, to make up the loss of earnings his absence from England would entail.

He wrote, very successfully, for a world-wide market; ironical, that—he was so insular a man. With the wildfire dissemination and translation of *Economic Consequences*, his audience included the United States and Europe, and even China and Japan. He employed a world-wide clipping service for reviews, and he very soon had agents who would place his articles in the important newspapers of the major countries. He quickly learned to make sure of his copyright. He had a good idea of the price he could ask and get in each quarter and he acted accordingly.

But money was not what made Keynes a journalist. He was a crusader, a teacher and a preacher. With his eyes 'turned towards the possibilities of things,' as he put it, the world seemed infi-nitely remediable. All the world had to do was to adopt his prescriptions—offered with an air of energetic daring and cheer-ful optimism which added to their attractiveness.

If moral indignation and reforming zeal made Keynes a jour-nalist, his own proficiency—the satisfaction of doing the job so well—kept him at it. He thought of himself as the intellectual persuader, but he also was a natural charmer, even a seducer—he had a syren's voice. He charmed with words, words which represented logical ideas and precise thinking processes. But the words he used so logically and precisely also represented strong emotions and subtle shades of feeling. Words were his journeyman's tools—and he could use them as an artist. He took a natural pleasure in using his tools so well—in his performance, that is, in the skill and the power of the persuader.

The skill came with practice but the bent for putting things right he possessed from the start. As a junior in the India Office he approached each new problem as a maladministered mess which he could correct. 'If you at all agree . . . I could throw it into a minute,' he volunteered, ready to clear up the complicated difficulties of the jute trade and deference to a superior only just masking his cockiness. Most people lose this élan as the years pass, but a Treasury colleague of World War II, Dennis Proctor, recalled in the King's College memoir of Keynes that his instinctive attitude to any new situation was to assume, first, that nobody was doing anything about it, and, secondly, that if they were, they were doing it wrong. It was a lifetime habit of mind based on the conviction that he was armed with superior brains—which was undeniable—and, Cambridge Apostle that he was, gifted with superior sensibilities.

This assurance shows in some strikingly pithy opening sentences:

'The Budget and the Economy Bill are replete with folly and injustice.'

'One blames politicians, not for inconsistency, but for obstinacy.'

It shows, too, in some dismissive sweeping statements:

'There are only three lines of policy to which it is worth the Cabinet's while to direct their minds. . . . All the rest is waste of time.'

'In Great Britain our authorities have never talked such rubbish as their French colleagues or offended so grossly against all sound principles of finance.'

He has the answer. Successive French finance ministers have done their utmost to revive the franc. 'What more could they have done?' asks Keynes.

Simply: 'I will tell you.'

Keynes could damn a whole group of people or a profession: 'There are limits to permissable misrepresentation, even at the hands of a lawyer,' he jibed in reply to an old adversary who had written a critical review. Statements like this sometimes carried him overboard into his own variety of outrageous rudeness. Describing a Chancellor of the Exchequer as 'endowed with more than a normal share of blindness and obstinacy' would not be so insulting if it were not so strikingly well put. His most successful portraits—for example, those of Woodrow Wilson and Lloyd George—balance a tight-rope eerily above bad taste and cruelty.

But Keynes in a didactic rather than a reforming frame of mind could take a more sober, measured tone. The beginning of *How to Pay for the War* is arresting without being combative:

'It is not easy for a free community to organize for war.'

Sometimes the opening sentence is simply very workmanlike: 'The report of the Economy Committee can be considered from several points of view.' This article closes plainly, with a summary of recommendations.

In the civil service Keynes learned the technique of presenting an argument by numbered paragraphs or steps of reasoning. He often itemized his own arguments very effectively, demolishing his adversaries and marshalling his remedies. The technique, perhaps deceptively, makes his solutions seem very simple, rational and only common sense.

When the issue to be presented to the lay public was very complicated, Keynes sometimes hits on a deliberately homely metaphor. In his 1930 article diagnosing 'The Great Slump,' he wrote, 'I doubt whether I can hope to bring what is in my mind into fully effective touch with the mind of the reader. I shall be saying too much for the layman, too little for the expert. . . . We have magneto trouble.' In *The Means to Prosperity*, the image was two drivers meeting in the middle of a highway, unable to pass each other without knowing the rule of the road. (There is something self-conscious about this; Keynes's own car was chauffeur-driven.)

He made conversation with the reader, posing and answering questions, concluding 'If, then, I am right. . . .' He was adept at this expansive style of unbuttoned cosiness, especially in his radio talks, making his talk so confiding that one almost forgets that the dialogue was one-sided. Part of it was the placing of his words which was faultless. If something is out of the usual order, it is for a purpose. Describing the discomfort of one born a political animal finding himself without a party, he could write 'cold and lonely and futile it is', and never put a word wrong.

He had what was called an English classical education, which gave him a knowledge of the precise meanings of words and a respect for them. He was very particular that translations of his work should carry his exact meaning. He was a master of the brilliant use of the esoteric word. But his use of language only occasionally sends one to burrow in the dictionary; it is the appropriateness of his ordinary vocabulary that is noticeable.

Conscious of the precise meanings of words, he was also conscious of their overtones. 'Words ought to be a little wild,' that is, emotive—and he used these overtones with great skill. A lovely example is his 'short view' of Russia—'The beautiful and foolish youngest son of the European family, with hair on his head, nearer both to the earth and to heaven than his bald brothers in the West.' It is East o' the Sun and West o' the Moon, but must have been beautifully evocative to the European inhabitants of the 1920s.

His announcement to the world in the *Tract on Monetary Reform* that the gold standard was a 'barbarous relic' combines sense and emotion in a single memorable phrase.

He took pleasure in words and in playing with them, and his humour and fantasy are both very verbal. Seeking to define the function of gold as a garment of respectability, he produced the phrase 'furtive Freudian cloak', then, turning to the small stocks of coins belonging to individuals, evoked the presence of 'the little household gods, who dwelt in purses and stockings and tin boxes'—the detailed minutiae of which reminds one very much of Virginia Woolf.

Like Virginia Woolf, he could freeze a figure in a single snapshot, as when he wrote of young Alfred Marshall, forbidden mathematics by his father, surrepticiously concealing Potts' Euclid in his pocket as he walked to school. 'He read a proposition and then worked it out in his mind as he walked along, standing still at intervals, with his toes turned in.'

Keynes much enjoyed writing his memoir of Marshall, which he said grew under his hand. 'Mathematics represented for Alfred emancipation,' Keynes explained, his own enjoyment soaring into fantasy: 'No! he would not be buried at Oxford under dead languages; he would run away—to be a cabin-boy at Cambridge and climb the rigging of geometry and spy out the heavens.'

His fantasy was never far from tumbling him into the absurd: he pictured the Russian Communists as 'early Christians led by Attila . . . using the equipment of the Holy Inquisition and the Jesuit missions to enforce the literal economics of the New Testament.'

A large element in his verbal humour is ridicule—generally a lighthearted rejoicing in human absurdity, usually with no bad aftertaste. He was fond of the device of *reductio ad absurdum* in which ideas are piled impossibly like a house of cards until they come sliding hilariously down. Such is the sudden descent of his mock lament in 'Am I a Liberal?' for the 'old battle-cries' which 'are muffled or silent. The Church, the aristocracy, the landed interests, the rights of property, the glories of empire, the pride of the services, even beer and whisky—will never again be the guiding forces of British politics.'

His keen eye for the absurd made him a mordant satirist. Frequently the satire is expressed in a concrete physical image—the Americans shipping all the bullion in the world to the United States and erecting there a sky-scraping golden calf—the overly-optimistic bank chairman like a rash spring robin, chirruping amongst the bushes.

Irony pervades these word-pictures. Only recall Keynes's depiction of the Mitty-like day-dream of the average American graciously receiving the love and gratitude of his European debtors and overwhelming them with forgiveness. Again, with irony, some years later, he dropped intuition for arithmetic, and made the calculation of the good works that could be done in England with the money represented by Britain's debt to America.

The style of Keynes's early articles and letters to the editor is sober, no-nonsense, but effective. At that time he thought of himself as an academic whose excursions into the press were simply to put the record straight. The Treaty of Versailles, with its attendant personal repercussions, was the catalyst which converted him into a journalist by applying the emotional heat that was released in *The Economic Consequences of the Peace*. In writing it he learned that it didn't hurt to let go and pull out all the stops; and he grew comfortable with the magnificent organ voice he could produce. A purist might complain of flamboyance. Along with excesses of taste, it is possible to find, as his output swelled and he wrote in haste, an impatience leading to carelessness and to awkwardness in construction—but, considering the output, not often.

Economic Consequences combines two methods in a way which came to be his trademark. The process is somewhat like this: we are first presented with a sort of apocalyptic vision, clouded with foreboding and prophecy, a broad sweep through history lit up by flashes of insight and wit displayed in brilliant vignettes of individuals. Following this we are treated to a barrage of statistics to convince the hard-headed, number piled on number, the bombardment of heavy guns—it is very impressive.

In *Economic Consequences* Keynes used these two techniques to combine his appeals to heart and to head. In writing regularly for the *Nation* later he would sometimes follow one week's emotional reasons with the facts and figures next week. So a con man typically snows his victim.

Was he a con man or do you prefer to look on him as a conjurer—a conjurer of words?

Pigou, writing in the King's memoir, complained that Keynes was too ready 'to hoist the flag of intellectual revolution,' stressing disagreements over agreements—as he said,

> By defining common words in uncommon senses, as with savings and income in his earlier book, and 'full' employment—which was compatible with a large volume of unemployment—in his later one, he caused much confusion among persons less agile-minded than himself.

Pigou's criticism was perhaps well-taken. It is ironical that Keynes, so concerned with the precise meanings of words, so desirous of being properly understood, and with such a facility for and firm command of language, should succeed in effect in dazzling and blinding some of his colleagues. His style in writing is a mirror for his style in economics, and economists have had to sort and weigh his words. His other readers—of the essays and the two memoirs—are free to indulge the delight that comes in watching the seemingly effortless, painstaking art of an old pro.

4
Keynes's Attitude to
Compulsory Military Service

Clive Bell described Keynes during World War I as a conscientious objector 'of a peculiar and . . . most reasonable kind'.[1] The description was challenged by Sir Roy Harrod in a review of Bell's *Old Friends* in the pages of the *Economic Journal*, in which he denied that Keynes was a conscientious objector in 'any sense, peculiar or other,' dismissing his behaviour as 'just a little gesture of appeasement to his Bloomsbury friends'.[2]

According to Clive Bell, Keynes was a conscientious objector *to conscription*. This version of the matter is borne out by a draft letter, written and signed in Keynes's own hand, which gives a considered statement of his personal view. This letter and other evidence in Keynes's own papers support Bell's interpretation of Keynes's opinions and actions.

Conscription came into force with the Military Service Act of 27 January 1916, by which all men between eighteen and forty-one who were unmarried or widowers without dependent children were 'deemed . . . to have been duly enlisted.' Keynes had from the first disliked and opposed conscription, not as a pacifist, which in contrast to some of his friends he never was, but as a liberal who denied the right of the State to abrogate to itself a decision which he and many other liberals believed should be a decision for the individual. For some time before the passing of the Act he had been increasingly concerned about the morality of conscription, about its possible economic effects, about his own personal duty in relation to it and about its consequences for some of his friends.

Among Keynes's papers are copies of memoranda written by him towards the end of 1915 in which he argued that the country could not afford the dislocation to industry and shipping which would result from conscription, and that the financial help which Britain could give her Allies as an alternative was both more economical and more valuable politically. The Chancellor of the Exchequer, Reginald McKenna, accepted this view and argued it with his colleagues, though without success, as Lloyd George related in his *War Memoirs*.

It was this stand that Keynes took in a long letter published in the *Daily Chronicle* of 6 January 1916, under the pseudonym 'Politicus'. The final paragraph reads:

> Those who believe that the true Englishman is one who throws himself not where he is most efficient but where his personal sacrifice will be greatest, who believe that our duty to the Allies is not to help them most effectively but to impress them with the nobility of our self-sacrifice by getting as many of our men killed or maimed as we plausibly can, or who believe that the chief test of patriotism is an eagerness to dissipate the national resources at the maximum possible rate, will find much moral solace in compulsory service. But in the business of war there is no room for such sentimentalities. That is not the way to beat Germany.

Keynes appears to have followed this attack on the proposed Conscription Act by suggesting amendments to it, which he sent to Philip Morrell, a Liberal Member of Parliament and a personal friend, while the Bill was being debated. A reply over Morrell's initials, thanking Keynes for his letter and amendments, is in his files.

John Neville Keynes commented in his diary during January 1916 on his son's thinking at this time:

Jan. 6 (The two elder Keynes were visiting J. M. K. in London) . . . The Government have decided on compulsory service for single men. Maynard talks of resigning his post at the Treasury, and we are very much worried about him.

Jan. 14 Maynard writes, 'Things drift on, and I shall stay now, I expect, until they begin to torture one of my friends. I believe a real split now and a taste of trouble would bring peace nearer, not postpone it; otherwise I'd swallow a great deal. I've been very busy and with occasional excursions into high life,—met the P.M. at dinner on Saturday, refused to dine with the old scoundrel on Sunday, banqueted with the Lord Mayor yesterday.'

Jan. 16 Maynard is home today . . . I am afraid he takes an extreme view on conscription.

Jan. 28 Florence [Mrs. Keynes] . . . saw Maynard in London. He is still thoroughly interested in his work, and Florence does not fear his throwing everything up in consequence of the Compulsion Bill.

Under the Military Service Act of 1916 there were two methods by which exemption could be granted:

(i) The individual could make application to a local tribunal on the grounds of: (*a*) national importance of his work; (*b*) hardship; (*c*) ill-health; (*d*) 'a conscientious objection to the undertaking of combatant service.'

(ii) Certificates of exemption could 'be granted by any Government Department, after consultation with the Army Council, to men or classes or bodies of men, in the service or employment of that Department, or, in cases where it appears to the Department that certificates can be more conveniently granted by the Department than by the local tribunal, to men or classes or bodies of men who are employed or engaged or qualified for employment or engagement in any work which is certified by the Department to be work of national importance and whose exemption comes within the sphere of the Department.'

It is clear that Keynes had been thinking in advance about his own personal position and duties. One can trace the events of the next few months in a small file among his papers which contains the documents concerning both his exemption and his special application to the Holborn Local Tribunal. It begins with a letter from Sir Thomas Heath, Joint Permanent Secretary of the Treasury, dated 23 February 1916. This is accompanied by a certificate of exemption for six months from the provisions of the Act, issued the same day by the Treasury, 'being a Government

Department under Section 2 (2) of the Act.' Heath's letter states:

> I understand that you have not attested under the Derby Scheme and I have had consequently to take into consideration your position with regard to the Military Service Act. It has been decided to issue in your favour the enclosed certificate of exemption from the provisions of the Act, limited to a term of six months from the 2nd of March, 1916, on the ground that you are engaged on work of national importance.
>
> It will rest with yourself to make any representations which you may desire to put forward to the Local Tribunal on any of the grounds enumerated in Section 2 (1) *(b)* *(c)* and *(d)* of the Act.

(The Derby Scheme was the final attempt to recruit by voluntary means before the adoption of compulsory service in January 1916. Men in vital industries were urged to attest that they would serve in the forces when they were called, but were not to be enlisted.)

Thus, Keynes was given a temporary exemption by the Treasury, so empowered by the Act, and he was informed that it rested with himself to make any claim on other grounds, including conscientious objection, to his Local Tribunal.

It is clear that he did wish to put himself on record. If he had not so wished, there was no reason why he should have approached his Local Tribunal at all. He was exempted in virtue of his work. His approach to the Tribunal must have been made because he wished to be exempted *in addition* on one or other of the grounds of hardship, ill-health or conscientious objection.

That his approach was on grounds of conscience is clear from a completed draft of a statement of his case to the Local Tribunal. It is addressed to 'The Tribunal' and written on King's College writing-paper in Keynes's own hand-writing, dated 28 February 1916, and signed by him. It is as follows:

King's College,
Cambridge.
28.2.16

I claim complete exemption because I have a conscientious objection to surrendering my liberty of judgment on so vital a question as undertaking military service. I do not say that there are not conceivable circumstances in which I should voluntarily offer myself for military service. But after having regard to all the actually existing circumstances, I am certain that it is not my duty so to offer myself; and I solemnly assert to the Tribunal that my objection to submit to authority in this matter is truly conscientious. I am not prepared on such an issue as this to surrender my right of decision, as to what is or is not my duty, to any other person, and I should think it morally wrong to do so.

J. M. Keynes

No words are crossed out or changed in the draft, but the word 'morally' in the last sentence is inserted with a caret. Keynes typically wrote only one draft, although he might correct it extensively, but occasionally, at this stage of his life, when the matter was important, he would write out a fair copy as this appears to be.

There survives no absolutely certain evidence that Keynes sent precisely this statement to the Holborn Tribunal. But we do know that he was asked to appear before the Tribunal and that must imply that he had made an application to do so. The next item in the file is a postcard, post-marked '24 Mar 1916' and addressed to him at 3 Gower Street, from the Clerk to the Holborn Local Tribunal, notifying him that the application in respect of J. M. Keynes would be considered on the 28th day of March 1916 at 5 p.m.

This postcard is presumably what Harrod referred to in *The Life of John Maynard Keynes*, and later in his review of Bell, as 'the calling up notice' to which Keynes 'replied on Treasury writing-paper that he was too busy to attend the summons.' In *Old Friends*, however, Bell had said that it was a *tribunal* to which Keynes had sent word that he was too busy, and following Harrod's review he explained in a private letter that Keynes had been summoned to a conference 'of considerable importance' at the same hour.

That Keynes's application actually came to a hearing is clear from the fact that the postcard from the Tribunal is followed in the file by a letter addressed to Keynes at Treasury Chambers, from the Clerk to the Holborn Local Tribunal, dated 29 March 1916, referring to a letter from Keynes of 27 March and informing him that his application for exemption was dismissed, 'having regard to the fact that you have already been exempted for six months by the Treasury.' He would be entitled, if he desired, to put in an application for further exemption after six months. Thus it is beyond doubt that Keynes's application was heard *in absentia* on the basis of some written statement of his case, similar, if not identical, to that which remains among his papers.

In fact, the Treasury renewed his exemption, conditional, without apparent time limit, on his remaining in their employment. The certificate, dated 18 August 1916, was kept in Keynes's files and it was this document, and not Keynes's letters, which settled the matter.

The final document that Keynes kept in this collection was a certificate of registration under the National Registration Acts, 1915 and 1918, dated 16 March 1918. There is no certificate in the file for Keynes's registration in 1915. Registration under the 1915 Act—in effect a census used as an instrument for the Military Service Act—was far from complete, and the Act of 1918 was tightened up by placing an obligation on employers to require all male employees to produce a certificate of registration. One can speculate whether Keynes, like many others, had neglected, possibly in protest, to register under the earlier Act.

We know less from Keynes's papers of his views over the following years. His application had been rejected by the Holborn Tribunal on the ground that he had already been exempted by the Treasury. When the Treasury in August 1916 exempted him without limit of time, conditional on his remaining in Treasury employment, he may very reasonably have assumed that he had no grounds on which to go back to the Tribunal and to ask it to reconsider its decision. What we do know is that Keynes's grave concern regarding the morality and wisdom of compulsory service was not ephemeral, and that his attitude had not changed substantially before his case came up for hearing.

A letter to Dennis Robertson, dated 18 June 1916, several months after the Tribunal had dealt with Keynes's case on 28 March, included the following passage:

> The Tribunal crisis is getting over now, as concessions to the C.O.'s are impending. But it has been a foul business, and I

spend half of my time on the boring business of testifying to the sincerity, virtue and truthfulness of my friends.

Thus Keynes's own papers reveal that, in Clive Bell's words, he was indeed a conscientious objector to conscription 'of a peculiar and . . . most reasonable kind.' The statement of his views which remains among his papers, even if it was not sent to the Tribunal in precisely that form, unquestionably shows his thinking at this time, and it is wholly consistent with his fundamental personal philosophy as described in 'My Early Beliefs':

> We entirely repudiate a personal liability on us to obey general rules. We claimed the right to judge every individual case on its merits, and the wisdom, experience and self-control to do so successfully . . . we repudiated entirely customary morals, conventions and traditional wisdom . . . we recognised no moral obligation on us, no inner sanction, to conform or to obey. Before heaven we claimed to be our own judge in our own case.

While it professes a special kind of conscientious objection, it is exactly the kind attributed to Keynes by Bell:

> He was not a pacifist; he did not object to fighting in any circumstances; he objected to being made to fight. Good liberal that he was, he objected to conscription. He would not fight because Lloyd George, Horatio Bottomley and Lord Northcliffe told him to (*Old Friends*).

As with all else that Keynes wrote, the words of his Tribunal statement are carefully weighed. It is clear that he was not claiming exemption as a pacifist: he did not argue that there were no conceivable circumstances in which he would voluntarily offer himself for military service. But he was 'not prepared on such an issue to surrender my right of decision.' His attitude was that of many honest and sincere liberals of the time. His aquaintance Sir John Simon resigned from Asquith's Cabinet on precisely this issue and then volunteered for military service. It is a view of the rights of the individual that is in danger of extinction today. In Keynes's case it amounted to something more fundamental than a sop to Bloomsbury.

5

Dr. Melchior

Keynes was intensely preoccupied during the five years of his life following the First World War with the treatment of Germany, and the problem continued to concern him for a decade thereafter. His devotion to this cause was not a blindly partisan action, but the pursuit of something he felt, in justice and in reason, had to be done. In this he was much affected by the personality of one man, the subject of his posthumously-published memoir, 'Dr. Melchior: a Defeated Enemy'—with whom Keynes wrote that he had 'one of the most curious intimacies in the world, and some very strange passages of experience.'[1]

The year 1919 was an extraordinary one for Keynes. In that year he bore great responsibilities and laboured under intense stress, suffered disillusion and disappointment, and 'in a sort of a way', as he put it, fell in love—idealistically—with a former enemy. He might have had a nervous breakdown, but being the sort of person he was, he thought better of it and wrote a best-seller, *The Economic Consequences of the Peace*, instead.

It was a dramatic change in style and *modus operandi*. The proper, capable *Economic Journal* editor and contributor, the coolly efficient draftsman of Treasury memoranda, broke away from his established academic and official audience and stepped out on a larger stage—to address himself to the civilized world, no less. The changed style still expressed Keynes's fundamental polemical attitudes evident in all that he wrote from his first self-confident minutes for the India Office—his indignation at injustice and championship of the oppressed, his optimistic reliance on the appeal to common sense, and his faith in the final triumph of the intellect. These attitudes had become somewhat broadened and refined by time and serious responsibility, but what happened at the Paris peace conference set all their elements afire.

Keynes himself admitted that *The Economic Consequences of the Peace* was the child of much emotion. For four years he had performed efficiently, and at times brilliantly, as the perfect civil servant, forgetting his scruples towards a conscriptive government in the heady excitement of managing millions. He was like the young officer proving his mettle and learning to enjoy his war. But the deliberations at Paris turned out to be a different sort of experience for him—a scarifying return to the battlefield to pick up the dead and dying.

Keynes came to Paris in January 1919 as the Treasury's chief representative at the conference and their acknowledged expert on reparations. He was immediately caught up in the problem of financing food supplies for Germany, which brought him face to face with the German financial representatives. He first saw Carl Melchior, his opposite number, across a bridge-table in a crowded railway carriage at Trèves, in company with the other Germans 'with drawn dejected faces and tired staring eyes, like men who had been hammered on the Stock Exchange'. Then,

> from amongst them stepped forward in the middle place a very small man, exquisitely clean, very well and neatly dressed, with a high stiff collar which seemed cleaner and whiter than an ordinary collar . . . his eyes gleaming straight at us, with extraordinary sorrow in them, yet like an honest animal at bay. . . .
>
> This Jew, for such, though not by appearance, I afterwards learnt him to be,* and he only, upheld the dignity of defeat.

Although the British and the Americans had every intention of

---

* Keynes seems to have shared the commonly accepted anti-Semitism of the British middle and upper classes of his time. In the thirties the editor of the American *New Republic* was shocked by one of his milder *obiter dicta* and protested that the readers of this journal would never stand for it. Keynes's attitude was curious, considering the important and influential roles that several Jewish friends played at different periods in his life. It also appears that on his visits to the United States he moved to a large extent in Jewish intellectual circles. The hitherto unpublished memoir of Einstein (in *Essays in Biography, Collected Writings*) casts a little light on this paradox.

delivering the food in question, the French made obstacles and the Germans were loathe to pay for it by giving up their gold and their ships. As the meetings dragged to a standstill, Keynes sensed in Melchior his own feeling of hopelessness and on impulse asked permission of the senior British representative to speak with the head of the German delegation privately. Terrified out of his wits—in his own words—with what he was doing, he protested his sincerity and that of his government. Melchior promised to ask Weimar for more discretion to act but said he had little hope of success. Speaking 'with the passionate pessimism of the Jew', he voiced his fears for the future of civilization. Both men were much moved. 'In a sort of a way,' Keynes wrote, 'I was in love with him.'

After a second private exchange with Melchior the desired transfer of food was accomplished. Then, at Keynes's instigation, the German representatives were brought together with their allied counterparts at the Chateau Villette near Paris in an attempt to exchange information that would further understanding on both sides and enable a wiser settlement. With Keynes as a sympathetic chairman the Germans were asked to present their views. As described by one of them, Max Warburg, in privately published memoirs, Keynes was punctiliously correct; only by his manner of listening did they sense his desire to enter into their problems.

During the Paris conference Lloyd George encouraged Keynes's moderate opinions on reparations as a political counter-weight to the wild expectations of some members of his Cabinet. When Keynes revived his own pre-armistice proposal for an all-round cancellation of inter-allied debt backed by a bond scheme for the restoration of German and European credit (his 'grand scheme for the rehabilitation of Europe', as he proudly described it for his mother),[2] the plan was adopted and presented to Wilson, Clemenceau and Orlando as official British policy. Wilson, wanting to get the United States out of the banking business in Europe, rejected the scheme outright; he accurately pointed out that the allies were in the process of taking away from Germany all her sources of wealth, her very means of recovery. It was a bitter pill for Keynes who had recognized what was happening all too well.

The Economic Consequences of the Peace gives some measure of Keynes's horror at the cumulative stripping of right after right from Germany and the imposition of obligation on obligation on her generations to come. 'Certainly if I was in the Germans' place, I'd rather die than sign such a peace,' Keynes wrote to his mother, 14 May 1919. Depressed by the fate of his brave proposal and exhausted by five months of overwork (the Treasury representation had been chronically short-staffed)—and in what he could still call years later 'an enraged and tormented state of mind'—he warned his superiors of his intention to resign. For a while he stayed on to protest against a similarly harsh and unreasoning treatment of Austria. Before he left he produced a final memorandum for Lloyd George showing how Germany could undertake the physical restoration of France and Belgium as an alternative means of reparation.

General Smuts told Keynes that one could only leave the field of battle *dead*. Keynes preferred to leave it alive, and to retire to that haven and stronghold of middle-class Victorians and Edwardians in search of peace and quiet, the bed. 'I . . . only rise for interviews with the Chancellor of the Exchequer, Smuts, the Prime Minister and such', he reassured his mother (3 June). What would have signified a nervous breakdown to a later generation was simply a strategic retreat. By the end of June he had started his book.

Keynes was urged in several quarters to tone down parts of the book before its publication but he changed little, feeling that for better or worse he had to tell the story as he saw it. When it was published, the most telling criticism came from American representatives at the conference, who looked to a gradual re-working of the treaty in accordance with the economic facts, rather than the drastic revision that Keynes called for. Keynes acknowledged the strength of this position, but he had burned his bridges and would not retreat from his moral stand.

It is interesting to speculate on the intensity of that commitment. He had championed causes before but with no worlds lost. A. C. Pigou, Bertrand Russell and Gerald Shove suffered obloquy and, in the case of the latter two, damaged careers as conscientious objectors, while Keynes was lucky enough to be able both to take a stand and collect a C.B. The Cambridge Apostles of

Keynes's 'early beliefs' endeavoured to explore and face such moral dilemmas as honestly as was humanly possible, and Pigou, Russell and Shove, who with Keynes were all Apostles, made an outright commitment to pacifism in 1916. Keynes, who was not a pacifist, was excused from military service by a government that recognized he was more valuable in the Treasury than in the trenches. Although he certainly intended to attract attention in the considered declaration that he wrote for the military tribunal, the circumstances robbed him of making any practical point. So it was not until the ordeal of Paris, and the age of 35 going on 36, that he was confronted with an over-riding emotional necessity to commit himself.

The final clue to Keynes's commitment is to be found in the memoir 'Dr. Melchior', rather than in his early beliefs. The drama of those early meetings must have intensified for Keynes the profound effect that Melchior's personality had on those who knew him. 'Who is that German with the room-filling modesty?' a French politician who was an astute judge of men was known to have asked. This suggests an arrogance, however, that was belied by the affectionate evidence of Melchior's friends and associates.

Melchior was indeed an extraordinary human being—if by no other testimony than that thirty-four years after his death his surviving Hamburg friends collaborated to publish a collection of essays in his memory.[3] Early in his career he had been a judge, before he joined the banking firm of M. M. Warburg as a partner and became an international banker of high reputation and skill. Officially and unofficially during the succession of negotiations over what Germany was to pay and not pay, he laboured selflessly for the good of his country and the cause of what was right. The bankers and civil servants who knew him wrote without self-consciousness of his purity and nobility of spirit, of his disciplined objectivity in search of truth and justice, his fastidious and cultivated mind, and the inherent personal reserve that yet allowed him to be humanly and delightfully approachable, especially to his younger colleagues.

Wounded as a captain early in the war, he became director of the central government food purchasing agency where his skill as a negotiator was clearly apparent. Anti-Semitism caused him to

resign in 1917, but he had won both the respect of the Kaiser's
Government and of the Socialist grain-controllers of Roumania
and the Ukraine whom he had been charged to placate. The new
republic at Weimar trusted him to represent them in the armistice
proceedings. With the other members of the German delegation
he recommended rejection of the conditions of the draft treaty; as
they left Versailles they were stoned by a French crowd. When
the Weimar officials signed the treaty as an expedient, Melchior,
like Keynes, resigned.

From the start Keynes was attracted and fascinated by Melchior
and quickly came to have a great respect for him, a feeling which
was reciprocated. He spoke of 'my dear Melchior', as their friendship steadied and grew in affection. They were alike in so many
ways: sharing an empathy with others, a devotion to the cause of
truth, love of country, generous hospitality, art collecting. There
was also an attraction of opposites. Keynes's mind was like
quick-silver; it ran here, there and everywhere and could never
be caught and bottled up. But Melchior was steadfast—his mind
arrived at truth like the needle of a compass, held calm and
unwavering by the strength of his will.

So, I believe, Melchior for a time became a touchstone for
Keynes's conscience. This was the reason that, 'on impulse', he
asked Melchior in October 1919 to meet him in Amsterdam. At
the house of the Dutch banker Vissering the two for the first time
were able to talk naturally as friends. Melchior, who had declined
an important government office (as he often did thereafter), had
returned to private life and banking in Hamburg. Keynes had
finished his book. Now he read Melchior his chapter on Wilson,
holding it up to his alter ego for confirmation. As Keynes wrote in
his memoir, his friend was deeply affected, apprehending in the
failure of the President

> . . . neither profound causes, nor inevitable fate, nor magnifi-
> cent wickedness. The Tablets of the Law, it was Melchior's
> thought at that moment, had perished meanly.

This sharing of understanding and goals led to another
'strange passage of experience' which Keynes did not relate. It
was on a more prosaic level than were the high emotional

encounters of 'Dr. Melchior', but it was no less unusual as an experience and it also had important consequences.

Melchior wrote with deep seriousness of the profound impression that *The Economic Consequences of the Peace* had made on him (in contrast to the titillation felt by Keynes's gossip-eager English acquaintance). Keynes and Melchior continued to correspond.[4] As Keynes pursued his journalistic crusade for revision of the treaty he wrote to Melchior for information that could be obtained only from the German side, and when he undertook the editorship of the *Manchester Guardian* series of supplements, 'Reconstruction in Europe', he asked Melchior to suggest and approach German contributors. Melchior performed this task with modest efficiency (he was a very quick worker), producing the kind of distinguished names and co-operation that Keynes sought to give prestige and authenticity to his venture. In April 1922 they both attended the Genoa Conference, Melchior as an adviser to the German delegation and Keynes as correspondent for the *Manchester Guardian*. They both disapproved of the secret diplomacy of the Treaty of Rapallo between the Germans and the Russians manoeuvred there, and when Keynes heard that Melchior had left the conference he wrote that he was not surprised.

In August 1922 Keynes visited Melchior's Hamburg during that city's Overseas Week. He addressed an economic congress, saw his friend, and renewed acquaintance with Wilhelm Cuno, manager of the Hamburg-Amerika shipping line, who had been another of the German advisers at Paris. Keynes was alarmed by what he saw of the German inflation and the threat of its political consequences, and he wrote two reports describing conditions for the *Manchester Guardian*. In November he was invited to Berlin as one of a group of foreign experts asked to pronounce on the possibility of stabilizing the mark.

Late in November 1922 Cuno became the head of a new German government, an insecure coalition—Keynes mentioned it to Melchior as 'a wretched affair'—in which industrialists predominated. Melchior, apolitical as always but close to the counsels of the new Cabinet, saw hope for a more active policy regarding the reparations situation, which had reached a dangerous stalemate with France. In England Lloyd George's coalition had been ousted by the Conservatives. Andrew Bonar Law was the new

Prime Minister and Stanley Baldwin the Chancellor of the Exchequer; Keynes knew both personally from working with them in the Treasury. Both Keynes and Melchior were close to the seats of power.

Their correspondence became increasingly active. Melchior wrote, 5 December, of trying in Berlin to bring about 'a clearer, more detailed and more concrete declaration' of what payment Germany could offer in the diplomatic note that was planned for presentation at the approaching conference of allied premiers in London. He said that he had shown the contents of two of Keynes's letters to Cuno and his Foreign Minister and Minister of Finance in the hope that 'your words may contribute to clear the exceedingly menacing and possibly tragic situation.'

In the first of these letters (17 November) Keynes had criticized an earlier German proposal to intervene in support of the mark on the foreign exchange instead of stabilizing it (as had been advised by the majority of the invited experts, Keynes among them) and emphasized the impossibility of Germany's obtaining a foreign loan without stabilization of the mark. In the second (1 December) he had decried the German government's habit of putting forward ambiguous proposals; the only chance of progress, in his opinion, was for Germany to make a very clear-cut offer which could be supported by some of the allies, who could then demand that those who did not accept it should put forward a workable alternative.

The new German note, although still vague and hurriedly put together, was considered a positive improvement, even by the francophile *Times*. Premier Poincaré, however, attributed the improvement to his own threats to annex the Rhinelands and occupy the Ruhr.

During the autumn of 1922 Sir John Bradbury, British representative on the Reparations Commission and Keynes's former chief at the Treasury, had drawn up an elaborate plan for settling both the German liability and the inter-allied debts. Keynes had seen all four versions of this, produced his own version, and discussed Bradbury's plan with Bonar Law. Bradbury's proposal was finally adopted as British policy for the Paris conference of prime ministers in January 1923. Although Keynes was sceptical of any settlement resulting at this stage, he praised the British proposal to

Melchior (5 January) as 'a fine intellectual performance, making an honest attempt to settle the whole question on more or less rational lines.'

The French refused to consider the Bradbury plan and the conference broke down before this letter was posted. Keynes added: 'We have now got, all of us, to be very cool and careful. I'm not sure I don't envy Cuno his job!'

'So you see,' Melchior remarked, forwarding this extract to Cuno, 8 January, 'there are even people in the secure position of Cambridge professors who envy you. May this be a good omen!'

Melchior had visited the Paris conference unofficially. On 9 January he wrote to Keynes at length about the British proposal, his own fears for what France would do, and the moral crisis ahead for Germany.

On 11 January the French entered the Ruhr. 'I wish I could guage the depth of German feeling,' Keynes replied (17 January).

> . . . the extent of the sacrifices which the average citizen is prepared to make rather than give way is going to dominate the eventual result, as against any possible political or economic considerations.
>
> The proceedings of France are viewed by almost everyone in England with anger and disgust. . . . Our sympathies are profoundly with you.

Again Melchior forwarded Keynes's remarks to Cuno, with the comment that he was convinced that Keynes's letters 'even though addressed to me, are not intended exclusively for me.'

As these events were unfolding early in 1923 Keynes was involved in taking over the weekly journal, the *Nation and the Athenaeum*, with the aim of establishing a voice for more progressive Liberal opinion. In the first issue under his chairmanship of the editorial board Keynes began a series of his own articles on Britain's foreign policy, calling for more definite and vigorous action by the government. France now controlled the economy of the Ruhr; supported by the rest of Germany, the Ruhr's inhabitants had adopted a policy of passive resistance. There was little sympathy in Britain for the behaviour of the French, but a few Cabinet die-hards made the Conservatives hesitate to take a stand.

In a new note Germany attempted a fresh departure by offering to submit the amount of her liability to an impartial tribunal—unfortunately clouding the issue with muddy language, the result of internal compromise. ('Heaven knows that propaganda is a sinful thing!' wrote Keynes in the *Nation*. 'But there is nothing wrong in writing a short sentence.') France remained intransigent while the British Foreign Secretary, Lord Curzon, was only mildly encouraging. Keynes evidently transmitted his impatience in a letter to Melchior, who replied (14 May), 'I should heartily welcome it, if you would carry out your intention to come over to Germany and lift the veil.'

Keynes did something even more quietly dramatic. He wrote privately and directly to Reichschancellor Cuno, 'suggesting' with all due humility, the form that the German answer to Curzon should take.

Dear Dr. Cuno,

I have of course been following recent events with deep pessimism and profound sympathy for the efforts you have been taking. Nothing, in my opinion, is of any utility at present, except something which makes clear to the average Englishman and the average American the true purposes of France and Germany respectively. It is hopeless to attempt to satisfy France. Any further reply you make to Lord Curzon can have no object except to affect favourable British and American opinion. It may be useless to say anything. But I venture, very humbly, to enclose a suggestion of the line which a further reply might take. I have shown this suggestion to no one. The reply must be short and simple and dignified. What I suggest does not amount to anything novel. Please excuse my presumption in sending it. A foreigner naturally feels much delicacy in making a suggestion.

Yours sincerely,

J. M. Keynes (16 May 1923)

Keynes's enclosed 'Suggested German Reply to Lord Curzon' consisted of four paragraphs. It stated: Germany previously offered payment in terms of a loan because she understood that this was what the allies contemplated. She was willing to comply with the British proposal of payment by an annuity, provided that the amount was determined by an independent tribunal and was one she believed she could fulfill. She was willing to discuss the question of securities. She could not agree to occupation of her territory beyond the limits of the Treaty of Versailles and regretted that reparation payments were impossible as long as occupation continued.

Keynes sent his letter to Cuno the 16th of May. On the 22nd Melchior wrote:

I had occasion to see our mutual friend—who spent the Whitsuntide holidays in the country near Hamburg—and to discuss matters fully with him. He showed me your letter . . . [which Cuno asked Melchior to answer.] I would mention that besides him and myself nobody else knows of this correspondence, and that he is most grateful to you for your letter and your exceedingly important suggestions.

Melchior 'imagined' that the German offer would be a maximum of 30 milliards, probably too optimistic, he said, in view of her real capacity. She desired to raise the amount by a loan, but if this was impossible would assent to an annuity. She would repeat her willingness for arbitration. Keynes, replying (24 May), said that he was worried by the mention of a specific sum and particularly of 30 milliards which he said would seem too small to the allies, but he urged that Germany should stand fast and not undertake what she could not carry out.

Baldwin had succeeded Bonar Law as Prime Minister—'a very nice and sensible man who will always behave well and fairly (I know him intimately),' Keynes confided in the same letter.

He continued,

Lord Curzon is a bad influence and only behaves as well as he does because the French have irritated him intensely. (If the French were sensible they would flatter him to the utmost and they could then do anything with him.)

On 26 May the new Cabinet was announced. Lord Robert Cecil was appointed to head British representation at the League of Nations and Reginald McKenna designated as Chancellor of the Exchequer—'two very influential figures who do *not* believe in huge figures,' Keynes, who again knew both men personally, wrote to Melchior the same day. Keynes counselled that Germany now make a conciliatory reply asking for a conference:

> I can see very well what lines such a reply might take. I have half a mind to pay you a flying visit in Hamburg next weekend, leaving London on Thursday or Friday evening. If this would be convenient and not undesirable in your judgement, will you send me a telegram to 46 Gordon Square? I could collect some important opinions before leaving here.

Among his papers from this time Keynes left a brief draft, clearly his idea of the sort of private appeal Curo might make to Baldwin as one businessman to another, which Keynes wrote with his knowledge of both their characters. It makes explicit his pressing desire to cut through diplomatic protocol and meaningless formulae. 'Dear Mr. Prime Minister,' it begins.

> Perhaps it is permitted in the unusual conditions of to-day for one holding my office to write a few words to one holding yours, as a private man, yet expressing feelings of public consequence.
>
> I have held my office six months. It lies outside the scope of my career and my ambition. I would gladly lay it down. I accepted it with the thought that I might contribute something, because as a business man I have been trained to discuss frankly in international negotiations. I hoped to meet face to face those who speak for the Allied countries. But time passes by. Great misfortunes accumulate. I am imprisoned in Berlin, powerless to escape from the sterile interchange of diplomatic notes. I still think that we can only get out of this impasse by establishing a direct contact.

Melchior urged Keynes to come to Hamburg. Keynes saw Baldwin for an hour on Wednesday 30 May. ('I have something I want badly to ask you,' he wrote the Prime Minister in a note. 'I have had certain communications with Germany in the last few days. They may be going to do something not very helpful, yet might be influenced into more fruitful paths.')[5] He dined with McKenna the same day. In the meantime Cuno had asked Melchior to come to Berlin, where Keynes met him on Friday, 1 June. The only known account of this episode was dictated by Melchior for his diary. Asked by Cuno and the Foreign Minister, von Rosenberg, to comment on a draft reply to the Allies, he prepared a version requesting oral negotiations, the kind of informal diplomacy at which he himself was so skilled. He obtained permission to discuss the draft with Keynes, who suggested some changes. The next day Keynes talked with Cuno and Rosenberg privately and again with Melchior. Melchior and Keynes were able to dissuade the Chancellor and the Foreign Minister from making the offer in terms of a specific figure, the strategy being urged on them by some of the political elements on whose support they depended, as being sure to be rejected out-of-hand by the French.

On Saturday evening, 2 June, Keynes, Melchior and Rosenberg were dinner guests of Cuno; on Sunday, 3 June, Cuno, Keynes and Melchior had tea with Rosenberg. While the four had become convinced that the note in the form that they had decided was right, they were not confident of success. The Germans emphasized to Keynes that an unfavourable reaction in England could cause the downfall of Cuno's government—which they were sure would be followed by Communist outbreaks and even civil war. His task would be to influence the British press, especially *The Times*, which under the new editorship of Geoffrey Dawson had become friendly to him and less biased towards France. Keynes's own hope was that a favourable reception of the note would result in Britain calling a new inter-allied conference at which it would be possible to prepare for a meeting with German participation.

Back in London in time for his fortieth birthday, Keynes described 'The Situation in Germany' for his 'Finance and Investment' column in the *Nation* and remarked anonymously in the same journal's 'Events of the Week' on the change in tone and method of approach of the new German Note and the extraordinary unanimity of approval in the British press: *The Times*, the *Manchester Guardian*, the *Spectator* and the *New Statesman* had all agreed that it offered a fair basis for negotiation. He also wrote the *Nation and the Athenaeum's* unsigned leading article of 16 June 1923, urging Baldwin to make a firm statement in favour of accepting a settlement based on the German proposal and suitably generous to France.

Cuno wrote thanking Keynes for 'all the support you gave our memorandum. You were very successful indeed. I do whatever I can to keep the German people quiet. . . .' He said that he was astonished at the strong determination of those in the occupied areas to continue their passive resistance (a tactic with which Cuno in particular was associated). He feared hostile attempts by Poincaré to break their morale before the British could succeed in opening the way for negotiation.

> . . . you know our very difficult situation and therefore it is of the utmost importance that your government will not permit the French government to ask us for conditions which we are not able to accept. You know I am ready to do whatever I can to bring the problem to a *fair* solution but I never can accept conditions which I cannot fulfil, even if I would have to resign and to leave my place to anybody else, who may be willing to promise but never would be able to meet those conditions (16 June 1923).

During the summer Keynes wrote again in both the *Nation* and *The Times* calling for a more decisive British attitude. Poincaré remained unbending but the British Note of 11 August came out in favour of an impartial inquiry into Germany's ability to pay. Although Cuno's government fell the same day, a stronger government succeeded him. In the *Nation* of 15 September Keynes anonymously suggested that Britain make a friendly offer to collaborate with the Germans in studying their financial problem.

Passive resistance was given up in the Ruhr but the stalemate continued and separatist movements seriously threatened the break-up of Germany. Keynes asked Melchior what England could do; in a letter for publication he wrote, 'We are most of us oppressed and terrified by the developments in central Europe, enraged by what appears to be the policy of France, and disgusted by the weakness and ineptitude of our own government.' Evidently he asked Melchior to come to London during the Imperial Conference in October. Although he was no longer a confidant of the German Cabinet, Melchior came, ostensibly on business, and Keynes arranged for him to meet and talk with Smuts, who was in London for the conference and was much concerned with reparations at this time.

This conference led to the British proposal of another inquiry into Germany's capacity to pay and a train of events which finally culminated in the Dawes Plan, a complex compromise. In the *Nation* Keynes prophesied its eventual break-down; he said that Germany could not make the transfers to pay for the foreign loans allowed by the plan without grinding down her workers impossibly. This was the argument for his *Economic Journal* article on 'The German Transfer Problem' of March 1929. Melchior, who was for a time a member of a committee safeguarding German interests under the plan, also perceived the danger of these loans. On 4 March 1929 he wrote to Keynes agreeing with the article, his letter—the last of his kept among Keynes's papers—as always slightly formal, in the custom of the time, beginning 'My dear Keynes,' and ending 'Please remember me to Mrs. Keynes./ With kindest regards,/ Yours very sincerely,/ C. Melchior.'

Keynes saw Melchior when he visited Germany with his wife Lydia Lopokova in 1926 to lecture on 'The End of Laissez-Faire' and again with her on the way to and from Russia in April 1928. From 1928 onwards Melchior was much involved in the succession of meetings which led to the final settlement of reparations at Lausanne. The 1929 and 1930 conferences at Paris and the Hague preparing for the adoption of the Young Plan were periods of great strain for him. At the conclusion of the meetings at The Hague he was appointed as a German representative on the administrative board of the newly-created International Bank at Basel.

It is thought that Keynes probably read 'Dr. Melchior' to the Bloomsbury Memoir Club in the summer of 1931, or at least before January 1932. He would have had opportunities to see Melchior within that period. Melchior was in London as an adviser to Chancellor Brüning at the time of the German 'standstill' on foreign payments; as Brüning's adviser he attended three important financial meetings during 1931. In January 1932 Keynes briefly visited Hamburg and had a talk with Brüning in Berlin, presumably arranged by Melchior.

The sight of Germany 'in the grip of the most terrible deflation that any nation has experienced,' of Hamburg with 'many miles of ships laid up silent in its harbour', haunted Keynes on his return. He wrote in the *New Statesman* of a Germany still spick and span as ever . . . like a beautiful machine at a standstill, ready to spring to life at the press of a button, but meanwhile inanimate. But while the machine sleeps, its crew cannot sleep.

We need to have an imaginative apprehension of all this. The reparations problem has become a matter of human feelings, of deep popular gusts of passion, and, consequently, of very simple reactions and decisions. It is high time for the 'experts' to leave the room. . . .

This visit must have been the last time that Keynes met Melchior, who, partly as a result of the strain of these meetings, was fatally ill. He lived to see the settlement at Lausanne that spelled the end of reparations in June 1932, but the future was clouded. His last months were spent in trying to work out some means for protecting German non-Aryans from persecution. As a lover of his country he still hoped to find a temporary compromise by which German Jews and others could survive. In the Hamburg memoir his friends wrote that they were glad he did not live to see what happened.

Melchior had been a bachelor, but during the last year of his life he married a French woman from a distinguished family, with whom he had been emotionally involved for some time. Their son was born after his death. In 1945, after the war, Marie Melchior de Molènes wrote to Keynes from the Dordogne to inquire about the possibility of arranging an au pair holiday in England for the twelve-year-old boy and herself. Keynes had never met her, and his letter to her reads[6] as if aeons of time had elapsed since he had last seen and written of his old friend.

'Dear Madame Melchior de Molènes,' Keynes replied (9 February 1946),

I have been much interested to have your letter and hear from you and to know that you and Carl Melchior's son are still well and in reasonably good conditions. I shall never forget the intimate relations I had with your husband after the last war and how greatly I respected his character and his mind.

I wish I could help you and the boy to a holiday in this country. But I am afraid that the practical difficulties in the way are still very great. There is an extreme shortage of house-room, and pleasant holiday quarters are practically unobtainable unless you are prepared to give a great deal of time to searching for them. And, as for living with families, since few families have any servants worth mentioning, their whole job is to keep the numbers in the house down as low as possible. The old conditions in which what you suggest would have been so easy and advantageous have simply faded away. I am afraid I should be giving you bad advice unless I should suggest anything but that you should wait for better times.

Yours sincerely,
Keynes

Much had been consumed by time and the gas chambers of the Nazis. Keynes had lived through the stratagems and the depredations of another war. Within a few months he too would be dead.

Part II
Keynes
and His Environment

6
The Social and Intellectual Origins
of *The General Theory*

Understanding of *The General Theory*—its motivation, definition of problems and style of presentation—can be illuminated by consideration of the personality of Keynes himself and of the social and intellectual milieu in which he made his career. It is a particularly rewarding exercize for the practising economic theorist interested in the ideas that shape economic policy-making.

Our treatment of this subject is necessarily and admittedly impressionistic and open to the charge of overgeneralization. We discuss it under the following topics: the economic problems of society as Keynes saw them; Keynes's political stance; his concept of the social role and professional duty of an economist; Keynes and the Marshallian tradition of economics; and some characteristics of *The General Theory*. We conclude by speculating on the question of whether, had circumstances been different, there would have been another *General Theory*, and commenting on Keynes as a subject for research in the history of economic thought.

The General Theory is no seamless garment of tightly woven theory. It is a variegated patchwork applied to the classical coat, which had become frayed and torn by the wear and strain of a society growing and changing too rapidly to be well suited with the same old clothes. The patches are of many cloths and colours; like garments churning in a washing machine they rose to the surface, to be pulled down again by strong currents which again forced them up to the light of day—in the variety and multiplicity of ideas circulating in Keynes's head. A surfacing idea would be picked out—perhaps tossed back, only to be chosen again before being pressed into use—or again discarded. The patches were applied to the coat, which was held up for the scrutiny of colleagues; often stitches were unpicked and all was to do again. But from the worked-over patches evolved a new coat, dazzling those unwary of its origins with the brightness of its colours and the commodiousness of its cut, and distracting them from appreciating the painful working and re-working of the materials that went into its making.

That is probably more than enough for the time being of that particular metaphor. But Keynes and his 'Circus' of the early 1930s, following the example of Dennis Robertson, had a penchant for working out fundamental theory in terms of examples using bootmakers, tailors, and other mundane personages of everyday life, so the metaphor may be excused.

Let us begin by contemplating the very drastic and far-reaching changes undergone by European society in the 1920s and 1930s. Keynes's life spanned those years: he watched the funeral of Queen Victoria as a member of the Eton College Officer Training Corps and he presided at the birth of the International Monetary Fund and the International Bank for Reconstruction and Development, which, it was hoped, would make possible a new era of peace and prosperity among nations.

Keynes's Cambridge and Bloomsbury friends questioned and challenged the manners and morals inherited from middle-class Victorian England; in the aftermath of the 1914–18 war their reaction, if not their questioning, became general. In Chapter 2 of *The Economic Consequences of the Peace* Keynes depicted the seemingly comfortable middle-class order and stability of pre-1914 Europe; few people realized, he wrote, 'the intensely unusual, unstable, complicated, unreliable, temporary nature' of the economic organization which the war swept away. Whole countries were made paupers and faced famine—while elsewhere flappers cut short their skirts and their hair and smoked cigarettes to prove their emancipation. Steadily increasing unemployment impoverished and demoralized the workers, and inflation consumed the income and the capital of the business and professional classes. The worst inflation occurred in Germany, where a pair of boots bought one week cost as much to resole the next.

Keynes visited Germany to advise on stabilization of the mark and was deeply struck by the disintegration of public confidence that accompanied the collapse of the monetary standard of value. In *The Economic Consequences of the Peace* he had quoted Lenin as saying that the best way to destroy the capitalist system was to debauch the currency, and demonstrated how inflation arbitrarily confiscated the wealth of some citizens and rendered windfall profits to others. Dark tides of Communism threatened to sweep in from the East. Fear of the Bolsheviks seemed almost the only unifying force at the Paris Peace Conference, where the statesmen of Europe allowed a continent to be carved up to satisfy their immediate narrow political goals.

Keynes's first concern in 1919 was for the restoration of the fabric of European society. His own articles in the *Manchester Guardian* 'Reconstruction in Europe' series focused on the problems of inflation and deflation and the state of the foreign exchanges; out of them came *A Tract on Monetary Reform*, published in 1923, preaching orthodox theory in favour of the regulation of money. It is interesting that at this time he regarded his country as part of the Continent; but his involvement with the Liberal Party's soul-searching during the 1920s in connection with their 'Industrial Inquiry' soon directed his attention to problems peculiar to England. The glaringly immediate problem was unemployment, which affected one third of the population and was to become the crux of *The General Theory of Employment, Interest, and Money*. Along with unemployment, Keynes identified the arbitrary and inequitable distribution of wealth, another serious fault in the social and economic structure, for which he also set himself to find a remedy.

A number of Keynes's writings from the 1920s explore his own attitudes towards society and what he saw as the political possibilities for social and economic reform. In *The End of Laissez-Faire* (1926) he contradicted the Benthamite teaching that private interest coincided with the general good: the giraffes with the longest necks got the tenderest leaves.

If we have the welfare of the giraffes at heart, we must not overlook the sufferings of the shorter necks who are starved out, or the sweet leaves which fall to the ground and are trampled underfoot in the struggle, or the overfeeding of the long-necked ones, or the evil look of anxiety or struggling greediness which overcasts the mild faces of the herd.

Keynes wanted a society that was at the same time economically just and economically efficient. With this in mind he laid down his 'Agenda' for government: not to attempt to do things that private enterprise or semiautonomous public bodies were doing well already, but to apply itself to those things that were not being done at all. Here at different times he proposed some far-reaching areas for government activity, but a central and common factor in all his prescriptions was the management of savings and investment. He was careful, however, not to recommend measures that would discourage business—'For it never pays to render the entrepreneur poor and seedy'—and would not starve 'the goose that lays the golden eggs before we have discovered how to replace her. We must tax her eggs instead.' The businessman would be encouraged to make his profit; instead of receiving higher wages, the workers were to be benefited by social insurance, pensions, state-provided recreation and education, housing and family allowances—to be paid for by the businessmen's taxes.

Keynes's general iconoclasm misled some people into thinking that he would support socialism; but its tenets were too doctrinaire for his free spirit. 'I fancy that I have played in my mind with the possibilities of greater social changes than come within the present philosophies of, let us say, Mr. Sidney Webb, Mr. Thomas, or Mr. Wheatley,' he wrote, comparing himself with leading Labour lights. 'The republic of my imagination lies on the extreme left of celestial space. Yet—all the same—' he added, recognizing that his free-wheeling thoughts always winged their way back to roost, 'I feel that my true home, so long as they offer a roof and a floor, is still with the Liberals.'

With the hard days of the 1930s, economic nationalism became general as the countries of Europe turned inward to take care of their own and the totalitarian states solved their problems by regimentation of their peoples. At that time, Keynes's views reflected the trend towards policies of national self-sufficiency, in his advocacy of a revenue tariff, but he seemed not too comfortable in this posture. Both *The General Theory* and *How to Pay for the War* were answers to totalitarianism; Keynes placed the highest value on individual liberty of choice and would sacrifice variety to no man.

During the 1920s he took an active part in Liberal politics, speaking on platforms, editing the *Nation*, and framing election programmes based on government spending to relieve unemployment; but 'a certain coolness of temper' that seemed to him 'at the same time peculiarly *Liberal* in flavour, and also a much bolder and more desirable and more valuable political possession and endowment than sentimental ardours' intervened. In 1928, speaking at a conference on price levels, he remarked that the theory of money and credit policy was in a deplorable state and that he did not except himself from such criticism. He thought that economists should concentrate on this problem without too close an eye to current events. At this time he was struggling to get the *Treatise on Money* off his hands in order to clear the way for *The General Theory*. One suspects that all the time he was talking about politics he was more intensely and fundamentally interested in economics, and as he approached his main work he threw off his other guises and donned a high priest's robes.

Keynes liked to say that in the future economists would become humble competent specialists called in to make repairs, the big problems of maintaining a healthy economy all having been solved. But this throw-away line does not really correspond to his sense of his own importance and the importance of the task on which he was engaged.

Proposing the establishment of an 'Economic General Staff' to serve under the Economic Advisory Council set up by the Labour Government in 1929 (of which he was a member), he envisaged an expert body that would

> mark a transition in our conceptions of the functions and purposes of the State and a first measure toward the deliberate and purposive guidance of the evolution of our economic life . . . a recognition of the enormous part to be played in this by the scientific spirit as distinct from the sterility of the purely party attitude, which is never more out of place than in relation to complex matters of fact and interpretation regarding technical

difficulty . . . it would be an essay in the art of combining
representative institutions and the voice of the public opinion
with the realization by Governments of the best technical
advice in spheres where such advice can never, and should
not, have the last word or the power, but must be a necessary
ingredient in the decisions of those who have been entrusted
with the last word and with the power.

The economist so described is on the one hand buttressed by
his professional expertise, and on the other hand controlled by
the structure of responsibility in a parliamentary democracy. But
Keynes himself would never have filled the bill: although he
recommended (as many others have since) what he thought the
government of an orderly, well-functioning society should equip
itself with—it was not what he himself provided, welcome or not.
On the one hand, he was not an academic scientific economist,
but an all-purpose intellectual. His preparation was narrowly
Marshallian and lacking in knowledge of the literature of the field
of macroeconomics in which he chose to specialize. He devoted a
relatively small part of his time to economics as such, and for the
purpose relied heavily on conversations and exchanges of notes
and manuscripts with a few junior Cambridge colleagues and
students—just as he relied on intimate acquaintance with the
politically and financially powerful to keep himself informed on
world affairs. On the other hand, of course, he was no dispassionate scholar to be lured from his study only by a sense of duty
to his country and to its duly elected political leadership; instead,
he showered both public and politicians with his own diagnoses
of their problems and his own practical prescriptions for solving
them.

Keynes's own mandate can best be described as a simple matter of *noblesse oblige*. The evenings of uninhibited philosophical
discussion with his Apostolic brethren, which are the subject of
'My Early Beliefs,' gave him confidence in an audacity of thought
soaring into realms where anything was possible, that might
otherwise have been an equally arrogant confidence in the traditional attitudes of his class. Aside from the assurance of impeccable family background and education, he had the confidence
that comes from belonging in the inner circle of power, the

assurance of one who knows what is going on from the inside. He maintained the contacts made at the Paris Peace Conference; and was often consulted by former colleagues. He carefully cultivated influential acquaintances in politics and in the City of London. In 1930 he was a member both of the Government's backroom Economic Advisory Council and of the important Macmillan Committee on Finance and Industry. This latter group he immediately proceeded to instruct on how to think about economic problems according to the ideas he was evolving out of the *Treatise* in preparation for *The General Theory*. (Regarding one of his interventions, Professor T. E. Gregory was moved to write grumpily that he 'certainly obtained the impression that we were being presented by an ultimatum. "If you do not accept the explanation of the trade cycle as set forth by me, the alternative is to say that there is no explanation of the trade cycle at all . . ."').

So powerful was he, unofficially, that when he advocated public spending to reduce unemployment as part of the Liberal election campaign of 1929, the Treasury felt it necessary to go to the extraordinary length of issuing a white paper officially asserting that such a policy could not work—the so-called 'Treasury view' that later became a catchword for Keynesian caricature.

And all this power was directed to fulfilling the obligations to society implicit in conception and definition in his beginnings in turn-of-the-century Cambridge, where the family home was indeed a castle that protected its own, equipped them with both the best education available and a strong sense of moral responsibility to the less fortunate, and sent them out to do battle against the forces of evil and stupidity. That stupidity and ignorance, not malignant evil, were the chief villain to combat was a major principle of late nineteenth-century English social thought, along with faith in the resolvability of social problems by the application of intelligence and the obligation of charity to the unfortunate poor. Keynes's approach to the economic problems of his time was deeply rooted in this late-Victorian English ethic. He had a propensity for producing on any occasion a plan designed to kill any number of popularly wanted birds with a single stone, and a far less flattering tendency (documented in the Moggridge edition of his papers) to treat scholarly critics of the *Treatise* as either inherently or wilfully obtuse or as too petty to deserve his considered attention, or to pester them to define out-of-context terms that he claimed to be unable to understand.

The late-Victorian English ethic permeates the writings of Alfred Marshall, Keynes's main teacher and chief academic patron, and its social philosophy was brought to its economic apotheosis in the monumental work *The Economics of Welfare* produced by Marshall's successor A. C. Pigou. The influence of these two remained dominant in Keynes's scientific economic work, despite—or perhaps as evidenced in—the fact that *The General Theory* was the culmination of a 'long struggle of escape . . . from habitual modes of thought and expression.' The social philosophy that underlay Keynes's political stance, and which appears scattered throughout *The General Theory*, often in the form of unmotivated digressions, is essentially late Victorian and Pigovian in character. Had the late-Victorian world survived further into the twentieth century, Keynes might well have made his ultimate career in the civil service and his circle of Bloomsbury friends, though he might instead have become another one of those brilliant Oxbridge dons, maintaining academic respectability by dabbling in his subject when other calls on his time permitted, and unknown outside Oxbridge except for the occasional dazzlingly superior newspaper article or review. As it turned out, however, the Victorian world collapsed into monetary instability, followed in England by a decade of mass unemployment which made the Victorian (and Pigovian) concern with ameliorating the distribution of income in favour of the working classes pale into social irrelevance. Keynes retained it as super-cargo; but mass unemployment offered a far superior challenge to his talents. His Victorian background made him sublimely confident he could overcome by Victorian methods of reason and reform.

As was said, Keynes's general approach to economics was deeply and rather narrowly rooted in the Marshallian tradition. This was true, first, of his general social philosophy—which was strongly Victorian not only in its concern (already mentioned) with transferring income from the rich to the poor by the provision of social security and public goods through fiscal policy rather than through intervention in wage and price fixing, but also in its general optimism about the capacity of a limited further amount of capital accumulation and a great deal of intelligent policy-making between them to produce the good society in a reasonably short space of time. And it was also true (far more disastrously from some points of view, including that of a fair assessment of Keynes's ultimate place in the history of economic thought) of the technical equipment he had at his command in tackling his chosen area of specialization, macroeconomics.

To put the point briefly, the Marshallian tradition in micro-economics, so far as it went—that is, in the partial equilibrium formulation preferred by Marshall as suitable for conveying his message to his intended audience of businessmen and men of affairs—was both sound and subtle, a remarkable intellectual achievement. But it did leave some awkward lacunae. Notable are the failure to distinguish clearly between the welfare implications of increasing and decreasing returns—over which Pigou stumbled in the first version of *Welfare* and was censured by Frank Knight—and the fudging by Marshall and Pigou of the reconciliation of perfect competition at the industry level with the theory of the firm—which provided the opportunity for the independent development by Joan Robinson and Edward Chamberlin of the theory of imperfect or monopolistic competition. Most important from the macroeconomic viewpoint however, were on the one hand the theory's suppression of the concept of general equilibrium into a complication that should be kept in the back of one's mind whenever one engaged in partial equilibrium analysis, and on the other the absence of any very serious effort to deal with the fundamental complexities of capital theory.

Yet Keynes, as is well known, kept very close to the Marshallian tradition, not only in his use of the concepts of demand and supply as the framework for his analysis of the determination of aggregate output and employment in *The General Theory*, but in many points of detail. Of these, the assumption of perfect competition in the determination of prices from wages is worthy of note (unlike many of his followers, Keynes was never a convert to imperfect competition theories of industrial pricing), as is the assumption of a declining marginal real product of labor as employment increases. The latter gave him much trouble in distinguishing his analytical conclusion—that an increase in aggregate demand must reduce real wages—from the Pigovian proposition that a reduction in real (confused with money) wages was necessary to increase aggregate output and employment in the first place. His treatment of the marginal productivity of capital was also fairly conventional, though disguised by relabeling the concept as 'the marginal efficiency of capital'; and in consequence it left open the question of what determines the rate of investment. (As subsequent theorists have frequently rediscovered, however, he did have a scientifically useful theory of the rate of investment, carried over from the *Treatise*, in which that rate is determined by the supply response of new capital goods set by a broad variant of 'liquidity preference.')

The most fundamental reflection of the Marshallian tradition appears rather paradoxically to be Keynes's choice of the wage unit as the unit of measurement, since this permitted him to identify money prices with real prices and conveniently apply large chunks of Marshallian microeconomics to monetary theory—though at the expense of having to stuff the whole question of price-level expectations into the determination of the schedule of the marginal efficiency of capital, where it is only too easily forgotten. (To this day, the tendency to assume that money prices are stable and to identify real and money rates of interest, at least as a first approximation, distinguishes the Keynesian tradition in monetary theory, as represented most prominently by the Yale School, from the neo-quantity-theory tradition.)

The crucial limitation of the Marshallian tradition, however, from the standpoint of tackling the macroeconomic problems with which Keynes was concerned academically, lay precisely in its concentration on microeconomics, based on the assumption that monetary disturbances could be ignored in a first approximation. This was a reasonable assumption for the late-Victorian era, in which business cycles were generally short and sharp and affected trade and commerce rather than industry and employment; but it left a disastrous vacuum for economists concerned with Britain's post-World War I macroeconomic problems to fill for themselves from what they could make of the master's fragmentary discussions of the subject.

Specifically, Marshall never got around to writing the book on money that was to have accompanied and complemented the *Principles*; what he left instead was mostly the quantity equation,

modified to bring it within the umbrella of marginal utility theory
by means of some largely undeveloped insights into money as a
form of wealth the holding of which in relation to income could be
explained by the convenience of the services it yielded. It was, of
course, Keynes's great theoretical contribution in the *Treatise* and
The General Theory to build on and extend these insights into an
explicitly capital-theoretic approach to the demand for money
based on distinguishing the characteristics of money from those
of other forms of wealth—and that achievement has been
absorbed, with insufficient and grudging acknowledgement,
into the rival neo-quantity-theory tradition. But the quantity
equation is only the first step in the construction of a satisfactory
monetary theory, and as such serves mostly the non-monetary-
theoretic purpose of establishing the neutrality of money in the
long run and thus clearing the way for the safe elaboration of a
general equilibrium theory cast in terms of the real factors of
wants on the one hand and limited resources and available technology on the other; in other words, it serves to establish that in
the long run money serves merely as a veil over the self-
equilibrating processes of the real economy.

The more interesting and important question from the
monetary-theory point of view concerns the conditions under
which money will function merely as a veil *in the short run*, that is,
will function so as to facilitate the processes of real adjustment to
real economic change without injecting monetary disturbances
into the real economy. An alternative way of putting the question
is in terms of how money should be managed so as to ensure its
short-run neutrality. The quantity equation is of no help in answering it, but is rather, a hindrance; what is necessary is a theory
of monetary dynamics and disturbance, focused on the concept
of what became established in the literature as 'monetary equilibrium.' This was the concern of Wicksell and a number of contemporary and subsequent Continental writers on money, including
Hayek, who moved to the London School of Economics at the
beginning of the 1930s on the strength of his demonstrated mastery of the European tradition of monetary theory. In England,
however, only Robertson at Cambridge went into the subject
with any thoroughness; and his writings on it were tortuous in
the extreme, whether necessarily so or not is a question not

pertinent here. The common concern of this literature in its later stages was the problem of 'hoarding' and its converse 'dishoarding,' which we would have no difficulty nowadays in accepting in Robertson's defined sense as a shift in the desired money-to-income ratio. It may be noticed in passing that in the hands of Hayek in particular the analysis led to the conclusion that the quantity of money should be kept constant—a conclusion which has its modern counterpart in the proposal of Friedman, Shaw, and others for a rule imposing monetary expansion at a constant rate on the central bank, and to the conclusion in the growth model literature that if the golden-rule conditions are satisfied, constancy of the quantity of money will optimize the holding of real balances.

Be that as it may, Keynes identified the quantity theory with the quantity equation, following Marshall; and in his early writings, notably the *Tract on Monetary Reform*, he stuck very closely to that equation. But his practical policy orientation towards the problem of mass unemployment in Britain led him increasingly to the view that there was something seriously wrong with the quantity theory—hence his 'long struggle of escape.' He had no sympathy or patience, however, with the convoluted superstructure of the theory of monetary equilibrium and its identification of the causes of depression with 'hoarding.' Instead, he set out in the *Treatise* to recast the quantity equations to capture his insight—which was a valid if limited insight into the 1920s Britain of his experience and concern—that the key to the problem lay in the behaviour of the entrepreneurs. This led him to fall afoul of the monetary theory specialists, who insisted that the phenomena he was analysing must be describable in terms of hoarding and dishoarding and found fatal flaws in his 'Fundamental Equations.' In this they were technically correct, though he could not or would not see their point and instead increasingly ridiculed, and encouraged his 'Circus' at Cambridge to ridicule the concept of hoarding and the Robertsonian 'loanable funds' approach to interest theory in which it was embedded. (Part of his counterattack, incidentally, rested on the non-operationality as he saw it of the concept of hoarding, in terms of identifiability with observable changes in monetary statistics; hence his reiterated and irritating requests to Hayek and Robertson for an explanation of definitions. A modern econometrically oriented monetary theorist would not find that a cogent objection.) The debate thus, as a result of Keynes's inability to understand what the monetary theorists were driving at, became embroiled in unnecessarily acrid and personal controversy, which divided Cambridge from the London School of Economics and Robertson from Keynes and his junior colleagues within Cambridge. In fact the theory of liquidity preference (which as mentioned originated in the *Treatise* and lost some important elements in the transition to *The General Theory*) provided a theoretically much more sophisticated alternative to the concept of hoarding, which was formulated too primitively in terms of shifts in a parametric ratio of money to income without a well-explicated theory of a demand-for-money function to support it; but one does not win enthusiastic acceptance of a new approach by describing it as a somewhat better formulation of an old theory, but by claiming that the old theory is fundamentally mistaken in all respects. Keynes's own new theory was itself crudely formulated, and this enabled Friedman subsequently to turn the tables on the Keynesians by claiming the concept of a stable demand function for money as the essence of the Chicago quantity-theory tradition. (Since modern Keynesians have also turned liquidity preference into a stable demand function for money, it may legitimately be noted that both modern schools have ignored a key assumption on which Keynes and his contemporary neoclassical theorists were agreed, the instability of the demand for money.)

In the meanwhile Keynes, probably as a result of the concern for operationality that had led him to reject the concept of 'hoarding,' abandoned the dynamic approach of the *Treatise*, which rested on the possible inequality of saving and investment defined *ex ante*, in favour of *ex post* statistical identity and a Marshallian-style short-period equilibrium analysis highlighting the problem of mass unemployment as an equilibrium outcome of the capitalist system of economic organization. This switch of course generated further confusion among the monetary-theoretic opposition: Robertson's question about the *Treatise*—does this mean that the quantity theory, besides being a tautology, is not true?—became the complaint about *The General Theory*: why is it necessary to prove that saving and investment must be equal in equilibrium if they are always identically equal by definition?

At the level of scientific analysis, the outcome of the 1930s debates would have been far different—and twenty years of hard effort at re-synthesis rendered unnecessary—if Keynes had recognized, as he did in other contexts, that a major monetary disturbance injected by a major error of monetary policy (the decision to return to gold at an overvalued exchange rate after the First World War) was largely responsible for the mass unemployment he blamed on the separation of decisions to save from decisions to invest under capitalism, and if he had set himself to convince his professional colleagues that they were taking a theory designed for an economy in which wages and prices adjusted rapidly enough to maintain full employment and mis-applying it to an economy in which severe monetary disturbance had made this assumption false, instead of setting out to demonstrate that that theory was wrong from the bottom up and that a new theory which he was providing was necessary for the understanding of reality. But then there would have been no 'Keynesian Revolution.'

In selecting some characteristics of *The General Theory* for discussion, we intend not to belabour theoretical details that have been thrashed over thoroughly by economic theorists in the nearly forty years that have elapsed since the book was published, but instead to comment on some general aspects of the content and thrust of the book, aspects which on the one hand can in our view best be understood in terms of Keynes's social origins, role in British society, and preoccupation with Britain's contemporary economic problems, and on the other hand constitute a surprisingly great contrast to the legacy left by Keynes as embodied in present-day conceptions of Keynesianism as a guide to economic policymaking.

A few minor points may be dealt with first. It is not surprising, given Keynes's very narrow base of contact with economic scholarship through his affiliation with King's College, Cambridge, that what is presented as an attack on classical theory is basically an attack on the recent writings of Pigou, Hayek, and Robertson; not, given Keynes's life-long bibliophilia, that he should have chosen as predecessors worthy of commendation the list of long-defunct, predominantly mercantilist underconsumption-ists that he did. It is also not surprising that (as reported in *The New Economics and the Old Economists*, by J. Ronnie Davis)[1] *The General Theory* interpreted as an argument for public works to increase employment should have received a cool reception in the United States: the American economists were a pragmatic lot, and their opponent was the well-recognized sheer stupidity of the government in Washington, whereas Keynes was a self-confident flower of Cambridge theoretical training seeking for intellectual victory over the best academic brains of his time—an engaged political animal who had long been trying to sell a programme of public works in the teeth of the best counterargu-ments a highly trained civil service could produce. Nor, finally, is it surprising that a man who led a busy life divided between the academic isolation of Cambridge and the world of finance and politics should have built a theory of capitalism centred on the mysterious behaviour of business confidence, making economic theory a sort of multiplier analysis applied to a sociological multi-plicand—the extreme example of which is the dependence of Joan Robinson's, and to a lesser extent Nicholas Kaldor's, theoriz-ing on ultimate reference to 'the animal spirits of the entre-preneurs.'

A far more important observation concerns the role which the target of full employment has come to play in Keynesian policy thinking and policy making. On the face of it, full employment is an extremely crude definition of the economic requirements of the good society, which in most conceptions would include a host of other desiderata, including equality of opportunity, social mobility, a fairer distribution of income and wealth, and a much more interesting and richer life for all. In addition, there is the problem of inflation associated with the maintenance of full em-ployment, which Keynesian policy theorists at first did their best to ignore and which they have since come to recommend resolv-ing by the application of an incomes policy.

The primacy of full employment in *The General Theory* obvi-ously owes a great deal to the traumatic disruption of the tranquil-ity of the Victorian era in Britain after the First World War, the natural reaction to which was the desire to get everyone back to work in his accustomed place in society and resume business as

usual. On this point Keynes was undoubtedly strongly conditioned by the preconceptions of the natural order of the world
inherited from his Victorian background. Moreover, to one who
had grown up in a world of full employment with price stability,
and passed through a brief historical interlude of acute inflation
clearly associated with the aftermath of war and with instability
of monetary management into a period of prolonged mass unemployment, it was probably ludicrous even to contemplate the
question of whether full employment, once the political leadership had been converted to acceptance of it as a policy objective,
would lead to inflationary wage and price pressures that the
political process would be powerless to arrest. Keynes seems
simply to have assumed that the working class would be grateful
enough for the favour of full employment he promised them to
return cheerfully to work at the accustomed level of money
wages—by no means the only instance of his patronizing the
working class by attributing middle-class values to them.

But there was more to it than that. As already mentioned, the
pages of *The General Theory* are liberally garnished with a Victorian philosophy of social betterment, to be achieved by policies
of income redistribution presumed not to threaten to strangle
British enterprise and burden Britain's international competitive
position. There is a strong flavour of the assumption that the
middle-class—people of Keynes's own type—not only know best
what the distribution of incomes should be—and the tone is as
patronizing about the level of business profits necessary to induce
entrepreneurs to carry on happily with their entrepreneurship as
it is about the level and especially the composition of consumption that is seemly for the working class to enjoy—but can contrive to implement its judgements through the power of the
State.

Allied with this is the idea, belief in which presumably owes
something to Keynes's own impatience to get things done, that
no more than an extra generation of capital accumulation would
suffice to satiate the economy's needs for capital and open the
door to a relaxed and ample life for all. This belief is clearly
untenable except on the implicit assumption that the standard of
life now enjoyed by the masses—provided that all can enjoy it by
virtue of full employment—is already close to the maximum they

deserve and should be allowed to have. Once one scraps the notion that the current middle-class standard of living constitutes the legitimate summit of decent aspiration, and that the masses could and should be content with something substantially less, in favour of a more democratic belief in providing the opportunity to achieve unlimited affluence to all willing to work at it, the nineteenth-century belief in imminent capital saturation has to be scrapped as well. The alternative necessarily imposes the rat race of struggling for sustained rapid economic growth, the mechanisms of which are nowhere comprehended in *The General Theory* or in Keynes's other economic writings. In fact, about all that can be said about it is that post-World War II British experience of attempting to stimulate economic growth by nominally Keynesian policies under the aegis of political leadership and exhortation while insisting on distributing the fruits of past and prospective economic growth according to an egalitarian ethical standard is disappointing. Such efforts are incapable of turning the trick. Nevertheless, the incorporation of economic growth as a policy objective of modern states along with the Keynesian objective of full employment demonstrates a crucial shortcoming of Keynes's Victorian philosophy as a guide to contemporary economic policy-making.

In personal recollections of Keynes, Hayek writes of having put a great deal of labour into a review of *A Treatise on Money*, only to be told by Keynes that he had changed his mind and no longer believed what he had said in that book.[2] Hayek did not return to the attack with the publication of *The General Theory*, fearing that before he had completed his critical analysis Keynes would have changed his mind once again. In fact, with his habit of continuing revision and rethinking and almost instant publication of ideas in progress, a second *General Theory* was a fairly safe prediction. Keynes wrote to Ralph Hawtrey, seven months after *The General Theory* was out, that he was thinking of producing in the next year or so 'what might be called *footnotes* to my previous book, dealing with criticisms and particular points which want carrying further. Of course, in fact the whole book needs re-writing and re-casting. . . .' A draft table of contents for the proposed volume dates from this time, and half a dozen journal articles give some indication of its intended nature. But in the summer of 1937

Keynes suffered the first of a series of heart attacks, and in 1939 came the war, which took him back into the Treasury for the last intense, dedicated, prolonged brain-storming session of his life. If the war had not intervened, how many more *General Theories* might there not have been?

Keynes felt himself continually pressed by the need for re-assessment and re-adaptation of the ongoing stream of economic thought. Writing to Dennis Robertson, for whom everything was to be found in Marshall and who refused to slough off his skins 'like a good snake,' he admitted to being 'perhaps . . . too ready to take pleasure in feeling that my mind is changed.' Robertson, he said, was 'too ready to take pain' and walked about in his un-cast skins 'with the whole lot on from the earliest until the latest, until you can scarcely breathe, saying that, because your greatcoat was once your vest, your present vest and your greatcoat are the same.' Keynes paraded his patchwork coat; in his brain the brightly coloured stuffs of ideas kept circulating. Who knows what theoretical garment, rich and strange and dazzling to behold, he might have paraded on the next occasion?

Keynes would seem to offer an excellent subject for research in the history of thought, not only because of the on-going publication of his papers by the Royal Economic Society and the fact that his major professional contribution coincides with a fairly well-demarcated period of British and world economic history, but because the work on his papers has been done by non-specialists in economic theory and the history of economic thought, directed by avowed and proud disciples of the master with a hagiographic purpose clearly in mind. There is therefore much work of interpretation of the evidence thus made available still to be done; and the passage of time has at last made it possible to approach the subject in an objective historical fashion, rather than as a contribution to contemporary scientific polemics. Again, as has happened before in the history of economic thought, the success of a revolutionary 'school' apparently stamped out the ideas and reputations of a number of serious and worthy scholars; but in this case there has been a counterrevolution, and subsequent scholars have rediscovered, or retrieved by reconstruction from the literary tradition of the subject, the problems and the con-

cepts with which those scholars were concerned. Historical-
theoretic research into the contributions of Keynes in relation to
his contemporaries could therefore add appreciably to current
understanding of the foundations of monetary theory.

7

Cambridge as an Academic Environment in the Early Nineteen-Thirties: A Reconstruction from the Late Nineteen-Forties

This chapter was inspired by a conversation with Don Patinkin. He was anxious to talk about the relations between the (relatively few) economists with whom Keynes was personally and intellectually concerned during the transition from the *Treatise* to the *General Theory*, most of whom (especially if Hayek and Robbins at the London School of Economics are excluded as targets or butts representing 'orthodoxy') were Cambridge acquaintances, and most of those Cambridge colleagues. Patinkin was especially intrigued by the narrowness of the age differences among Keynes, Pigou, Robertson, and some others—a narrowness attributable to the appointment of the youthful Pigou as Marshall's successor over the much older Foxwell (whose many Cambridge supporters Marshall outgeneralled) and the interruption of the academic careers of Pigou's immediate juniors by the First World War. What, then, was Cambridge like, as an environment for economic discussion and research, in the period of the writing of *The General Theory*?

I have long been interested in the influence of the physical and social geography of economics departments on their character and their style of economic research. By physical geography here I mean what the terms imply—the spatial relationships and dimensions within which economists carry on their work. 'Social geography' is a more ambitious and far vaguer concept. I mean by it generally the social relationships among members of the same department, as influenced on the one hand by the hierarchy of tenure, remuneration, and power of decision or of influence over collective decision, and on the other hand by the activities and responsibilities of the department—especially teaching responsibilities, but sometimes also research responsibilities—and the co-operative efforts they may entail; also the social relationships of the department with its clientele—mainly its students; with its colleagues (peers) in departments in the rest of the university or similar institution in which it exists; with the professional academic community at large; and with the larger society of which the university is a constituent and into which most of its students graduate. All these relationships have an influence on both the style and content of economic discussion with colleagues in and close acquaintances outside the department, and the choice of audience and style of addressing it for oral (usually unpublished) and written (published) communication at the academic and professional level.

To illustrate briefly and casually the kind of influence I have in mind: my first teaching post was as a one-man replacement for a two-man department at Saint Francis Xavier University, Nova Scotia. I was very lonely, being a stranger in all relevant ways; and the effect was to press me strongly into reading, and writing lengthy, serious letters to distant friends. My predecessor, like my current colleagues in other fields, belonged to the community and was clearly exclusively a teacher of the young in the ways of the world as he understood them—I was shocked by his boast that he 'used the textbook only as a whipping-boy,' because I was too inexperienced to realize that what he had to whip it with was his (and the students' parents') social and economic experience. *His* quondam colleague, a very cultured German refugee, had like myself taken refuge in prodigious reading, and became a figure of student fun for his inappropriate scholarship. We were both misfits: the place demanded a concern with low-level teaching and the formation of adult character, and identification of economic and social interests with those of a generally poor community of farmers, fishermen, and coal miners, as against an

exploiting class of shop-keepers, equipment-suppliers, local
bankers, and the coal and steel company.

My next teaching position was at the University of Toronto, as
an Instructor (below a Lecturer, and therefore not a member of
the voting department). The department was housed in an old
building (formerly the McMaster University building) on the
northern fringe of the campus between the football field and the
Ontario Museum, so that one tended to eat in nearby cheap
restaurants and not to consider oneself as part of a university
community. Large offices and lecture rooms were on the ground
floor, small offices on the fourth floor, with stairs and no elevator
connecting them. Senior and much older staff members had the
ground floor offices, junior untenured staff the fourth-floor cub-
byholes. The vertical geographical distance between the two
faculty groups corresponded to an age difference, a tenure and
rank difference, and a social distance between them. Communication was difficult and almost nonexistent. One saw the
Department Head briefly on appointment, to discuss teaching
duties, and any difficulties one was foolish enough to voice, and
once at one of two Sunday tea-parties he offered to junior staff
late in the year, one for sheep possibly on their way down from
the fourth floor to the ground floor, and one for goats definitely
on their way down from the fourth floor to the exit door. Apart
from that, one saw him only by appointment under strain, usually for advice or a reference in connection with a possible job for
next year; his stock response to an implicit request for reassur-
ance was 'Well, we wouldn't want to stand in your way.' As a
result, the ethos of the fourth floor was one of gossip, rumour,
and sometimes panic, of needlessly hard and unfocused work,
and of conviction that one was not good enough to be a scholar,
that if one were one would not produce anything for hopeless years ahead, and that if one did produce something it
would be read only by a handful of other scholars, all of whom
would be devastatingly critical. No wonder so many used the
exit!

As a final example before I return to my main theme, I would
contrast briefly Harvard and Yale with Chicago in the 1960s,
both, I admit, from a Chicago standpoint. The economics faculties
of Harvard and Yale were not (and are not now) Departments of

Economics in the same sense as Chicago's, in my objective judgement. They were congeries of small personal departments depending from individual senior professors, to whose seminars (their main activity) transient Assistant Professors attached themselves. The number and the transience of the Assistant Professors reflected the labour-intensive undergraduate teaching responsibilities of the Departments. The relatively small quantity, and the policy orientation, of the published output of the tenured staff reflected the social position of the two Ivy League schools in the American society, and particularly the reliance of Democratic Party government on the advice and participation of established academic figures. Chicago's much larger published output, by contrast, represented the position of the social 'outsider' and, in a general way, the lesser role of the academic in the Republican Party's approach to government. Chicago's department, also, had no undergraduate teaching responsibilities, hence no need for numbers of transient Assistant Professors, and hence the ability to absorb a few transients into a much larger (but still numerically small) professional and social community. In addition, the Chicago academic community mostly lived within a mile of the campus, which both made encounters in the course of out-of-hours visits likely, and informal social gatherings at home easy to arrange—in contrast to the far-flung suburban living patterns of Harvard, M.I.T. and Yale. Physical geography was also important: the Harvard and Yale economists were scattered among widely separated buildings, whereas the Chicago economists lived on one floor, the fourth, with a single elevator around and in which they automatically met frequently and informally.

To return to my theme, Cambridge as an academic environment for economics in the early 1930s: as my subtitle indicates, what I have to say is based on my own experience, as a student in 1945–46 and an Assistant Lecturer/Lecturer from January 1949 to March 1956 (especially the first year or two, while Cambridge was still living the life and carrying on the fights of the 1930s). This was before the Department of Applied Economics shifted from its temporary building on the courtyard of the Downing Street science buildings complex, and the Faculty of Economics and Politics and the Marshall Library shifted from the meagre facilities the

Faculty had occupied in that complex since 1912 and the Library since 1925, respectively, to the present reconditioned old house on West Road (the Department) and the modern buildings, complete with library, lecture rooms, auditorium, and most noticeably individual faculty offices and common room, they now occupy on Sidgwick Avenue, across the river near the University Library. For simplicity of writing, I describe Cambridge as it was prior to the geographical shift and concentration of location, and ignore the Department of Applied Economics, which was not in existence anyway in the early 1930s.

The dominant fact of Cambridge physical and social geography was the Colleges, and the system of (predominately undergraduate) teaching based on them. Most of the serious teaching was done by supervision, usually by a Fellow of the College specializing in the relevant subject. This consisted of an hour a week per individual student (or for as small a group as could be managed, the numbers being vastly enlarged in the years of the postwar bulge), the supervision being based on an essay topic (either invented, or drawn from past examinations) assigned one week, and written, turned in, read, and discussed the next week. Holders of university assistant lectureships and higher posts were limited to twelve hours of supervision a week, except for Professors, who were not allowed to supervise undergraduates. Fellows of Colleges without university appointments, of whom there were some even in economics, such as Gerald Shove (long discriminated against as a conscientious objector in the First World War), were subject to no such restriction; and some, such as Shove, bore a very heavy teaching burden. Some Colleges, notably King's, restricted their Fellows to teaching their own College's students only; other Colleges were easier on this point. Colleges without Fellows relied on the services of University teachers without Fellowships, such as Maurice Dobb, my own undergraduate supervisor at Jesus (long denied a Fellowship because he was an avowed communist); and, in the postwar period at least, on graduate students and staff members of the Department of Applied Economics, though usually mainly for first-year-student supervision. University teachers without Fellowships had a lonely life; on the other hand, they were not obliged to take all the students admitted by the College Tutor and his admission advisers (I remember a friend who was shocked when Richard Kahn told him that a certain first-year King's student he was supervising was certain to fail at the end of the year—but my friend had to teach him through the year anyway) and could instead, if good enough, 'shop around' for good students—as Joan Robinson did very shrewdly in my day.

A University appointment was not necessary to a successful Cambridge career. In some ways, indeed, a University position could be an inhibiting responsibility, since some of the College jobs were much better paid than University teaching posts but required either very long hours of extra work, or the sacrifice of ambition extending beyond the lectureship level, or too much effort to be consistent with a teaching post; on the other hand, a Professorship involved resignation or abstention from any College post, as well as sacrifice of income from undergraduate supervision—a fact about which Richard Kahn protested bitterly when he became a Professor and had to cease being Bursar of King's. In addition, a University appointee was required to live not more than five miles from Great St. Mary's, and to be in residence a stipulated and fairly large minimum number of nights per term. By regulation, a University teacher who had a Fellowship received (in the early 1950s) only £100 a year of his Fellowship stipend above his university salary, though of course he also got a room or rooms, free dinners, and an entertainment allowance (and, if I remember, free postage). In the inflation after World War II, however, and with the spreading tendency of Cambridge academics to marry young, the University gradually came to dominate the College as a source of income—one result being the initiation and subsequent improvement of social and catering facilities for non-College-Fellow teachers and researchers.

The University appointment, as such, was a very minor part of an individual's teaching responsibilities—that obligation Brian Reddaway at one stage used to refer to as 'the forty-hour year.' One's forty hours, approximately, meant a two-lecture-a-week course in each of the two major teaching terms of eight weeks, and the same in the teaching part of the examination term (the first four weeks of the third eight-week term, the rest being for student reading, and examination week). It was, however, possible in some cases to take classes with less per-hour credit; for a few years, my load included eight classes in money for third year, shared by rotation over three groups with Joan Robinson and Richard Kahn (I had to make up the reading list, and explain to Kahn that once we decided the first person's first rotation we had fixed the whole programme, each year) and five lectures on the theory of the balance of payments. The lectures were mostly held in the Mill Lane lecture rooms (opened in 1928), though sometimes in other odd rooms in university buildings; and one of the classes was held in a room in King's. In other Faculties, lectures were frequently given in a room in the individual instructor's own College (or, when classes were small, in his own College study); and I suspect this was probably true of some of the lecture courses offered in the interwar period (the 'special lectures' offered in the early 1930s were presented in a University lecture hall). In any case, the fact that one gave so few formal lectures, and made a special trip away from one's own College or home to make them, in buildings intended for lecturing and not for loitering, meant that one had very little, if any, regular contact with other Faculty members outside of one's own College. There were, in fact, only four kinds of occasions on which one met non-College colleagues academically.

First, one might be appointed to one of the Boards of Examiners. There were three of these: Tripos Part I, Preliminary Examination, and Tripos Part II. One was not allowed to examine in the subject on which one lectured for the year to which one taught it. The examinations were by papers, not by courses; all examiners (including two external examiners in Part II, usually Oxford or London dons but occasionally provincial professors) had to agree on the presence and the wording of all questions on all papers, each contributing some questions to other papers as well as the one for which he was primarily responsible; all papers had to be read by two examiners, and by one or more additional examiners in case of disagreement in marks or serious disparities between a candidate's performances on different papers; and the decisions on 'classes' (I, II(i), II(ii), III, and 'Special'—meaning failed this examination but would probably pass it on a re-trial, hence allowed a degree anyway) had to be agreed by all examiners and the list made out and signed, all within a couple of weeks' time. It was in the process of setting the questions, and even more in the grading of the candidates' performances, that doctrinal disputes and philosophical differences among Faculty members, and between them and non-Cambridge economics as represented by the external examiners, came into confrontation most seriously—elsewhere they could be studiously ignored, or steered on inconclusive non-collision courses. (The emphasis on the undergraduate final examinations and the marking and outcome of them, incidentally, explains the concentration of Joan Robinson and Nicholas Kaldor on criticism of what the undergraduate textbooks and the professors teach the young, and of 'orthodoxy' more generally.)

Secondly, one could get elected to the Faculty Board. To do so, however (for an economist, as distinct from an economic historian or politics specialist), required considerable seniority and/or, in the late forties, strong attachment to the left or the right political wing of the Department. The Faculty Board was a strongly political body, in the sense of both academic and party politics. It controlled the committees that selected new Assistant Lecturers and Lecturers, and the Faculty representation and Faculty nominations for outside economist representation on the University Committees that appointed Professors (and, I believe, Readers). It also of course decided the day-to-day Faculty business.

Third, there was the Political Economy Club, founded by Keynes and continued by Robertson in my day. Student membership was by invitation, automatic for Part I Firsts and almost so for II.1's, that is, for A or top B students. Faculty were free to attend by implicit open invitation, visiting economists by explicit invitation only. Meetings were on Thursdays in my day; papers were written and read by students, mostly third-year (sometimes second-year students from the Commonwealth taking their second B.A.'s via the second and third (part II) years of the Tripos). Students drew slips to determine the order in which they were obliged to comment on the paper. Faculty were free to choose the point at which they spoke about the subject; visitors spoke by invitation. In Keynes's time, I was told, more than one visitor who chose to speak was told in no uncertain terms that he was a fool; Robertson was invariably gentle and polite. The proceedings were formal—set speeches rather than cut-and-thrust—but occasionally one found it worthwhile to carry on discussion with a colleague after the meeting formally ended.

Finally, in my day but I am fairly sure not before World War II, early in each autumn term the Faculty put on a large sherry party, to which were invited all faculty and their wives, and all academic visitors to the Faculty and their wives. It says something for the lack of academic and social integration of the Cambridge Faculty that at one of these parties I met Claude Guillebaud (Marshall's nephew, and a life-long Cambridge man) who asked me, 'Who's that fellow over there?' I looked, and answered with surprise, 'Why, that's Andrew Roy. He's been a member of the Faculty for three years now!' Of course, Roy taught statistics ('applied economics') and was therefore somewhat out of the main stream, though he was regarded by the King's group as one of the Robertson-Guillebaud mob, and for that reason they tried unsuccessfully to refuse him tenure, in spite of the fact that he had already produced some first-class articles and been co-author of a good book with Alan Prest.

With the exception of the few unlucky enough not to have won a College Fellowship, one's academic as well as social life lay within one's College (and in Keynes's case also in London), and not in the Faculty and among one's professional economist colleagues. There were of course some possibilities of social connections outside the College within the University community, such as D. H. Robertson's interest in acting, and Keynes's membership in the Society of Apostles. But the Society had in the post-World-War-I period become largely a King's College group—there was a certain connection between the Society's homosexual orientation, veiledly disclosed in Keynes's *Two Memoirs* ('Dr. Melchior' and 'My Early Beliefs'), and King's College's reputation as the centre of homosexuality. (Before I became a Fellow of King's, I remember being shocked by hearing a Cambridge Professor of Archaeology refer to King's College Chapel as 'The First Church of Christ, Sodomite;' he was right—but the faithful did not proselytize their religion among mature adults.) The connection was symbolized by E. M. Forster's posthumous novel *Maurice*, with its theme of the unthinkable transformation from intellectual to physical homosexuality.

The College was the centre of life, especially for the unmarried Fellows to whom college was home (with possibly a family or devoted mother located elsewhere as a vacation home) and who did not participate much if at all in the home entertainments of the group of married dons; there were far more bachelor Fellows in the interwar period and early 1940s than there have been since.

Before I pursue this point, it is worth commenting on why there was so little personal contact between economists in different Colleges, even men of the same age group. One reason was presumably an indirect result of the long reign of a bachelor, and after the first war a distinct misogynist and misanthrope, Professor A. C. Pigou. Pigou, as his *Times* obituary (attributed to D. H. Robertson) rather acidly informs us, took little interest in Tripos reform and related teaching matters. Another reason was the very busy Term timetable of a don—one bought a specially printed diary for the academic, not the calendar, year, already containing printed information on various University calendar events, and one quickly filled it with one's teaching and College fixtures and further crammed it with various kinds of meetings and appointments. A third reason was the emphasis on the privacy of one's College rooms; one opened them for one's pupils, and a few College familiars and cronies, but casual dropping in on or by colleagues was unwelcome on the one side and known to be presumptuous on the other. A final reason was the unfamiliarity and usually the inconvenience of the telephone, which so far as I can judge was generally installed in the Fellows' rooms only after the second world war. In any case, the telephone was feared and shunned by the older generation—as was mentioned to have been the case with Keynes, so far as casual contact with strangers and casual acquaintances was concerned, though we are told he did speak with the brokers every business morning by telephone. In place of the telephone and personal visits, communication with colleagues was carried on by hand-written notes—the 'done thing.' This was very efficient, in its way, since not only did the Cambridge post office make deliveries on the same day (at least three deliveries a day, I understand, in pre-World-War II days) but also the University had its own internal postal system, manned by the college porters. The college supervision and university lecture system was congenial to this system of communication. The lectures were very formal—Robertson and Dobb, to my personal knowledge, and in my generation Robin Matthews, wrote out their lectures in full and read them (in Robertson's case, it was a reading in a theatrical sense); and the students did not ask questions, but sat in respectful silence to the end—or did not come at all. The supervisions involved more personal contact and meeting of minds with the students, but they were basically a playing of the formal roles of instructor and instructed, and their essence was formal interpretation, criticism, and defense of a written document. It was natural enough—and incidentally a great boon subsequently to the editors of Keynes's papers—to request a written statement on a point of disagreement, and to give a written reply, among people who had little or no experience of open public argument, except perhaps in the artificial form of formal debates in the Cambridge Union.

I had two experiences, in my early days at Cambridge, of this system of academic communication, before it fell out of fashion with changing personalities and communications technology and habits. Just before I arrived there, I had published a short note in *The Quarterly Journal of Economics* on 'An Error in Ricardo's Exposition of His Theory of Rent.' It was a typical case of overgeneralizing a particular arithmetical example into a general principle. On arriving in Cambridge I found Dobb and Piero Sraffa much excited by my note, which they were sure was wrong; Sraffa even proposed to publish a criticism of my note, thereby breaking nineteen (I think) years of silence. They were then both Fellows of Trinity College, with rooms not too far apart. Nevertheless, I was shown a stack of notes that had passed between them, notes replete with such phrases as 'Johnson's fallacy is. . . .' I would have been overjoyed to have smoked Sraffa out of his long silence, especially as I knew for sure that my mathematics were correct. But unfortunately, or fortunately, Sraffa eventually looked up Edwin Cannan's history of thought and found the error already noted there, whereupon he dropped the subject. (That taught me two lessons: one about the scholarship of Cambridge, and the other about the scholarship of Joseph Schumpeter, who had got me to write up and publish the note. On balance I far prefer Schumpeter's style: if one does not know the literature, and a young man can prove an error one had not noticed, it is better to encourage him than to assume that he must be wrong; better still, of course, to check the literature to guard against unnecessary originality in the establishment of errors.) Joan Robinson also attempted several times to engage me in economic discussion by return of post; the difficulty with her was that she proceeded directly to differences in conclusion, without exploration of the logical sequence by which she had reached hers and with obvious contempt for the processes of reasoning by which I had reached mine. Also, I never learned to fling the word 'fallacy' about with Cantabrigian abandon; and notes ending 'I challenge you to . . .' made me quail. But Joan Robinson was a natural public debater, not an ivory-tower academic correspondent. She would send me a handwritten note in the morning, and I would scribble an answer by noonday; and then I would get a note back in the evening saying, 'Where you made your mistake is as follows . . .' I could keep that up for two days, but I soon wearied of the game. Why was I the only one who made hopeless mistakes in pure theory?

Underlying the reasons just given for the isolation of Faculty members in their Colleges, however, was a fundamental fact of physical geography, left implicit in the discussion so far. This was that the Faculty had effectively no geographic administrative and business centre. Geographically, it existed only as a staircase in the science building on Downing Street, just inside and to the right of the entrance archway. The location was about two blocks from the Mill Lane Lecture Rooms (themselves, as mentioned, no favourable venue for intra-Faculty encounters), and much more distant than that from any of the important economics teaching colleges—King's, Clare, Caius, Trinity, and St. John's. Most of the space was taken up by the Marshall Library, over the archway: while Faculty members met there occasionally *en passant*, collecting or returning books or browsing over the new journals displayed on the open shelves, the librarians naturally discouraged conversation in the Library's single large hall, and there was no place outside to congregate except the stairway and entrance hall. (Also, there were unlimited borrowing periods for faculty, and most had substantial personal libraries and regularly bought the new books in the local bookshops.) Above the Library was a

large room used for the weekly meetings of the (general undergraduate) Marshall Society, and during the day for a few classes
and lectures, especially in statistics, the hand-calculators being
used at other times by a few hard-working graduate students.
Apart from that, there was the Royal Economic Society office on
the first floor *en route* to the Marshall Library—a place swamped
with new books received, R.E.S. publications awaiting sale, and
stacks of manuscripts and galleys, presided over by Austin
Robinson and his editorial assistant from time to time. On the
ground floor, tucked under the stairs, was the Faculty Office, a
poky little room with one secretary in charge during my day. (I do
not know whether there was even one, before World War II.) The
secretary was theoretically—but not in practice—free to do
Faculty member typing when not busy on Faculty business typing for the Faculty Secretary. In fact, those who had letters or
(much more rarely) manuscripts to be typed used their college
offices or a famous Cambridge institution, Miss Pate's, which did
typing and sent in girls to take dictation of letters. (I remember
Kahn once telling me that he had a girl in one morning a week
from Miss Pate's, because otherwise his correspondence would
get out of hand.) I was unique at that time inasmuch as I could do
my own typing. Fortunately, the prosperity of the Department of
Applied Economics under Richard Stone's direction enabled one
to wangle professional typing of statistical or mathematical papers free of charge from time to time.

There is one other relevant fact—the automobile was virtually
unknown to the academic, even in the early 1950s. (The only
car-owners I recall were Ruth Cohen, who had been corrupted by
a travelling fellowship in the United States prewar, and Nicholas
Kaldor, who was independently wealthy.) The automobile vastly
encourages spatial mobility, partly by saving time, and partly by
removing the boredom of slowly traversing space on foot. Without it (and without the convenient telephone), spatial movement
requires calculation of the time-cost of movement of personal
physical location, and estimation of the probability of a journey
being fruitless. In short, the absence of the automobile, and the
resulting need to go by foot or bicycle for short distances and by
train for longer ones, powerfully reinforced the other incentives
to make one's college rooms the focus of one's academic

activities, and to communicate with colleagues by postal notes.

Thus, one's professional and social life was concentrated inside one's college. That meant that one was more or less entirely on one's own as an economist; and this was true even of the few large Colleges, and not-so-large ones such as King's, which either needed more than one economist for teaching, or had one to spare as a by-product of some College administrative position. The reason was that, even though the Cambridge Economics Faculty (and other Faculties) made a great point of democratic equality, and everyone called everyone else by his first name (I remember Kahn being so distressed by my persistence in calling him 'Mr. Kahn' that he finally asked me point-blank to please call him Richard), there were very definite age-and-generation differentials that were respected by great formality in people's behaviour to one another even if they were Fellows of the same College. Insistence on the outer forms of democratic equality is, to be sure, not unknown in North America. Both at Harvard, when I was a graduate student there, and later at Chicago, I remember being struck by the habit of referring to colleagues as 'Mister —', partly because it was the American equivalent of Cambridge first names, but also because in Cambridge, and in the United Kingdom generally, one was careful to describe colleagues in front of non-colleagues as 'Doctor' or 'Professor' when they actually held the title. In the less eminent Departments in the United States, however, rank is noticed and described fairly punctiliously. The important difference, in any case, was that in Cambridge it was age-group rather than rank that segregated Department members hierarchically; and this was related on the one hand to the fact that the archetypical Cambridge or Oxford don made his career from matriculation to retirement and ultimately death or senile incarceration in the same college, and on the other hand to the related fact that each succeeding year's crop of B.A.s made their subsequent careers and positions in British society on the basis of their relative competitive performance on that one year's examinations. Thus the peer-group and the rivals were defined once and for all, and naturally included only a few individuals close in age to oneself.

My own experience, in any case, was that I received no assistance whatsoever from my seniors in the Faculty, and especially those in my own College, in the way of comments on my early professional papers. In fact, though I continued to give them copies, I got used to having Kahn ask me, some six months later, whether the paper I had given him was going to be published, and when I said 'yes' he would express gratitude that he would now not have to read it. Others in the faculty, in their turn, occasionally remembered to give me a copy of something they had written, but I 'was not expected to reply' (to quote the standard King's College High Table rule when a guest's health was proposed); I remember once pointing out to Kaldor that in a paper on policy theory he had forgotten his own past demonstration that after a certain point increasing a tariff to improve a country's terms of trade would make the country worse and not better off; only slightly and momentarily embarrassed, he admitted that the paper had already been sold to the F.A.O., but would be published where no one would notice it.

Since the so-called 'Circus' played a significant role at one stage in the transition from the *Treatise* to *The General Theory*, it is worth recording perhaps that in 1949–50 or 1950–51 or so we junior Cambridge Lecturers did run an informal seminar, for the purpose of reading Samuelson's *Foundations*. But it was always difficult to arrange a time at which we could all meet, and for us individually to manage to do our homework, and the effort eventually petered out. Instead, the Department of Applied Economics seminar, run by its full-time research staff, became the centre for mathematical-theoretical and econometrically inclined junior Faculty staff.

The isolation of a career centred on the individual's college, with contact with comparable professional economists being derived almost exclusively from the reading one chose to do, and with only a small number of such economists, almost exclusively located in Cambridge, Oxford, and London, being considered as worthy of attention or criticism, obviously had a number of conditioning effects on professional academic writing.

To begin with, apart from the reading of literature and the pursuit of controversy within Cambridge by note-of-hand, there were three main types of personal participation in everyday economic discussion. One, already discussed, was the formal lecturing. Here there was essentially no feedback from the students—except the dropping off of auditors, which was expected, and attributable to a variety of causes, not easily translatable into a judgement of professional competence in general, let alone a judgement on the validity of particular arguments or formulations of problems. (Where it might seem to be so, it could be claimed that political bias motivated supervisors to advise their supervisees against attending.)

Also not very useful professionally, was the conversation with other, non-economist, Fellows, especially at High Table (dinner). In this connection, College practices differed greatly in the extent to which regular dinners at High Table meant a random alternation of dinner conversationalists. In Jesus College, for example, where I was attached to High Table before I won my King's Fellowship, one assembled always in order of seniority, and could escape one's lifetime dinner companions only by bringing a guest to sit at the Master's right hand, or arriving apologetically too late for the procession and the grace, and sitting at the bottom of the table with the hope of having a neighbour outstanding enough to compensate the sodden drag of the ever-present College Chaplain. In King's, on the other hand (thanks partly to the geographical accident that Senior Common Room was not directly adjacent to the High Table end of the Hall, but at the opposite end), one entered in a straggling mob after the Provost, and could with luck select one's table neighbours; it was also respectable, thanks to Pigou's example, to arrive consistently just after the grace for vaguely agnostic reasons, and thus be able to sit among kindred unreligious spirits. In any case, the rule was that one must not 'talk shop.' This meant, in practice, that one talked either about cultural events or about government social and economic policy, in either case relying for level and topics on careful reading of *The Times*. *The Times* was, and for that matter still is, the British economist's only really seriously required reading; and a steady diet of it has a profound influence in shaping British economists' concepts of both economic policy problems and feasible ('politically acceptable') solutions to them.

This is, incidentally, an important point about British economic policy discussion both past and present. It has certainly been important (and dangerous) in recent years, when *The Times* leaders on economic policy have been written by bright young

Oxford B.A.s in Politics, Philosophy and Economics, who believe in the standard Oxford panaceas of a higher price for gold (for the international monetary system), incomes policy (for inflation and the balance of payments) and international commodity agreements (for economic development and international justice). The influence of *The Times*, and for the early part of the period the *Manchester Guardian*, and perhaps also the *Telegraph*, on British economists' conceptions of Britain's economic problems in the interwar period has not so far as I know been seriously discussed: I would like to recommend it as a subject for serious study in British economic history and the recent history of the development of economic theory, one aspect of which would be the influence of the quality British press on Keynes's economic writings.

The third, and by far the most serious and important, personal exposure to economic discussion came through the supervisions. These, however, were only very rarely exacting in the sense that one had a pupil both able and argumentative to deal with. In addition to the fact that one taught all three years or levels and that the pupils naturally varied in quality, there were two main reasons for this. One was that the tutor or tutors, in deciding admissions, tended to be guided both by the desire for a representative sample of students likely to fill the various positions of social and economic success in British industry, government, landed estate agriculture, and so on, and by an ideal concept of the type of young man that should represent what the College stood for, an ideal which stressed all-roundness, good family, or sophistication rather than solid academic excellence. In my time, they were fighting a losing battle on behalf of the nonintellectual indifferent student; but in the interwar period, I understand, they were both short of revenue and students, and willing to stretch admission rules very far in favour of the progeny of previous undergraduate members of the College.

The other reason was that in contrast to other Triposes Economics had a one-year Part I and a two-year Part II, and so tended to attract many more students for the Part I than continued into Part II, the students switching to a preferred Tripos for their Part II and their degree. In particular, intending Law students could avoid the horrors of Roman Law, compulsory in the Law Part I, by taking Part I Economics instead. Part I Economics was also used, sometimes, as a means of obtaining a B.A. for a really dim but blue-blooded student, in combination with Part I Agriculture (or Estate Management). In consequence, the preponderance of one's supervisory activities was occupied by Part I teaching of elementary principles. (The Faculty exploited this situation by minimizing the lectures for Part I students by offering no optional lecture courses at that level, and using its Part I student numbers to justify appointments of lecturers who gave Part II optional courses; there was also some evidence of professional discrimination against Part I lecturing, which tended to be assigned to the weaker colleagues.) College fellows with special administrative responsibilities in their colleges, or with special bargaining power, could, however, manage to confine their supervisory work to supervisions or classes with selected high-quality students, as presumably Keynes did and as Kaldor managed to do in my time.

This kind of audience for one's everyday teaching and discussion of economics necessarily forms and distorts one's concept of the audience one is addressing through one's written work—if, that is, one does not, as many Oxford and Cambridge dons do, content oneself with oral communication through lectures, supervisions, and discussions with economist and non-economist academic cronies and colleagues. The most obvious example of this process is actually a common Oxford style, related to the character of the Politics, Philosophy and Economics course and examination tradition, and best exemplified in the work of R. F. Harrod, J. R. Hicks, and many other lesser luminaries, which can best be described as a sort of conversation with oneself, a dramatic monologue performed for a somewhat dim audience of economic amateurs, in which one works one's way laboriously through a succession of false starts and red herrings, eventually winding up with the more or less obvious and correct approach and solution to the problem at hand. It is a style presumably effective for instruction of a captive audience of bashful undergraduates, whom one is committed to instruct for an hour on some basic principle that could be communicated in a few minutes to anyone with a logical mind and a distrust of the economic pronouncements of the socially powerful but academically illiterate; but it is tedious in the extreme for a professional economist to have to wade through. The Cambridge equivalent is a little less tedious but equally irritating to a professional. It posits a nameless horde of faceless orthodox nincompoops, among whom a few recognizable faces can be discerned, and proceeds to ridicule a travesty of their published, presumed, or imputed views in the process of revealing the unorthodox truth in a simple encapsulated form suitable for the average undergraduate to swallow without gagging. This is the extreme form of the modern post-Keynesian-Cambridge style, which unfortunately *The General Theory* did so much to implant. It has three major elements in it, traceable directly to salient characteristics of Cambridge as an academic environment: the belief that fundamental questions of social and economic policy are ultimately determined by debate among a handful of academic economists, in Cambridge and at most two other British universities; that policy failure is the result of bad—and bad means orthodox, or more generally pedestrian, tedious, and unimaginative—economics; and that the world is to be put right by instructing the undergraduate students at Cambridge and elsewhere in the complex fallacies committed by orthodox economics and the simple truth as derived by anti-orthodox economic theory. The older, pre-*General Theory* Cambridge style was much gentler and more sophisticated, though it had the same basic ingredients: concentration on criticism of the work of a few eminent British economists, often not identified directly by name and reference (a scathing and extremely unscholarly attack on Hayek in *The General Theory*, for example, is indexed, necessarily, under 'wild duck'); allusions to the economic views and pronouncements of leading contemporary political figures; digressions into speculations of a vaguely philosophical or historical nature, of a type appealing to cultured undergraduates; and the basic assumption that the principle aim is to instruct undergraduates and guide them through the literature. A further noteworthy characteristic is the tendency to eschew both mathematics, except for illustrative purposes, and statistical analysis going beyond the capacity of an intelligent layman. In this respect, the Cambridge style was heavily and lastingly imprinted by the views of Alfred Marshall on the writing of economics, though Marshall's desire to write for the instruction of the average intelligent businessman has long since been abandoned in favour of writing for the instruction of the ebullient undergraduate, the sole remaining exception being the efforts of James Meade (Oxford-trained) to write formal economic theory in a form relevant to the concerns of the economic policy-maker.

In conclusion, I would like to raise briefly two subjects which thought about Cambridge as an environment for academic economists suggests to me, but which I have not had time to pursue further. First, I have mentioned that the examination framework of P.P.E. at Oxford tends to produce a particular, philosophy-oriented, style of economic writing among its professional economist products. It seems to me that Cambridge philosophy had a similar influence on Cambridge economics thinking, discussion, and writing, despite the separation of economics from philosophy, and largely also from politics, in the structure of the Cambridge Tripos, an influence mediated through Keynes as a result of his membership in the Society of Apostles, his early work on probability, his interest in collecting old books, and his friendship with Frank Ramsey and other King's College philosophers. What I have in mind here specifically is Keynes's use, particularly in the early 1930s (e.g. his reply to Ohlin in the controversy over German reparations in June 1929, and his correspondence with Robertson and others just after the *Treatise* was published) of a particular philosophy discussion device, which can be paraphrased as 'I cannot answer your question until you explain to me what you mean by the words . . .' (or, 'I cannot be sure I have understood your question because I do not know what you mean by the words . . .'). This device became discredited during the Second World War by the Brains Trust philosopher C. E. M. Joad's stock answer to a question, 'It all depends what you mean by . . .' (some crucial word in the question). This device is of course a very attractive one for turning an undergraduate's awkward questions into an opportunity for teaching him what one knows and dismissing other peoples' analyses as unsatisfactory. But I suspect that it, and the philosophical approach underlying it—which stresses semantic analysis of statements to the neglect of the operational and scientific purpose of the logical analysis of which the statements are constituents—had a great deal to do with both the obvious logical inconsistencies in *The General Theory* (which can also be explained by a rather amateurish but on the whole commendable desire to provide empirically observable referents for the theoretical constructs) and the heated semantic debates that ensued on its publication (especially about the savings/investment identity/equality).

The second subject is the influence of the nature of the Cambridge and Oxford College as an economic institution on the ideas of academic economists resident therein. The Colleges are, or largely were until the 'student troubles' of the late 1960s, fundamentally feudal institutions, based on landed property owned by the College, administered cooperatively by the Fellows collectively, and specifically, by a subgroup among them semi-self-selected by administrative interest and loosely controlled by a system of semi-egalitarian semi-gerontological personal-participation democracy, functioning to turn out qualified members of the elite or the establishment (including their own replacements) and dependent on the organized supporting services of the College Servants, or porters and kitchen staff. Keynes, as Bursar of King's, was one of the pioneers in shifting the financial base of the College system from landed property to industrial stocks and bonds. (He was also the innovator of the shift by his College from dependence on land rents to direct farm management, a story not relevant here but which ultimately proved a very expensive mistake for the College.) This shift involved, in Keynes's hands, an emphasis on speculation and capital gains, which had an obvious influence on his professional work: Robertson indeed criticized the theory of liquidity preference as 'a College Bursar's theory of interest,' referring particularly to Keynes's neglect of interest as the productive return on capital. More generally, it is possible to relate Keynes's social philosophy to the nature of the College as an economic institution, in two major ways. One concerns the working class and its welfare: if one thinks of the attitude of a College governing body towards its College servants, it seems natural to think of guaranteed employment as the main obligation of the employer towards its employees, together with the payment of wages just competitive with going market wage rates or slightly below, and with gratitude and loyalty assured by the conferment of extensive fringe benefits (notably sports facilities, subsidized housing, and free food and drink). The other concerns attitudes to the entrepreneurial class: it would be natural for college fellows who had trained the business executive class, usually at the lower end of the spectrum of academic capacity and performance, to regard businessmen as a class as rather inferior to college fellows, people for whom some reputable nonacademic nongovernmental employment should be found, but who should not be rewarded on an inordinate scale for success in their second-rate activities. It would also be natural for such men to believe that the messes into which the practical world of business and politics got itself resulted from the defect of inferior intelligence or the lack of a system of corporate decision-taking comparable to that of a College Fellowship body and its Council, and to look to intelligent academic discussion by dispassionate and public-spirited people as the obvious means by which to create a better world.[1]

Part III
Keynes's Early Work

8
The Early Economics of Keynes

The first two volumes of previously uncollected writings by Keynes which appear in the Royal Economic Society's comprehensive edition of his works contain a great deal of important unpublished material cognate to his early successive preoccupations with the problems of the Indian currency system and of British public finance during the First World War—preoccupations which culminated in the publication of his first two books, his eminently scholarly *Indian Currency and Finance* (1913) and his passionately critical *The Economic Consequences of the Peace* (1919).

These two volumes, *Activities and Associated Writings: India and Cambridge, 1906–14,* and *Activities and Associated Writings: The Treasury and Versailles, 1914–19,* (Volumes XV and XVI of *The Collected Writings of John Maynard Keynes*), throw a great deal of light on the character, personality, and intellectual development of Keynes, and on the nature of economics as conceived and utilized, in both the academic world and in government, in the period up to and including the First World War. One is impressed in passing with the strong moral passion that Keynes brought to his work, immediately attributable to his membership in the Cambridge Society of Apostles, but entirely congruent with the Cambridge ethos set by Marshall and Pigou—and with his concern for the collection and interpretation of both economic statistics and knowledge of institutional detail, as well as with the lurking problem of index numbers that concerned him in his later *Treatise on Money*. One is also reminded, incidentally, of the seriousness with which the Cambridge economists took the issue of free trade versus protection in the first decade of the century, to the point of going out on the hustings to advocate free trade, and that the issue of the effect of protection in encouraging investment in a country is by no means as new as it seems in some of the contemporary literature on economic development: witness Keynes's *New Quarterly* article of February 1910 on 'Great Britain's Foreign Investments.' One is impressed on the other hand with the tremendous power that an individual, and still very young, economist could exercise in the formation of public policy. Moving, as he did, in a very short time from the junior post which he left at the India Office to becoming that department's unofficial intellectual interpreter and public defender, and being catapulted by the outbreak of war to high responsibility in the Treasury, it is no wonder that he became enamoured—or so it appears—with social contact with the high and mighty, and left his Bloomsbury friends behind him. It is also likely that his early meteoric success, and especially its foundations in intellectual grasp and integrity, was responsible for his ability to resign and write in moral protest over the provisions of the Versailles Treaty, to cast himself in the role of Cassandra in relation to British economic policy, to present *The General Theory* as a boldly revolutionary and not merely a mildly revisionist document, and to press through as far as he was politically capable of doing so his plans for the financial reconstruction of the world economy after the Second World War. In spite of Keynes's public reputation in Britain of the interwar period as a brilliant but fickle and unreliable intellectual—'wherever there are six economists gathered together, there are seven opinions, two of them Keynes's—these books reveal him as a man who conscientiously sought for a superior grasp of the details as well as the essentials of a problem and was prepared to stand firmly behind his conclusions. As he grew older and busier, and as Britain's position in the world economy changed from the stable established order of his youth to the atmosphere of chronic crisis that has prevailed ever since, he undeniably yielded to the temptations to assume more knowledge than he could possibly have researched for himself, and to tailor his policy recommendations to his own judgement of what was politically feasible in his country. But these are temptations to which all economists interested in public policy are prone; and he redeemed himself magnificently with his contributions to postwar international economic reconstruction, the fundamental ideas for which harked back to his early work on Indian currency reform in the placid period of British greatness and his work at the Treasury in the exciting period of Britain's reluctant involvement in the First World War.

It is tempting, in a very brief review of Keynes's early economics such as this, to attempt to discover in that early work the seeds of *The General Theory*; or more modestly, and as the editors themselves invite us to do, to compare Keynes's ideas on war finance as they emerged in the First World War with the views set out a quarter of a century later in his *How to Pay for the War*. In the present context, however, it seems to me far more interesting to look into his earlier work for signs of the evolution of thought that led up to Bretton Woods, the Keynes plan, and the establishment of the International Monetary Fund system of international monetary organization. These signs are to be found in the two major incidents with which these books are concerned: his work on Indian currency and finance, culminating in his brilliant feat of persuading the Royal Commission to change its conclusions on a crucial issue in international monetary management; and the views on international financial relationships in the broad sense that led him to write *The Economic Consequences of the Peace*.

The Indian currency problem, as Keynes first encountered it, was very briefly as follows. In 1892, the Government had decided in favour of a gold rather than a silver or bimetallic standard, and had accordingly closed the mints to the minting of silver rupees on a full-bodied silver standard basis. The resulting monetary system involved the use of silver rupees and rupee notes as a token currency, the minting of silver rupees involving a substantial seigniorage profit for the government but requiring the maintenance of a reserve of silver and gold coins for exchange against inflows of domestic notes or of money from abroad. But gold was the standard, and maintaining the standard required two things: maintenance of a gold reserve in India, and maintenance of a reserve of liquid sterling assets in London, transfers between London and India being effected by sales in London of Indian bills and in India of London bills, the assets yielding interest to the Government of India and the transactions in both yielding a 'turn' on the difference between the buying and selling rates on sterling. (There were a number of technical problems, which need not concern us here, associated with the fact that until recently to that time the country had been divided into eight self-contained districts for the purposes of rupee note issue, that gold from different sources had different import and export points relative to the buying and selling margins on bills, that the Calcutta selling price of London bills was not a firm obligation of Government, and that the accounts for the various reserves were kept separately.) The central problem for policy was that those who had favoured, and still supported, the adoption of a gold rather than a silver standard believed that a gold standard required the actual circulation of gold coins, and wanted reforms designed to promote the use and circulation of gold coins in India; hence they were severely critical of the Indian currency arrangements that had developed after 1892 (the so-called 'Lindsay scheme').

Keynes's main contribution to the debate at this stage is contained briefly in an unidentified 'Memorandum on a Currency System for China', and much more extensively in a paper presented to the Royal Economic Society on 'Recent Developments of the Indian Currency Question' which grew into his book on *Indian Currency and Finance*. In the first, he advanced a gold exchange standard with a token silver coin circulation; in the second, he asserted that the existing Indian currency system was a gold exchange standard—in the process piercing through the veil of the system of accounts within which the various reserves were kept—and argued that, in line with the evolution of the gold standard elsewhere, it should become more so, rather than being forced to move towards a full-bodied gold standard. Notable among his arguments in this connection were that gold coins in actual circulation are the least available part of the total currency to the monetary authorities in times of difficulty, the public naturally preferring to turn in fiduciary currency for the acquisition of foreign exchange, so that centralization of the gold reserves in the hands of the authorities is the optimal policy—not only for this reason of maximizing available reserves but also because gold in circulation loses the monetary authority the seigniorage on the fiduciary issue it replaces; that the revenue obtainable by investing international reserves in liquid sterling assets rather than barren gold was a significant consideration for India;

and that it was inefficient to handle payments imbalances by actual physical movement of gold to and from India rather than by transfers of funds in London. In all these respects, Keynes's arguments foreshadow the structure of the post-Bretton Woods international monetary system, in which gold remains the reserve anchor of the system but the cost of holding it is reduced so far as possible by the substitution for it of interest-bearing credit instruments. His analysis also foreshadows recent interest in the whole problem of the creation and distribution of seigniorage implicit in the provision of credit rather than full-bodied international reserve money.

A financial scandal involving a secret but innocent purchase of silver bullion for Indian rupee reserves, and a series of articles in *The Times* by an anonymous correspondent whom Keynes strongly refuted with the above arguments, led to the establishment of the Royal Commission on Indian Finance and Currency, of which Keynes was nominated a member. Though the youngest member of the Commission, he took a very active part both in the questioning of the witnesses and in the preparation of the Report. It is quite clear from both his questioning and the acceptance of most of his arguments that, apart from Lionel Abrahams, his friend and mentor of the India Office, he was the only person involved on either side of the hearings who understood the monetary issues involved in the Indian currency system.

One of his most important contributions to the Commission's work was a lengthy memorandum on the proposal for an Indian State Bank eventually published as a separate section of the Commission's Report. This memorandum is remarkable, in view of the short space of time in which Keynes had to prepare it—though perhaps not so much so, in view of his work a short time before on *Indian Currency and Finance* and the years he had spent teaching money at Cambridge—for its exhaustive treatment of constitutional and operational issues and its command of relevant experience with central banking in other countries. (One might, however, criticize its rather superficial acceptance of the principle of the Bank Act of 1844 of dividing the central bank into a note-issuing and a banking department, and its close concern with the technical problem, paralleling the U.S. concern of a few years earlier that led to the establishment of the Federal Reserve

System, of providing an 'elastic currency' to meet the fluctuations in the Indian demand for credit as between the busy and the slack seasons of the year.) The main concern of the memorandum is with the problem of establishing an economical currency system, i.e., one that would not tie up an excessive amount of resources in barren reserves. Yet it is interesting, in view of the criticisms that have been expressed in recent years of both the Indian Government and of the Governments of the less developed countries in general for their failure to economize on international reserves and use expansion of the domestic money supply so far as possible to raise resources for economic development, on the basis of essentially Keynesian theory, to observe that Keynes the academic expert was roundly though politely criticized by Abrahams, the bureaucratic official, for his excessively conservative unwillingness to allow the resources accruing from seigniorage on the coinage and the expansion of the fiduciary issue to finance Indian industrialization.

Later in the proceedings of the Commission, Keynes was able to throw his weight successfully against those who wanted to expand the circulation of gold coin in India, and to write into the Report many of the arguments contained in the Royal Economic Society paper and in *Indian Currency*. Much of this argument, though it needs considerable re-interpretation, is relevant to contemporary debates about the international monetary roles of gold, dollars, and Special Drawing Rights.

Keynes's major contribution to the Report, however, was made in the penultimate stages of drafting it, when he was laid low in Mentone with diphtheria. His colleagues, only half-understanding his views, had arrived at a draft that both would have made it impossible to provide an elastic currency and would have accentuated the commitment of the resources backing the Indian money supply to sterile investments in reserves. The story is a complex one, both economically and diplomatically, and can only be understood by a careful reading of the editor's connecting text; and Keynes won his point largely because it could be met by two very simple changes of wording, the import of which his fellow Commissioners were presumably incapable of understanding.

The key issue, in very simple terms, was whether the fiduciary circulation of 20 crores of rupees to be permitted against the paper currency circulation should be a maximum, or whether the normal reserve of 40 crores of rupees should be considered a minimum; and in the latter case, whether the minimum reserve ratio of one-third should apply to the note circulation gross or net of the Government's own holdings of currency. By inducing the Commission to settle for a minimum normal absolute cash reserve rather than a maximum fiduciary issue, and application of the reserve ratio to the net circulation of notes, Keynes freed the hands of the Indian monetary managers to provide an elastic supply of credit through the lending out of seasonally surplus cash, and to invest money holdings above the normal at their discretion in domestic or foreign earnings assets. The final Report thus came out against a rigid gold-circulation or proportional-gold-reserve standard, and in favour of a much more economical and flexible minimum-absolute-reserve standard, or more briefly an intelligent gold-exchange standard. (Unfortunately, the outbreak of the First World War led to the shelving of the Report and to a rise in the price of silver that negated much of the seigniorage gain that Keynes had placed such store on; and India did not get a central bank until 1935.)

Keynes's activities in the period of approaching and initiated war, August-December 1914, present him in a not altogether attractive light as a young man anxious to obtain an important job in wartime economic management and not too scrupulous about taking sides with the Treasury and the Bank of England against the commercial banks and the City of London to further his ambitions. An alternative explanation would be that he shared the prevailing belief that the war would be short and limited enough not to disturb the prevailing order of things, that he was intensely patriotic, and that he had an Apostolic contempt for the second-rate minds that predominate among those engaged in the humdrum but economically necessary business of making money and protecting wealth from dissipation in bankruptcy. In any case, he surged forward with a memorandum and subsequent articles and correspondence against the proposal of the joint stock banks to suspend gold convertibility of sterling, arguing correctly (and consistently with his earlier ideas on Indian finance) that the purpose of reserve holding is external and for use in emergencies, and that the proper policy was to replace internal gold circulation by notes; and he was cock-a-hoop about Lloyd George's taking his point that suspension of the Bank Act with respect to the maximum on the fiduciary issue was not equivalent to suspension of gold convertibility, but instead a means of strengthening the ability to maintain convertibility. The general issue of whether Britain was well advised to go to such lengths to maintain the international monetary position of sterling was a moot point then, at least in the light of hindsight, and has remained an issue in British economic policy up to the present; suffice it to say that an important desideratum for Keynes was to strengthen the position of the Bank of England in relation to the London clearing house, and that he evinced towards the bankers a contempt, antipathy, and intellectual intolerance that remained characteristic of him throughout the rest of his career.

Subsequently, he busied himself in preparation for the hoped-for Treasury appointment in studies of the initial war-time financial arrangements of Germany, France, Russia, and other allied countries. A major theme of these studies, which recurs persistently in his later work for the Treasury on problems of inter-allied finance, is the irrationality of the approach of other countries to the domestic position and international use of gold. Gold was the focal point of all the problems of inter-allied finance with which Keynes was concerned during this period, through the American entry into the war and the peace treaty negotiations; and there are some interesting though not very direct parallels between Keynes's effort to induce the Americans to understand the reserve currency position of sterling in that period and more recent American efforts to induce the Europeans to understand the reserve currency position of the dollar. There can be no doubt that Keynes's prolonged grappling with the role of gold in the context of inter-allied finance in the First World War stripped his mind of any lingering remnants of the prewar mystique of gold, drove home to him the importance of proper management of international credits, and laid the foundations for his bold and brilliant proposal of the 'bancor' system as the basis for post-World War II international monetary reconstruction. At the same time, he remained thoroughly persuaded of the necessity of maintaining the convertibility of sterling into gold at a fixed parity—some of his arguments for specie now appear rather specious—and the ideas he formed in relation to Britain's special position among the allies as the only reserve currency country undoubtedly influenced the details of his 'bancor' plan—though by that time his experience of the adverse effects on British employment of an overvalued currency in the 1920s had converted him to the concept of the 'adjustable peg'.

Keynes's early work at the Treasury was hectic, heady, and highly varied, involving not only his main concern of inter-allied finance but also other issues such as inflation—contemporary Keynesian anti-monetarists would be well advised to read his memorandum on 'The Relation of Currency Inflation to Prices'—and an artful deal to relieve the Government of India, to the benefit of the British consumer, of the surplus of Indian wheat created by that Government's desire to prevent inflation of Indian food prices—and incidentally rob Indian wheat producers and the Indian economy of legitimate export income—by embargoing the export of wheat at a world price far above the domestic Indian price.

In 1915–16 Keynes became involved in the general issue of wartime economic management, which happened to focus on the issue of conscription—an issue on which his personal concern about his conscientious objector friends of Bloomsbury joined hands rather uncomfortably with his views on the economics of the situation. Briefly, his position was that unless Britain could drastically cut home consumption by increased taxation of the middle and lower classes, it had to choose between continuing to support its allies with munitions and material, and fielding a larger army of its own. He argued, rather emotionally but correctly in the light of subsequent history, that the former course represented the best course for beating Germany. (It would also have eased the problems of the peace treaty negotiations, which were intimately associated with the fact that Britain in effect supplied her allies with American goods financed by British debts to the United States.)

This piercing through of the veil of money and finance to the underlying real economics of the allocation of output and specifically of labour resources has generally been held to be the great contribution of 'Keynesian economics' to financial management in the Second World War; hence it is important to note both that

Keynes had arrived at this approach already in the early stages of the First World War, and that its application requires none of the novelties of *The General Theory*. Keynes was able to handle the monetary aspects of the approach quite satisfactorily with elementary quantity theory, including the concept of 'hoarding'. (The concept of the inflation tax appears in a 1915 memorandum.)

In February 1917 Keynes was made head of a new division of the Treasury, charged with responsibility for all questions of external finance, which in practice meant financial relations with the Americans. The details, which are hauntingly reminiscent of the same relations after the United States entered the Second World War, deserve only a brief comment here. Keynes encountered the same three major problems as recurred on the later occasion: difficulty in effecting firm bargains with Administration officials who had ultimately to wangle their bargains through a suspicious Congress, difficulty in winning U.S. understanding of the allied-war-finance implications of Britain's reserve-currency role, which centred on getting U.S. acceptance of the use of American loans to other allies to repay their loans from Britain, and the refusal of American opinion to allow American aid to be spent on goods from non-U.S. sources. In addition his haughtiness and impatience towards the Americans, which sometimes had to be restrained by his official and political seniors, gave him a reputation for rudeness that made him less effective than he might have been.

After the Armistice Keynes became concerned with the question of reparations, and subsequently with the negotiation of the Peace Treaty. (At the end of 1915 he had already prepared a memorandum on a possible indemnity, with Professor Sir W. J. Ashley, which was subsequently grossly misrepresented by Lloyd George.) The 'Memorandum By The Treasury on The Indemnity Payable by The Enemy Powers for Reparation and Other Claims', which he prepared, is a masterpiece of applied economic analysis, assessing both the claims that the allies might make for specific war damage and Germany's capacity to pay, finding the latter less than the former but in a comparable range of magnitude, and recommending quick rather than protracted payment, in the awareness that in the latter case Germany would have to build up her exports at the expense of Britain's traditional industries. A more important consideration, which dominated Keynes's reaction to the Peace Conference, was that no sovereign country had ever been or could be forced into a position of abject economic servitude for a substantial period of years.

Much of what he wrote in preparation for and during the Peace Conference is cannibalized in his *The Economic Consequences of the Peace*, and needs no summary here. What stands out from the record is his desperate humane effort to get Europe and especially the defeated enemies started on the path to reconstruction, in the face of the wildly unrealistic demands of the European allies for massive reparations and the growing incomprehension of and hostility towards these allies of the United States, which then as in the Second World War, in accordance with the anti-European and sport-oriented psychology of America, showed more love for the defeated opponent than for its own seconds in the ring. Keynes tried increasingly frantically to clear the financial problems of war debts and reparations out of the way of the relief of German and Austrian misery, first by a proposal to cancel out war debts (which for a time was an official British proposal) and then by a proposal for a joint guarantee of reparation bonds to be issued by Germany, only to be met by a U.S. refusal to recognize the problem or consider the proposed solution. The mood in which he resigned is illustrated by two letters both of which begin with the statement '. . . on Saturday I am slipping away from this scene of nightmare. I can do no more good here.' The one to Prime Minister Lloyd George continues 'I've gone on hoping even through these last dreadful weeks that you'd find some way to make of the treaty a just and expedient document. But now it's apparently too late.' The one to Norman Davis, chief representative of the United States Treasury, continues, 'You Americans are broken reeds, and I have no anticipation of any real improvement in the state of affairs.'

What does all this tell us, in the way of suggestion about the formative experiences that helped to lead Keynes up to his major role in the establishment of the International Monetary Fund system? Very little of specific substance, it must be confessed, apart from the fundamental idea that monetary and financial institutions and arrangements should be designed to promote the prosperity and progress of the people, and the belief that it is worth the while of an intelligent and knowledgeable man who has the opportunity to influence decisions to hang on and to keep proposing potentially negotiable plans so long as there is any hope of circumventing the blind unreasoning stupidity of the politicians. This latter belief of course has its dangerous temptations: Keynes had the character—and it must be admitted also the academic and financial independence—to be able to resign and to trumpet the reasons for his resignation, whereas many others in a similar situation have felt compelled either to resign quietly for inoccuously prevaricative reasons or to live with the noisy pretense that defeat is a novel form of victory. One might go further, stretching a point, and see in Keynes's concern for the milk-starved children of Austria the seeds of his later concern for establishing an international monetary system that would preserve and guarantee the priority of domestic full employment over the potentially hideous discipline of external balance, which was the original intention of his 'bancor' proposal, however far the IMF system in practice has drifted from that intention. But Keynes's concern in this period was with the problem of an impossible war-created structure of international debts and claims within a fixed-exchange-rate system (though already European rates had had to be floated, albeit intentionally only temporarily), rather than with the international monetary system itself. Later in 1919, he participated in a conference of bankers and others in Amsterdam, which among other things discussed the possibility of a new international currency; but that story is reserved for a subsequent volume in *The Collected Writings*.

9

Are Savings Male or Female?*

The English language, unlike many others, does not require the identification by sex of objects, activities and concepts described by nouns. Nevertheless, common usage and metaphor in English often attribute a sex to single and collective objects and activities; a ship is always 'she,' and a nation is 'she' when national policy interests are discussed. In economics, the latter usage is quite common; and a number of categories of economic actors or activities are typically thought of and described in male or female terms.

As a case in point, the two central concepts of macroeconomics, 'savings' and 'investment,' are typically visualized as female and male respectively. The maleness of investment is attested to by among other things the frequent references by Joan Robinson and other Cambridge writers to 'the animal spirits' of entrepreneurs; the femaleness of savings is evident in the passive role assigned to savings in the analysis of the determination of employment equilibrium.

In view of the established sexual identification of the two leading participants in the macro-economic scenario, it is interesting to note that in *A Treatise on Money*, the work which undoubtedly initiated the replacement of the quantity equation by the savings-investment equality in the English-language

---

* The passages from Keynes's *Treatise on Money* on which this note is based were called to my attention by Don Patinkin. He has, however, dropped reference to this intriguing puzzle from his *Keynes' Monetary Thought: A Study of Its Development, History of Political Economy*, Vol. 8, No. 1 (Spring 1976), and Durham, North Carolina: Duke University Press, 1976.

economics tradition, Keynes was himself ambiguous about the sexual identity of savings.

At the beginning of his chapter on 'Historical Illustration,' Keynes leaves us in no doubt as to how he saw the matter:

> If enterprise is afoot, wealth accumulates whatever may be happening to thrift; and if enterprise is asleep, wealth decays whatever thrift may be doing.
>
> Thus, thrift may be the handmaid and nurse of enterprise. But equally she may not. And, perhaps, even usually she is not. For enterprise is connected with thrift not directly but at one remove; and the link which should join them is frequently missing. For the engine which drives enterprise is not thrift, but profit.

Thus thrift—or savings—is clearly a female figure.

But at the end of this chapter—in the course of commenting on the lack of economic progress in postwar Europe—Keynes writes:

> Ten years have elapsed since the end of the war. Savings have been on an unexampled scale. But a proportion of them has been wasted, spilt on the ground, by the unwillingness of central banks to allow the market rate of interest to fall to a level at which they can be fully absorbed by the requirements of investment.

The allusion to Onan (who spilled his seed on the ground: *Genesis* 38:8–9) is unmistakeable. And as if to remove all doubt, Keynes goes on to predict a decline in the natural rate of interest—and to warn of the 'danger lest this consummation be delayed' by the aforementioned unwillingness of central banks to let the market rate of interest fall accordingly. And so savings represents a male figure!

This ambiguity in Keynes's conceptualization of savings raises many intriguing questions, personal, literary and economic. Did Keynes's love and respect for his mother, a very strong personality, lead him subconsciously to guard against criticism from an inevitable Women's Liberation Movement? Had he been reading his friend Virginia Woolf's *Orlando*? Is there an echo of T. S. Eliot's reference to Tiresias in *The Waste Land*? Does the eventual undisputed masculinity of savings foreshadow a return to neo-classical economics exemplified by the postwar development of Solovian in place of Harrodian dynamics? (Or, in the English economics tradition, the Leda of investment yielding to the Swan of savings?) Does the reference to the central banks in the second quotation imply that Keynes endorsed the 'monetarist' and not the 'Keynesian' school of thought on the instability of capitalism?

The reader is left to speculate for himself upon such intriguing questions.

Part IV
Cambridge in the 1950s

10

Cambridge in the 1950s

When I first arrived at Cambridge, the Canadian Army had excited a series of riots by its troops in Aldershot, due to its inability to claim the shipping to send them home immediately as expected, and then decided to cool them off by sending the longest-service of them home on ships that suddenly and not inexplicably became available, and as many as possible of the remainder who possessed adequate educational qualifications back to school on the spot. So I came to Cambridge in my corporal's uniform, which I wore for most of the rest of the year. When I finally tried to enter the college dining-hall in resplendent new mufti, the Head Porter stopped me and said 'Sir, you must wear a gown—otherwise the gentlemen will think you're a freshman'—and kindly lent me one for that evening. Fortunately I was not the only Canadian soldier there—there were nine other Canadian soldiers—or I might have felt either lonely or snubbed. There were also 150 American GIs there, and they bore, as usual, the brunt of discrimination against North Americans. (Nowadays, with no British-style uniforms and not much recognizable Canadian accent to distinguish them from Americans, Canadians often find themselves bitterly resentful at bearing the discrimination which the British love to inflict on ordinary Americans.)

Cambridge was quite a change from the academic background I came from, the University of Toronto, which functioned in those days with fairly small classes, and instruction mostly by informal lectures and seminars. Cambridge ran on a different system—and still does—whereby the lectures are few in number from any one individual staff member, and very formal. Most of the weight of the instruction is carried by a weekly hour one spends, alone or in small numbers, with someone known there as your 'supervisor' (and in Oxford as your 'tutor') for whom you write an essay every week for discussion in your 'supervision' or 'tutorial.' Moreover, examinations were set on the field and not on the lecture series, and would probably be dominated by what the external examiner happened to think were important current problems. This gave us an extra degree of freedom from attending lectures that was difficult for the more regimented North American to get used to. I played it safe, Canadian-style, and attended most of the lectures. My colleagues did not suffer visibly, given their ambitions and work capacity, from doing without most of the supervisions as well as most of the lectures.

I was allotted a room (actually a bedroom-study, living-room, and kitchenette for making tea and soup) in Jesus College. I had not been forethoughted enough to stipulate King's College, which shows something of my lack of understanding of economics at the time, since King's was where A. C. Pigou was and Gerald Shove was and J. M. Keynes still had rooms: in short, where the action was. Jesus College did not even have a supervisor. I was paired with a lively little American whose interest in economics was shown by his classical remark 'Cambridge is a great place: Yuh get yur own who'house' (referring to the fact that he could entertain girls in his room); but I soon arranged to halve my supervision with him and to be supervised alone.

It was a pretty miserable winter. There was no coal, and they managed also to contrive a shortage of bread. In England, then, with a lack of central heating, coal and bread were substitutes. One could heat oneself either internally with bread and marmalade or externally with coal. One ate starch five times a day and relished proximity to a roaring fire. I can remember doing my studying in my army overcoat and gloves and trying to leaf through the pages of The General Theory while I shivered away in my little set of rooms.

My supervisor Maurice Dobb, the well-known Communist intellectual, was probably the saving virtue of being at Jesus College, because everybody else was involved in the fight over liquidity preference versus loanable funds. Dobb, having no intellectual commitment to either side, was capable of being dispassionate when it came to discussing those issues. So I did not wind up brainwashed one way or the other on that fundamental issue, as it was put to us, of whether liquidity preference or loanable funds was the only possible approach to monetary theory.

Well, I went to lectures, not being able to shake off the habit of a North American education and the belief that lecturers somehow were there to teach us something—a great mistake, I now realize. And the first lectures I heard were by D. H. Robertson. They were brilliant lectures, but you had to know at least enough economics for a Ph.D. before you could understand them. In his youth he had been quite an eminent amateur actor, and his delivery was beautiful. It was not until you got to know him better that you realized that every single word had been written out. He allowed no questions. Toward the end of the year he would announce that anyone who wished to write out a question was welcome to do so, and he would take them home and write out his answers and read them to us the next time.

Robertson was in the habit, as many other Cambridge people were, of writing those lectures out fresh every year. They would take the whole month of September and spend it writing and rewriting. The lectures did not turn out all that differently from year to year, as I found out by going to some of Robertson's lectures after I returned to Cambridge. But it seemed to give them pleasure to do this and a feeling of assurance.

I asked Maurice Dobb about this after I became a lecturer, and he said that he wrote his out every time, every year. But in his case he did not have any elocutionary talent. He used to read these things in a flat monotone, and I went to those lectures out of a sense of duty, which was certainly required. They were supposed to be about the Economics of Socialism, which was a fairly hot topic in 1945–46; and he would start off with a large crowd of 40 or 50 students. Towards the end there would be nobody left except myself and a very small band of Communist Party members who felt obliged to reciprocate the services that he had done for the party by listening to the lectures. They were mostly about the 1930s arguments about socialism, which started with von Mises's assertion that socialism, simply 'could not work' because you could not 'coordinate all those decisions'. And quite a number of socialists had set out to challenge this by showing that 'Yes, indeed, you could coordinate decisions—by making a socialist economy work like a capitalist economy with prices serving as signals to decentralize managers. . . .' This was a rather abstruse debate involving at least three people who had published on the subject, and it took the whole term to work through it all. One never really discovered what would happen in a communist society except that it would indubitably be 'far better'—a matter on which, if you lasted the course, you would have at least a few doubts.

There was another lecturer who, while not involved in such fantastically fundamental issues, produced more or less the same impression. This was a man called J. W. F. Rowe, who was by way of being an expert on commodity markets. He would take a whole hour to explain to us the difference between retailers and wholesalers. This left one plenty of time for writing letters home; I cleared off most of my relatives during those hours.

The only exciting lecturer was Joan Robinson; and this, again, was a bit of a surprise. We had had female lecturers at Toronto who appeared nicely dressed and perfumed and wearing skirts and other kinds of recognizable sex symbols. But in strode this rather mousy-looking woman, wearing a sort of blouse-and-vest combination on top and a pair of slacks down below, and sandals. She proceeded to put an elbow on the lectern, peered out at us, and started off in a rather flat monotone. 'Well, it's very difficult these days to lecture on economic theory because now we have both socialist countries and capitalist countries. . . .' Everyone thought, 'Gosh, what a wonderful new idea!' I found out from one of my students some ten years later that he heard her start her lecture course exactly the same way, and he came to me and said, 'Gosh, what a wonderful new idea!' At any rate, you got used to the image that she was not recognizable as a female of the species and did not behave like one, and that was one of the main lessons one had to learn. Once she came to Chicago to talk to my students there; they looked at her and decided, 'Well, we'll certainly show this old grandmother where she gets of.' After they picked their heads up off the floor, having been ticked off with a few well-chosen blunt squelches, they took a much more respectful attitude.

Even at that time the fight between the liquidity preference and loanable funds groups was going on. Robertson had a little coterie of people who believed in loanable funds. Unfortunately for him, they were not really sharp theorists. They were mostly involved in peripheral subjects like industrial organization (on which the British have always been extremely weak), labour economics, and other similar subjects, so about all they could do was declare their faith and manoeuvre behind the scenes in the academic politics of the place, trying to get more of their kind elected to positions and keep out the opposite crowd. The Keynesians were the sharp theorists, and they made their points by caricaturing an orthodoxy that no one equally sharp (apart from Robertson) was there to defend.

Things went on like that. We were, I am afraid, not paying too much attention. It was too easy to drink beer and argue politics. As is well known, English public licensing hours are rather barbarous; but they do have the one great advantage that the pubs open at 10.30 in the morning, which makes it possible to cut a lot of lectures and feel no pain. They stay open until afternoon (when one was supposed to go out and play healthy field sports), and reopen an hour or so before dinner. Of course, one has to stop drinking at 10 o'clock at night, unless one can afford one's own private stock; but that did not make too much difference because in those days you had to be in by midnight or be gated or sent down (unless one knew how to climb over the walls). There were well-charted routes by which one could get into and out of colleges, including the female colleges, after midnight. Actually, the rule in the women's colleges was that, after 7 p.m., all men are beasts. Up until 7 p.m. they were all angels, and the girls simply had to learn to live with that routine and practise love in the afternoon.

It was during that year as a student that I saw Maynard Keynes for the one and only time. It was at the 'Political Economy Club' which Keynes had founded. The Club had a set of rules based on those of the society of 'Cambridge Apostles' one of which was that somebody would read a paper, and before the paper was read those present would draw numbers from a hat. The numbers would run from 1 to 6, and this would determine the order in which you spoke. If there were more people present than six then there were blanks in the hat, and if you drew one at the Political Economy Club you could heave a sigh of relief and devote yourself to getting close enough to Robertson's coal fire to keep warm. Robertson was something of a miser, and the coal fire was always lit but it never generated too much warmth. So that if you arrived a little late for the meeting you found yourself frozen, and you had to follow the lecture carefully as you shifted from foot to foot, or else you spent so much of your effort combating the cold that you could not follow what was going on. It made a great difference whether you had a number or not. If you had a number *and* came late, you were really in trouble.

I was eventually invited to join this club. At my first meeting Keynes was the guest. They passed the hat and I drew number one, which was a pretty daunting experience. I spent the time that Keynes was talking trying desperately to think of something that might be wrong with his argument; and failing that, something that might be right, but could somehow be still more right. My colleagues were kind and they offered to take my number and give me a blank, since it was rather unfair to put me up against Keynes the first night. But I refused manfully to accept this lifeline that was being offered to me. The paper he gave is the one that was published posthumously on whether or not there would be a long-run dollar shortage. He argued fairly convincingly (at least as far as he was concerned and we were concerned) that there would not be. His argument depended very heavily on an appeal to the long-run classical mechanism, basically the influence of balance-of-payments surpluses on money, wages, and so forth.*

Keynes was a brilliant phenomenon; he was a sparkling man

* Seymour Harris (whom I was to know but learn little from later at Harvard) got into the act very quickly with a denunciation of this; and that set off a whole wave of books on the permanent dollar shortage. The most unfortunate economist in that respect was Donald MacDougall, who managed to produce a very scholarly 400-odd page book, full of regression analyses of everything you could think of, demonstrating conclusively that there *was* a permanent dollar shortage. He had taken so long over the regressions that by the time the book came out there was clearly a dollar surplus, and the book had to be remaindered. And there has been a dollar glut virtually ever since, in more or less the same basic and mistaken sense.

Well, Keynes was right. In fact, we have been suffering in the American economy from an over-shooting of the mechanism he talked about, though the mechanism failed to grab hold for long enough for all those people to get their tenure and full professorships on the basis of 'the permanent dollar shortage.'

and a great experience for me. The speaker had the good fortune of sitting right beside Robertson's hearth fire, so he had no trouble keeping warm. Keynes sat there in an arm-chair with his legs slumped out in front of him—and he had very long legs; he was in some ways, physically, a slightly miniaturized John Kenneth Galbraith. He had some notes on the table beside him, but he never seemed to look at them. He have us a very elegant talk, beautifully constructed, every sentence a piece of good English prose and every paragraph cadenced—just a wonderful performance. But it was in the discussion afterwards that I learned so much from him. I got up and struggled through a rather lame argument. It was to the effect that, given the availability of lots of farm labour in the United States, it would take some time before the pressure of demand for American industrial products would force up the general level of wages, just because the labour could be drawn off the farms. I was not really convinced of this myself, particularly after having listened to Keynes. But he was very kind, and he picked up the point and made something of it. And I noticed that this was what he did. One of the secrets of his charm was that he would go out of his way to make something flattering out of what a student had said. If the student had made an absolute ass of himself, Keynes would still find something in it which he would transform into a good point. It might well be the very opposite of what the student had said; but the student was so relieved to find that he was not being cut to pieces that he was really impressed by the brilliance of what he was told he *had* said. On the other hand, when a faculty member got up—faculty members had the right to get up at any time, having interspersed themselves among the students, and at that time Joan Robinson stood up and attempted to argue with him—he simply cut their heads off. No matter how ingenious what they said was, he would make nonsense of it. And that, again, flattered the students, because they had been told that they were really incisive and then somebody they knew was really clever was reduced to rubble before their very eyes. That was a doubly flattering thing. I think that this has something to do with the various well-known reactions to Keynes as a personality. When he was out of the public eye, he could be extremely kind and charming, and could make somebody feel glad to be alive. On the other hand, when the chips were really down, he could be quite ruthless in the way he dealt with people.

I happened to meet Robertson a day or two after this, and I expressed my tremendous appreciation both for the invitation and for the paper itself. He said to me, 'Ah, but you missed something that used to be there—the impishness of his mind.' And that, of course, reflected Robertson's very long concern and intimacy, first as a student and then as a junior colleague, with Keynes. He missed the flash of brilliance, or penetrating remarks of an unexpected kind. The paper was impressive, but it did not have the cut and thrust and the mental agility that Keynes had formerly displayed. And, of course, it was only about two or three weeks afterwards that Keynes died.

After that first year at Cambridge, I went back to Toronto and then to Harvard. But in between I worked my way across the ocean on a cattle boat and returned to visit some Cambridge friends. I. G. Patel, I think, told me I should go to see Robertson. So I went to see him, expecting it to be a pretty lame encounter, a sort of visit of respect; and it was, more or less. We did not have too much in common, but at the very end he stunned me by asking whether I would like an appointment in Cambridge. I recovered enough to say, 'Yes, yes, yes, yes, yes,' and later after I got to Harvard, I received a letter from him, written in his own hand. He never used a stenographer except for typing papers, conducting all of his correspondence himself; and this had been true even when he was the secretary (or chairman) of the faculty. Everything was done by hand, and it was infernally difficult to read.

At Harvard, I was educated in Keynesian economics by Alvin Hansen and Seymour Harris. I cut a lot of ice around Harvard, since Cambridge was where they all would have liked to have gone. That eased my path as a graduate student considerably, and I duly re-crossed the Atlantic and went back to Cambridge.

By that time two other members of the cast had appeared on the scene, Richard Kahn and Nicholas Kaldor. That set up a situation for the next ten years or so, which became a situation of considerable strain. Without, I hope, going too far in personal terms, I think one has to understand what lay behind the bitterness of the controversies in terms of the personalities involved.

When you become a member of the Cambridge faculty, you are there for life; there's nowhere else to go. And each of you is attached to a particular college, and you teach that college's students. You give your lectures (but that is a rather minor part of the responsibilities). Is there anything more likely to generate personal bitterness (and a penchant for overstepping the bounds of civilized discourse) than the knowledge that you and that other person are stuck there for the next thirty years? You cannot really do them any harm: they are not going to apply for a job anywhere else, so your opinion on their incompetence will never be solicited. And the same applies to you. You can be as incompetent as you want to be; you still have most of the weapons in your hands, in the sense that you can tell your students what you like and carry on the war that way.

The physical environment of the colleges, and the nature of the academic appointment had quite a bit to do with the bitter personal animosity of Cambridge controversy. There is something of the flavour of it in C. P. Snow's novels, which refer to a college that is really a composite of Cambridge colleges and their gossip. That kind of situation makes for considerable acrimony and for dissatisfaction in the long run among the students, because they are being told one thing by one teacher and another thing by another. Then the examinations are not set by the individual teacher, which would make life easy: you could be a Keynesian in one examination and a 'Loanable Funds Man' in another. But you have somehow to straddle the issues in a paper which will possibly be marked by one of each, which means that the ability of one to influence the other is going to have a substantial influence on the outcome. There will also be an external examiner whose name you may not even know (since they make every effort to keep the external examiners secret until the last possible moment). He may well set you a question innocently, into which you can drag liquidity preference or loanable funds. All those traps lie in wait. In addition, most students at Cambridge were not planning to become professional economists; so spending a couple of years trying to master the ins and outs of liquidity preference *versus* loanable funds before going back to India as government planners was not exactly a wise investment of time. Nevertheless, that was the prevailing ethos.

Robertson, as has been mentioned, had been a supervisee (or a 'pupil' as they used to describe it) of Keynes, and there was a great personal attachment between them. It lasted through the 1920s, but broke up with the publication of Keynes's *Treatise* (1930). The *Treatise* introduced a great many new concepts and a few equations that turned out to have nothing very much in them. On one of the final-year examinations (these are compulsory examinations, incidentally, there is no getting around it), Robertson set the question, 'In the *Treatise* Mr. Keynes says—. . . Does this mean that the quantity theory besides being a tautology, is not true?' And that kind of thing would go on in the exams in my days as student and don.

Robertson had been very deeply attached to Keynes; they broke over the *Treatise* basically, but it became worse as *The General Theory* began to emerge. And Keynes had a group of young people around him—Richard Kahn and Joan Robinson, in particular, though there were a number of others who were involved who didn't stay at Cambridge but went elsewhere. He deliberately egged them on to attack Robertson—not that they needed much urging.

Now to understand the implications of that one has to know a bit about the characters of the persons involved. Robertson was a very shy, gentle person. I suppose he might be best described as 'an English gentleman.' He had served in the First World War and been awarded the Military Cross, though nobody ever spoke about this, and I never found out for what act of valour he received it. It certainly was not anything he ever talked about. He was a bachelor, and he lived all the time in his college. His attitude towards economics was pretty much of a gentleman's attitude and an Establishment attitude. He had been trained as a classicist and that, I suspect, was where his heart really lay. His attitude towards economics was that it was something one did lightly. And, of course, some people at least who have read his little book on *Money* (1922) will remember the quotations from *Alice in Wonderland* with which he started each chapter. This truly reflected his character: whimsical, somewhat withdrawn, and very shy, and it expressed itself in what I have already mentioned—his writing out every word of his lectures and entertaining no questions, the lectures being theatrical performances, scripted by himself. He was not any good at give-and-take. The most you would get out of him at the Political Economy Club was a sentence or two of a not very informative nature. And Keynes had egged his young people on against him.

Their attraction to economics, particularly in the case of Joan Robinson, was basically a radical political attitude. This led to Joseph Schumpeter's description of them as 'Marxo-Keynesians.' In that respect one has to accord an important influence to Michal Kalecki, who had arrived in Cambridge and become one of the group in the middle 1930s, and who had actually produced much of the General Theory in his own writings in Polish (which were eventually translated), though with a very strongly Marxist flavour. Where Keynes had an 'aggregate propensity to consume,' which is the key pin of his apparatus, Kalecki had the division of society into workers and capitalists. On the Marxist assumption that the capitalists save and invest most of their income and workers consume most of theirs, you can regard the capitalists abstractly as having a unitary marginal propensity to save, and the workers a zero one. In fact, some of the empirical work of that period was devoted to this problem. Much to people's surprise they found that workers *also* save, and that the difference in marginal propensities was not all that great (though it was certainly statistically significant).

Keynesian economics originally (at least on a majority interpretation of it) started out really as a way of saving capitalism from the stupidity of its managers, and this, I think, remains the majority tradition of monetary economics outside England. The general proposition—that policy-making does have to pay attention to macro-economic management (but once that is properly looked after, micro-economics comes into its own)—became, in the Cambridge concept, very much tied up with questions which go a long way back in the history of economics, particularly the question of the justification, if any, for the payment of interest. On that question the classical economists often showed their complete failure to distinguish science from emotion. That certainly survived in this tradition at Cambridge. It is one thing to say that people who own property 'do not deserve to own it,' that inheritance of property is 'a bad thing socially,' and so forth. It is another thing to say that property, therefore, must be *unproduc-*

tive—because we want to believe that the people who own it have no real social function.

This, of course, has been one of the major problems in Soviet Russian economic planning. The Russians are exceedingly good at developing human capital. One of the major sources of their rapid growth has been the attention they have paid to developing the characteristics of the individual as a worker, or as administrator, or whatever else, fostering human talent as far as possible by intensive emphasis on education. Their chief difficulties come from attempts to argue that interest has no justification and no meaning, that capital is not scarce, that you should treat it as if it cost you nothing (and naturally if it *is* scarce you get into trouble). The same sort of problem arises in Russia with respect to the rent of land, which again (according to the Marxist and pre-Marxist tradition of various writers such as Ricardo) implies there is something wrong somewhere since no work is being done to generate the rent of land. Much of the development of economic theory, of course, concerns the separation of the economic logic of prices being attached to things that are scarce from the question of *morality*. That confusion of logic still runs right through the Cambridge Keynesian school (and I will say a little more about that later).

My point of departure is this characteristic of Robertson: a man who was very aloof about relationships with other people and was not cut out for the rough life of politicking behind the scenes or for public debate. This was fully realized by the other chief protagonist in this argument, Joan Robinson. She—I would not say necessarily consciously—certainly used the attitudes of the opposite sex towards her as an excuse for behaviour which often would not have been acceptable from a male economist, I mean in terms of distorting arguments and abusing the privileges of academic discourse. It was her favourite ploy with the students to say, 'Well, I don't mind—I'll gladly have a public debate with Robertson on any issue at any time.' Well, take—on the one hand—Joan Robinson, whose forte in life has been standing up in front of audiences and announcing her political conclusions (with much economic nonsense) without feeling any compunction about it; and—on the other hand—Robertson, who had to write out every lecture in order to give himself the confidence to deliver it. This was certainly no contest, it was a giant challenging a baby to a boxing match. And this went on continually.

The background to all this was the harrying of Robertson through the 1930s both in print and personally; the latter was much more serious. He had been prevented from receiving what he (and many others) considered was the final reward of a serious academic career, namely the professorship at Cambridge; for that reason he had gone to the London School of Economics as a professor. Fortunately for him, the war broke out—and the London School of Economics moved to Cambridge. So he could be a professor at the London School and still live in his old rooms. At the end of the war, when it was clear that Keynes was never going to come back to academic life, these people got together and persuaded Robertson to take the chair on the basis of promises that they would 'stop the persecution,' would 'live and let live,' and so forth. But those promises were very quickly forgotten. The bitter controversy and intellectual guerrilla warfare resumed full sway.

I remember taking Anthony Scott, a friend of mine from Harvard (who is now a professor at the University of British Columbia) to one of Joan Robinson's lectures. She was holding forth about liquidity preference and loanable funds. One of her main remarks was first of all to call attention to some analysis of Maurice Dobb's (about the Benefits of Planning) in terms of an analogy. A man is walking along a road across the field from his dog, and the dog tries to catch up with him. It starts off and each moment it is aiming for the man; but as it goes along the man is also going along, so it traces out a sort of curve: the 'pursuit curve.' Yet, if it had the brains, it would realize that if it did its canine calculations properly, it could go in a straight line to the point where the man had now arrived and save itself a lot of legwork. Joan Robinson called attention to this analogy, and then she said, '. . . and loanable funds is the fly buzzing around the nose of the dog.' This may be a good polemical tactic, but it is not exactly very instructive to somebody who wants to know what the real economic issues are. A great deal of this sort of thing went into her lectures, and much of the controversy was concerned with debating issues which had been raised in the 1930s.

Here I would like to fill in some background history which, I think, would help to clarify the basic questions.

The quantity theory as we think of it now, thanks to the atavism perpetrated by my colleague in Chicago, Milton Friedman, is usually conceived of as $MV = PT$, or $M = kOP$, or whatever. We used to have a lot of fun as students with the Cambridge formulation $M = kOP$. We always referred to it as M *equals kOP*, where M is the nominal quantity of money, k is a functional relationship representing the ratio of money people want to hold to their money income, O is output, and P is the price level. If we go back to Knut Wicksell we notice that for Wicksell this was merely the starting point: interpreting what this equation meant and how it operated. But very quickly Wicksell, in his own work (and in the development of the theory, based on his work) got quite a way off from the equation of exchange, which was just a starting point, to a discussion of the conditions under which money will be neutral—that is, under which monetary developments will not interfere with the achievement of the real barter equilibrium of the economy. Now Wicksell stated the conditions for that in terms of three principles which he thought were equivalent: namely, that savings should equal investment; or that the money rate of interest and the real rate of interest should be equal; or that prices should be stable.

A young Swedish economist, Johan Åckerman, pointed out that in a growing economy these conditions are not the same—that, in a growing economy, keeping savings and investment equal (at least as these are commonly defined) would not necessarily mean stability of the price level, and in particular as output increases with a given quantity of money the price level will tend to fall. As this becomes expected, then the money rate of interest will lie below the real rate—because people who hold money will be getting the automatic benefit of an increase of the purchasing power of money.

That set the framework for the development of the general quantity theory tradition, particularly with the Austrian economists who came to be represented in England by Friedrich Hayek of the London School of Economics. It also characterizes Keynes's work up to and including the *Treatise*. The basic mechanism which determines whether the economy is going through a 'boom' or a 'recession' is whether Savings are *less than* or *greater than* Investment. But savings there are defined as voluntary savings out of a full employment level of income, and investment is defined as the investment that businessmen want to make. So that if you have an excess of investment over voluntary saving you will get a rise in incomes and increases in saving which will accrue to businessmen as windfall profits. Now, in *ex post* accounting terms you would count these as part of 'savings', as in *The General Theory*. But in the *Treatise* these are windfall profits and not part of savings as defined by Keynes. Similarly the other way around. If full-employment Savings tends to exceed full-employment Investment, then you get a fall in the price level with windfall losses for entrepreneurs. Again, the mechanism is inequality of Savings and Investment (in the special sense defined).

Robertson's major contribution to the development of monetary theory was concerned with this question of the conditions for monetary equilibrium, in which he introduced two kinds of factors. There was the balance of real savings and investment, but then there was also the balance between the desire to accumulate cash balances and the willingness of the monetary authority to create them. So you had a market for loanable funds in which (in the short run) equilibrium would require that the sum of savings and new money creation would be equal to investment plus hoarding, the desire to accumulate cash balances.

It is a feature of Robertson's writings in this field—and one which comes as somewhat of a surprise to someone who has read Keynes's frequent diatribes against central bankers—that he was very much in touch with policy-making. He was, in fact, the only economist in the country who could invite himself to lunch at the Bank of England. While the Bank of England is not quite as august or eminent as it used to be, still, there were many others who had to wait to be asked. In my own case it was only two years ago that they asked me, and then it was not the Governor, it was just one of the Court. (The lunch, incidentally, was rather austere, though the wines were good.) Robertson kept writing into his monetary theory an assumption which to our minds would seem very strange (particularly given the 20 years or so of criticism of the U.S. Federal Reserve System that there has been), namely that 'the monetary authority is pretty smart.' Robertson always assumed that the monetary authority was 'smart' enough to know whether a disturbance in the market is due to a change in the real factors, Savings and Investment, or due to a change in 'the hoarding factor', namely the desire of people to hold idle balances. So from place to place you find him remarking that a normally astute central bank will recognize this difference; and if people want more money because there is a scramble for liquidity, the central bank will provide it. That, of course, is good, standard, central banking theory. It even goes back to Walter Bagehot. But it makes a big difference to the model whether you assume that the authorities are 'smart' and intelligent or not. The consensus among American monetary economists is, on the whole that they are *not*, and that their efforts to be 'smart' cause more trouble than they are worth. Not just Milton Friedman, but a number of others (including the Joint Economic Committee of the U.S. Congress) have come out in favour of limiting the power of the central bank to introduce arbitrary disturbances in the market by subjecting it to some sort of rule (or band limits) on what it can do to the money supply.

Robertson's contribution, then, was to set the problem up *this* way with loanable funds and to take account of hoarding. But it was very easy to make fun of the concept of hoarding. When I was a student at Harvard, for example, it was not Robertson but Hayek that people were having great difficulty with—because he had the concept of 'forced saving.' This is a concept, which after 40 more years of monetary theorizing, we can understand pretty well. All it amounts to is that, if you inflate the money supply of an economy, this will drive up prices; and the rise in prices will cause people to try to restore their real balances; and, to do that, they have to spend less on goods and services. So, you are extracting goods and services from them through the inflationary process. This is known in the modern literature as 'the inflation tax.'

But it is very easy to poke fun at the idea of hoarding and forced saving—who has the money? who has the savings?—and all that kind of thing. This was what Cambridge in the early 1950s was spending most of its time on. Richard Kahn was giving his lectures on monetary theory; in fact, there were several series of lectures going on this particular kind of issue. That, frankly, is why I chose to specialize in money and banking institutions—and to leave monetary theory alone—while I was teaching there.

It was primarily Kahn who carried on the Keynesian tradition of liquidity preference theory. It is important for the understanding of Keynes to realize that he started his life as a lecturer—talking about the stock market and the financial markets generally—and that he kept on with those lectures through much of his career. Kahn took over from him both in lecturing on that subject and in managing the College's finances (where this analysis is really of great practical importance). Kahn was a rather peculiar lecturer. He would always spend something like twenty minutes of an hour summarizing what he had said the *last* time and then, by the time he got through that, of course he could not finish what he was going to do *this* time, so that had to go into the *next* lecture's summary. And so you went on from week to week, being told either what he said last week or what he was going to say next time, with a very thin sliver in between of what he was actually saying this time.

But Kahn's main function in Cambridge economics was not the contribution of his own subtle analysis of liquidity preference. It was (on the one hand) to direct the strategy and tactics of left-wing academic political manoeuvres in the Faculty, and (on the other hand) to marshal all the intellects in support of Joan Robinson's version of Keynesianism. For this purpose, he played the affable host to the self-styled 'secret seminar', which met in his King's College rooms virtually every Tuesday evening in the Michaelmas and Easter terms and increasingly became a forum for the advanced testing of the technical analysis of Joan Robinson's *The Accumulation of Capital*.*

Anyway, Kahn was lecturing on liquidity preference theory, and Joan Robinson was lecturing on aggregate demand theory.

---

* The description 'secret seminar', incidentally, was a violent misnomer: its existence was known to all, and non-invitation to attend was deliberately used to snub those who lacked the correct Keynesian qualifications and/or political orientation, even though their theoretical abilities were indisputably at least equal to the group's average. 'Included out' in this way were both the Cambridge economist P. T. Bauer and the American visitor Milton Friedman.

She, of course, lacked the rewarding subtlety of Kahn's mind. Kahn was juggling, long before anyone else, with the question of extending liquidity preference theory to allow for more than two assets—treasury bills and equities as well as Keynes's money and bonds—and grappling with complicated issues of portfolio management theory.

Robertson, meanwhile, was giving essentially what was by then very old-fashioned stuff. He began with $M = kOP$, went on to loanable funds, and wound up with 'the four crucial fractions' (which Paul Samuelson sneeringly dismissed in his *Quarterly Journal of Economics* obituary of Robertson).

Actually, the four crucial fractions, which I do not want to go into here, had a lot more sense to them than Samuelson allowed. Let me explain very briefly what the problem is. One has a banking system in a growing economy; and one has a certain rate of growth of the demand for money. The supply of money has to be provided by the banking system. The banking system has a desired relationship between the amount of commercial lending it wants to do and the amount of reserves it holds. The business community has desired ratios between financing by bank credit, financing by security issues, and financing by ploughed-back profits. Robertson's problem, which originated in the circumstances of the 1930s when bank lending dropped very sharply and banks came to be loaded up with government securities, was this: Is there anything in the natural course of evolution of a society that will make all these ratios work out correctly? Or will there be troubles because the money people demand does not match the money that they want to see supplied, as reflected in their borrowing from banks?

That formulation, again, was easy for a more mathematically trained generation to ridicule. Professor Samuelson, I think, behaved rather badly in using an obituary of Robertson to make fun of it and of other efforts by a subtle but hopelessly literary mind to tackle serious problems. If Samuelson had drawn the analogy with Don Patinkin's *Money, Interest and Prices*, which was by then available, he might have been more perceptive. And if we had studied Robertson more carefully ourselves, we undoubtedly would have understood Patinkin much better. Anyway, Robertson was lecturing away on pre-Keynesian quantity-theory lines, $M = kOP$ and loanable funds and the four crucial fractions; and Joan Robinson was slashing away at Robertson using a very simple version of liquidity preference theory; and Kahn was making liquidity preference theory a general—and difficult—exercise in the theory of portfolio management.

As I have said, the early part of that period was devoted to making fun of Robertson, who more and more did his writing in the form of interpretative essays, full of allusions and quotations. Richard Kahn once said that he wanted to stage a debate between Dennis Robertson and Thomas Balogh. The contest would impose only one condition: neither of them was to be allowed to quote or cite anyone else—they had to make a straightforward argument. That might have been a good competition, except that neither would have made it past the starting point without being disqualified. The Keynesians all amused themselves by asking what 'hoarding' meant, and travestying Robertson's 'period analysis' to show that, in the short run, the loanable-funds approach led to the conclusion that the rate of interest might go either up or down. This is a result easily achievable. One repeals Walras's Law (the law that all money must be either spent or held) or one incorporates a concealed change in liquidity preference along with a change in the real factors (saving and investment). Joan Robinson's famous 1951 *Econometrica* article on the rate of interest had played this game. But eventually they got tired of that, which was not very enlightening for the rest of us anyway. Then along came Roy Harrod with his dynamic growth equation; and Joan Robinson latched on to that and proceeded to create a new confusion which Cambridge has insisted on ever since in the realm of capital theory. It is the mistaken belief that to prove capitalism to be logically impossible is sufficient to dispose of its existence.

To understand that controversy, one has to understand something about the politics of academic debate in England; more particularly, to appreciate the sharp division between the London School and Cambridge over Hayek *versus* Keynes in the 1930s, which eventually led the younger people to start publishing *The Review of Economic Studies*, so that those interested in serious technical economics (rather than academic polemics) could publish their ideas.

Joan Robinson's work in this connection is essentially a criticism of the aggregate production function. (This relates total output produced by the economy to the total labour and capital it employs, *via* the technology which permits productive factors to be converted into products). It was developed by J. R. Hicks and R. G. D. Allen at the London School of Economics at the turn of the 1930s, and so implicitly carries on the Cambridge 1930s myth of a 'revolutionary Cambridge' battling a dinosauric London orthodoxy. But by the 1950s F. A. Hayek had departed from London for Chicago, and there was no one left in London either capable of or interested in debating 'capital theory' with Cambridge. Had it not been for Cambridge (U.S.A.)—I mean MIT not Harvard—responding eagerly to Joan Robinson's challenge to 'orthodox' production function theory in order to display its mathematical-economics muscle—Cambridge (England) would have been revealed—even to its own captive student audience—as a voice crying nonsense in an imaginary wilderness. It would long since have been a dead duck professionally.*

A major break-through in economics in the 1930s, as it appeared at the time, was the imperfect competition revolution. In the postwar period this was reconstituted in the proposition that prices do not reflect any rational profit-maximizing process, but instead are determined by the mark-up that entrepreneurs choose for their own unexplained reasons to add on to their prime costs. As a consequence, running through the works of Joan Robinson (and quite a few American Keynesians of the same 1930s vintage like Sidney Weintraub and others) you find the notion that we really have no theory of income distribution and price determination that has any rational basis. One, therefore, has to construct one out of whatever pseudo-sociological materials lie to hand. This position, among other things, provides the scientific vacuum from which recommendations for Incomes Policy as a cure for inflation are derived.

* Cambridge (U.S.A.), out of a misplaced sense of rivalry, an underestimation of its own intellectual capacity, and an abnegation of its own common sense, chose to engage with Cambridge (England) in debate about these allegedly fundamental issues in theory, and so kept Cambridge (England) in the zombie business. It is a sucker's game for Cambridge (U.S.A.). Nonsense is nonsense, no matter how prestigiously pronounced; so why take it seriously and reconstruct it to the point where you make mistakes yourself?

The two major Cambridge protagonists in the attack on the aggregate production function were Joan Robinson and Nicholas Kaldor. While they agreed on the utter imbecility of neo-classical production and distribution theory, they differ radically on what should be put in its place. Joan Robinson has put vast efforts of both analysis and personal assertiveness into developing the theory of capital to the point where she has proved conclusively to her own satisfaction that Capitalism Cannot Possibly Work.

Nicholas Kaldor once commented that if you really believe in capitalism, it is worth while doing all the work required to explain how it functions. If you do not believe in capitalism, it is not worth while exploring how it is supposed to work in order to show why it doesn't. But to do all that work in order to show that it cannot work is a waste of time.

Well, Cambridge is a very isolated place, and the message still has not reached there that, by and large, the world has enjoyed full employment and fairly successful capitalism for over a quarter of the postwar century and that, that being so, the fact that Britain had mass unemployment for 20 years and the rest of the world for about eight years of the interwar period is not really a very great violation of the long run of historical experience. Joan Robinson's effort (and that of many of her disciples) had been to prove that capitalism cannot work and to do this on purely intellectual grounds. This is not a scientific game at all; it is not even an interesting divertissement; but with enough prestige inherited from superior minds, and with enough vociferousness, you can make a lot of the profession think that it must be important. One of the major elements in the radical case is the ancient idea that the rate of interest really has nothing to determine it. It is modernized into the contention that what determines the rate of profit is whatever it is that makes entrepreneurs decide on various kinds of mark-ups (or else some extension of the concept of 'liquidity preference').

Nicholas Kaldor, on the other hand, being a man who rolls with the times fairly fast, decided early on that capitalism actually was working. So for him the problem was, given that it works, it cannot possibly work because the theory of it is right. It must work for some quite unsuspected reason which only people as intelligent as himself can see. He developed a great deal of new theory to that effect, opposing Joan Robinson on theoretical fundamentals but joining her in rejecting the production function. In particular he developed a new 'Keynesian' theory of income distribution to oppose to marginal productivity theory, and something called the 'technical progress function' to reconcile production theory with his new distribution theory, thereby scoring twice over orthodox theory while not violating the crude facts of empirical observation. So that, you will see, is having it both ways. I was wrong the first time in saying it did not work. Now I must be doubly right, because I can show you that it cannot possibly work for the reasons that people always said it works; but that it nevertheless works, after all, according to a new theory I have developed to replace the theory I claim cannot possibly work. The consistency of the results—i.e. with the obvious facts the others started with—irrefutably demonstrates the brilliance of my own contribution.

I want to return briefly to the 'production function' as the subject of the Cambridge debate. One of the leading figures at London was J. R. Hicks, who won the Nobel Prize in 1972. He was instrumental in developing 'general equilibrium theory' in the United Kingdom. As a preliminary, in his *Theory of Wages* he applied the aggregate production function to the determination of the distribution of income. I want to say two things about that.

1. If you use a single aggregative model, which produces only one 'product', of course demand has nothing to do with the distribution of income—it is purely technologically determined by the production function. The total amounts of labour and capital suffice to determine how much each contributes to total output, and hence receives under competitive market conditions. So naturally, anyone who does not like the distribution of income (and is not smart enough to realize that there is a difference between the economic functions of factors of production and the social function of the distribution of their ownership) has a natural incentive to attack the production concept as a way of laying an intellectual foundation—though a completely unnecessary one—for his beliefs about the just distribution of property and income.

2. If you go beyond the one-sector model to a two-sector model, demand does come in again. The distribution of income is

not determined by technology and factor supplies alone, as the one-sector model necessitates. In a two-sector model there are two goods—which may for present purposes be identified with Consumer Goods and Capital Equipment—and two industries producing them, these industries using labour and capital in different proportions. A shift of production towards the labour-intensive industry increases the demand for labour, raises its price, and lowers the value of the services of capital (and vice versa). Hence, to determine the prices of factor services to production and the distribution of income, we need to bring in the demands of the two groups of factor owners for the two goods, weighted by the distribution of income corresponding to the allocation of production between the two industries.

The Cambridge mind, however, never stretched to the two-sector model, until they began working on the line of proving that capitalism could not work. They then developed the production side of the two-sector model, but they never fed back the implications of that for demand through the distribution of income between labour and capital and the preference systems of these two factors of production for the consumption of goods. Instead they relied on the Keynesian assertion that investment is subject to no budgetary constraint. Investors can undertake any amount of investment they want; saving is a fixed proportion of income (the proportion differing between labour and capital owners). Then you arrive at a model which is 'overdetermined' in the sense that you have investors determining how much investment there is and, therefore, how much has to be saved. This, in turn, implies a distribution of income which sees to it that amount does get saved. On the other hand, you have a production side of the economy which implies typically a different rate of return on capital and wage rate than is consistent with the assertion that investment is not subject to a budget constraint.

My own view is that the Keynesian assertion is the one that has to go—because it is inconsistent with the observable facts. It implies that investment has nothing to do with the rate of interest, that entrepreneurs can always find all the money they want for investment, and that everything depends on their high animal spirits.

It was about that time—the 1950s—that I began to appreciate

the difference between scientific and ideological motivations for theoretical work. I began to realize that more and more Cambridge people in my judgement were perverting economics in order to defend intellectual and emotional positions taken in the 1930s. In particular, for them Keynesian economics was not a theoretical advance to be built on for scientific progress and improved social policy. It was only a tool for furthering left-wing politics at the level of intellectual debate.

So I decided to leave Cambridge and go somewhere else where I might learn something useful—namely to Manchester.

I eventually left Manchester to go to Chicago, in spite of the fact that my days in Manchester were probably the happiest in my life, professionally speaking. Over the years I became fed up with the intellectual poverty of English economics, which provided increasingly inadequate spiritual compensation for the material poverty that English academic life in the provinces imposed.

But that is another story.

11

The Shadow of Keynes

Most outstanding university academic departments, in economics as in other subjects, became that way through the teaching, research and publications of one or at most a few (necessarily complementary) scholarly personages; and almost invariably the academic style and authority of the dominant academic personage lingers on after his physical or mortal departure, to constitute the main threat of decay of academic excellence. The departments of economics of the major universities at which I have studied or taught have all been characterized by this problem. Toronto has continued to suffer from the aftermath of the greatness of Harold Innis and the 'Toronto School' of economic history. Cambridge remains a self-satisfied example of the virtually inexorable operation of 'the law of diminishing disciples' in the wake of the genius of John Maynard Keynes. Manchester, where I moved from Cambridge in response to compelling arguments from W. Arthur Lewis (only to find him departing, soon after my arrival, on a sabbatical leave that was followed by two years advising Kwame Nkrumah and, belatedly, his resignation) continued to be dominated during my tenure by memories of his ideas and his ebullient and sometimes abrasive personality. Chicago in its turn was dominated by the memory of the great 1930s days of Frank Knight and Jacob Viner, though in fact Milton Friedman was already clearly in the ascendant, along with George Stigler—and Chicago's main problem in the next half-decade will be to bear up under the weight of their tradition.

Harvard was the exception. It was already suffering in the immediate postwar period from an embarassment of riches in the form of conflicts between Alven Hansen and John Williams

(Keynesianism versus conventional banking wisdom), between Edward Chamberlin and Wassily Leontief (monopolistic competition versus general equilibrium), and between Schumpeter's cultured and Austrian school economic style and the emerging mundane formal mathematical-geometrical theorizing and empirical approach of American economics—a conflict he internalized, unsuccessfully, in his efforts to master and teach mathematical symbolism to his classes. And it dis-distinguished itself for some twenty years by marrying the law of diminishing disciples with the selection of the least common denominator of acceptability.

When I arrived in Cambridge the shadow of Keynes—who was still alive, but no longer a part of Cambridge—already lay heavily over the place. As an outsider, a member of Jesus College, and a supervisee of Maurice Dobb's, I heard only rumours of the intellectual struggles of my fellow-students who were fortunate, or unfortunate, enough to belong to King's, where to help his College A. C. Pigou had returned to supervising undergraduates after over thirty years of debarment from the privilege by the terms of his Professorial post, or Trinity, where D. H. Robertson had returned as successor to the Chair of Political Economy. But one major message came through. Early in my year I was told by a South African who was trying to recruit me to pull an oar for Jesus that economics was easy: all you had to do was read Marshall's *Principles* during the year, and *The Times* at breakfast every morning, with the rest of the day free for being 'out on the river with God', as he put it. Alas, this was no longer true: in addition to Marshall, for Part II Tripos one had to read *The General Theory* from cover to cover, making what one could out of the concept of user cost, and Mandeville's *Fable of the Bees*; and in addition one had to master what can be best described as 'Robertson's Commentaries'. The central issue, which occupied much of one's reading and thinking time, was the collection of arguments concerning Keynes's 'liquidity preference' versus Robertson's 'loanable funds' theories of interest. Later, during my early days as a don, at Jesus College, I remember losing my patience though not my temper with one of my supervisees, Dipak Mazumdar, who became, much later, a colleague at the London School of Economics, and asking him just how useful he thought a knowledge of the ins and outs of liquidity preference theory would be to him when he got back to India and had nothing but primitive capital markets to theorize about. I now realize I missed the point completely on that occasion: the point for Mazumdar, my earlier self, and countless other individuals was not to learn something useful, but to have been at Cambridge—or Oxford, or even the London School of Economics—and to have distinguished oneself in its examinations. From that point of view a debater's knowledge of the literature deemed relevant to local controversy was far more important than an understanding of economic principles. Incidentally, the most extreme example of forcing students to immerse themselves in the details of a controversial scholastic literature I ever encountered was E. H. Chamberlin's insistence at Harvard that every Ph.D candidate understand the precise differences between Joan Robinson's 'imperfect competition' and his own 'monopolistic competition'.

When I returned to Cambridge as an Assistant Lecturer in 1949, thereafter a Lecturer and a Fellow of King's College, Keynes's shadow continued to dominate, his influence being mediated through Richard Kahn, Joan Robinson, and Austin Robinson. Their roles were complementary in the service of Keynes's memory.

Austin Robinson, broadly, implemented as far as he could Keynes's conception of the role of the Department of Applied Economics in relation to the Faculty of Economics and Politics, of the role and functions of the Royal Economic Society and *The Economic Journal* as representing British Economics, and—though this was probably as much Austin Robinson's as Keynes's doing—of the role of Cambridge economics as the quintessence and fountain-head of the only economics worthy of the name. As regards the Department of Applied Economics, Keynes (like a number of subsequent British economists) conceived of applied economics as being the handmaid of economic theory, with the applied researcher as a subordinate of the economic theorist. Things did not work out that way under the first Director of the Department, J. R. N. Stone, who excelled both as an original mind and an academic enterpreneur, and attracted as staff and visitors economists who have have since become eminent in the world profession. But, thanks to faculty resentment of Stone's increasing power and with the help of some adroit manoeuvring by Austin Robinson, Stone was hived off into a Chair of Accountancy (defined to include social accounting, Stone's major interest) with a small research staff, and the Department gradually reduced to a service role performed largely for or in supplementation of government.

As regards *The Economic Journal*, Keynes's tradition of personal and entrepreneurial editorship worked decreasingly well in the somewhat eccentric hands of Roy Harrod, especially as the profession of academic economists grew in terms of numbers, mathematical and statistical competence, and location outside the confines of a strong Cambridge paired with a weak Oxford, while Austin Robinson was largely responsible for committing the wealth of the Royal Economic Society, created by Keynes, to the financially perilous production of a monument to him in the edition of his collected works. As regards Cambridge economics, qualified economists in other British universities never became resigned to the impression that Cambridge economists seemed assured of publication of everything they wrote in *The Economic Journal*, that often unfamiliar Cambridge names dominated the reviews section of the *Journal*, and that unknowns from Cambridge and its hinterlands were frequently chosen over acknowledged experts from elsewhere for the British contingent at the Round Tables of the International Economic Association, which Austin Robinson dominated through his dominance of the Royal Economic Society.

Richard Kahn's role was to manage Faculty politics in the service of the Keynesian interest. The heart of this operation was the 'secret seminar' for the Cambridge Keynesians and occasional like-minded visitors, which automatically separated the Keynesians from the conservatives and gave the former a base for continuing informal interaction. Within the Faculty, the politics were generally concerned with appointments, tenure, and promotions. Here Kahn's power in King's was a great asset, since he could sweeten a lectureship with the chance of election to an attractive fellowship. Faculty politics also included in the early 1950s the killing off of the proposal to include sociology as a subject in Tripos—an unexpectedly easy task of academic slaughter. It began with rejecting the proposal to give a Chair to T. H.

Marshall of L.S.E. Then, it having been decided to try with three
Visiting Professors, the task was made almost too easy by inviting
Talcott Parsons as the first of these, in which role he drowned the
subject in Germanic verbosity, and further by inviting him to give
the Marshall Lectures—in which role he asserted to his rapidly
dwindling audience that sociology is the master social science of
which economics is a special sub-case, and tried to prove it by
re-interpreting *The General Theory*, read without knowledge of
any surrounding literature, in terms of his *Structure of Social
Action*.

The intellectual leadership in the battle for Keynesianism
against 'orthodoxy' was provided by Joan Robinson, who was
supported by continual discussion with Richard Kahn, Piero
Sraffa, and Nicholas Kaldor. (They had institutionalized a long
country walk every Sunday, in which others sometimes participated by invitation, in the course of which they mainly discussed
issues in economic theory proposed by Joan Robinson. Kaldor
was personally excused from participation in the actual walking
part of the exercise.)

Until 1950 or so, the campaign was fought on 1930s issues,
concentrating on the complete unrealism of assuming full employment, the impossibility of explaining precisely how the quantity of money affects economic activity, the ludicrousness of the
Robertsonian concept of 'hoarding', and specifically the demonstration that Robertson's 'period analysis' could—by subtle and
unplacarded alteration of assumptions—be made to generate any
dynamic sequential connection whatsoever between a change in
the desire to save and the resulting effect on the rate of interest.
This phase of postwar Cambridge Keynesianism was epitomized
in Joan Robinson's commissioned article on 'The Rate of Interest'
in *Econometrica* in 1951,[1] in which much play is made, doubtless to
the confusion of non-Cambridge readers, with the Robertsonian
question of 'what happens if I decide not to buy a suit from my
tailor, but to increase my savings instead?'. (Clue to the answer: it
all depends on whether I spend my new savings on securities or
hold them in cash, and on whether my tailor finances the unsold
suit by selling securities or by running down his cash balance.
Clue to the economic significance of the answer: in each case one
alternative changes the demand for money, the other does not.)[2]

After the publication of Roy Harrod's *Towards a Dynamic Economics*,[3] however, the intellectual character of Cambridge Keynesianism changed very rapidly, though it retained in reserve much of the intellectual baggage of the 1930s (and 1920s) British monetary theory and policy debate, notably a contempt for and utter rejection of anything connected with the quantity theory of money. This was the extreme result of Keynes's increasing dissatisfaction with the inability of the traditional quantity theory to cope with the rule of money as an asset, and especially the influence of expectations about the future on the relative valuation of money and alternative assets.

Harrod's book is a classic, which changed the fundamental conceptions of economists about the economic nature and problems of a capitalist system, and more generally of a growing economy. It may fairly be said that it was the only really seminal idea contributed by British economics to the science in the whole post-Keynesian period, with the possible exception of the work on economic dynamics and problems of stabilization policy of A. W. Phillips (which has been quite unjustly caricatured as the invention of 'The Phillips Curve' and dismissed by American monetarists who have not bothered to study the original, but have instead fathered on Phillips the crude version of his theory presented by Samuelson and Solow to the American Economic Association meetings of 1959). The basic idea of Harrod's analysis is simple, and can be simply put for present purposes. Keynes's *General Theory* demonstrated that for an economy to experience full employment investment must be at a high enough level to absorb the saving (or fill the gap between income and consumption) that would occur at full employment; the purpose of *The General Theory* was to explain why this would not result automatically from the operation of the competitive price system. But the analysis of *The General Theory* was a short term analysis, in the sense that the effects of investment adding to productive capacity were ignored. Harrod pointed out that, in a longer term context, investment would increase productive capacity and hence the gap between capacity and demand that would have to be filled in future by further investment, and he produced a simple equation expressing the rate of growth of output and investment that would keep capacity fully employed over time—the 'warranted' rate of growth–thus satisfying the expectations of demand and profit that motivated investment in the first place. This equation expressed the 'warranted' rate of growth as a function of the community's ratio of saving to income and the optimal ratio of capital to output in production.

Following and indeed outdoing Keynes, Harrod ruled out any automatic mechanism reconciling saving and investment desires through movements in the rate of interest, with the result that his analysis cast up two central analytical problems.

The first was that his self-justifying growth rate was unstable, a faster growth rate than the 'warranted' rate justified by his 'dynamic equation' leading to pressure of demand on capacity, abnormally high profits, and an inducement to still higher investment, while slower than 'warranted' growth would produce stagnation, low profits, and still lower investment. The second was that the rate of growth 'warranted' by the savings and capital-to-output ratios was that which would maintain full employment of the capital stock, which rate would, in general, differ from the rate of growth of the 'effective' labour force determined by natural population increase and technical progress.

As Harrod, and, following him John Hicks, in *A Contribution to the Theory of the Trade Cycle*,[4] developed it, the central emphasis of the analysis was on the 'trade' or 'business' cycle in a capitalist economy. But the analysis was capable of application in a variety of different ways—the most important in practical application being the planning of economic development; and in Joan Robinson's hands it underwent a particular personal transformation embodying strands from her own past thinking which owed little, or little directly, to Keynes.

Various elements in Joan Robinson's version of the Harrod phase of extension of the short-run Keynesian theory of employment into a long-run Keynesian analysis of capitalist economic growth can be mentioned briefly in this connection. One is her early work on the economics of imperfect competition, with its emphasis on the irrationality of consumer behaviour that imperfect competition is assumed to reflect (wrongly, in terms of more recent theory and empirical work), and on the 'exploitation' of workers by entrepreneurs that imperfect competition (by contrast with Chamberlinian 'monopolistic competition') is assumed and asserted to entail. A second, related, element is the emphasis on the examination of the realism or unrealism of analytical assumptions as a test of the validity of a theory. This dates back to Piero Sraffa's classical 1926 article[5] demolishing the Marshallian theory of the firm, an article which led ultimately to finding the solution in the concepts of 'imperfect' or 'monopolistic' competition and its central implication of a downward-sloping demand curve for the product of the individual firm and provided a basic technique of British theoretical discourse in the 1930s and on well into the 1950s. A third element, for which the evidence is admittedly rather speculative, is Hick's *Theory of Wages*,[6] which depended heavily on the concept of an aggregate production function combining labour and capital as inputs to produce output of aggregate product, a concept which made the distribution of income between labour and capital appear to be determined entirely by technology and relative supplies of capital and labour, with human choice and social institutions, other than free market competition, exercising no influence on incomes and income shares. Much more fundamentally important in this connection, probably, is Gerald Shove's review article on Hick's book in *The Economic Journal*,[7] which demolished the logical foundations of its analysis by pointing out that capital is a 'produced' and not an 'original' factor of production, so that its quantity cannot (in the aggregate) be measured separately from the marginal product that the quantity is assumed to determine. At any rate, the style and content of Joan Robinson's first attack on 'orthodoxy' (which, incidentally, is a uniquely Cantabrigian economic pejorative) took the form of an all-out attack on 'the production function' with recognizably Shove-ian and anti-Hicksian origins.

The most important key to the transmogrification of Keynesian economics into something intellectually quite different in the hands (and writings teachings and preachings) of Joan Robinson, however, is the understanding that the dominant influence on Joan Robinson's Keynesianism was not Keynes, but the Polish economist Michal Kalecki, who had developed a Marxist version of Keynes's theory earlier in time than, and in some respects theoretically superior to, Keynes's *General Theory*, but was unfortunate enough to publish in Polish, his native language, and doubly unfortunate in that, when he finally arrived in Cambridge, he proved to lack all the social and cultural graces necessary for acceptance in the British academic system and establishment—graces with which Keynes was super-abundantly endowed.* In Joan Robinson's discussion of theory in the early 1950s, 'Keynes' was just the name of an author she had known at one time as a very senior colleague and was not always entirely patient with; but her eyes lit up with admiration whenever she mentioned Kalecki and his works.**

What Joan Robinson presented as Keynesian economics was as much Kaleckian economics as Keynesian economics, and increasingly Kaleckian as time passed, and certainly Kaleckian in its division of Keynes's aggregate propensity to consume into a weighted sum of capitalist income (assumed to be all saved) and

* It is ironical, if true—though the story may well be apocryphal—that Keynes could have found a position for Kalecki in Cambridge (as he had done earlier for Sraffa), but chose not to do so, on the grounds that Kalecki's personality was too different from the conventional for Cambridge to swallow. The irony is that, through Joan Robinson, Kalecki rather than Keynes shaped postwar Cambridge's 'Keynesian economics'. There is another ironical possibility, that had Kalecki been kept in Cambridge, he would have developed an economics far more relevant to, and capable of handling, Britain's postwar economic difficulties than 'Keynesian economics' as it developed at Cambridge, and more specifically at the Institute of Statistics at Oxford. My reason for thinking this is that, on the one occasion on which I met him in Cambridge (he being *en route* back to Poland), Kalecki delivered a lecture on inflation that employed a simple quantity theory of money together with expectations about the future trend of prices—and which met with a reception from his former admirers so hostile that he was discouraged from publishing it.

On Kalecki's life and work, see the full-length study by Georg Ralph Feiwel, *The Intellectual Capital of Michal Kalecki: A Study in Economic Theory and Policy* (Knoxville: University of Tennessee Press, 1975). A biography by J. Kowalik is included in *Problems of Economic Dynamics and Planning: Essays in Honour of Michal Kalecki* (Warsaw: 1964).

** The only occasion on which I ever saw Keynes—when he presented his posthumously-published paper on 'The Balance of Payments of the United States' (*The Economic Journal*, Vol. LVI, No. 222, June 1946, pp. 172–87) to the Political Economy Club early in 1946—is engraved on my mind partly on account of the extreme rudeness with which Keynes dismissed a question of Joan Robinson's on that occasion: and it is to that experience I owe my perhaps erroneous impression that his reference in that paper to 'how much modernist stuff, gone wrong and turned sour and silly, is circulating in our system, also incongruously mixed, it seems, with age-old poisons', was aimed partly at her, though he might have been referring to Thomas Balogh.

workers' income (assumed to be all consumed.)* Kaleckian analysis was admixed with a contra-Keynes conviction that the capitalist system is a nonsense that must be jettisoned because it cannot possibly work; this was a peculiar personal view which might possibly be attributed to Marx but it is nevertheless important to get the logic of the analysis of it straight, particularly the alleged logical contradictions that make the system inherently impossible (mountains of empirical evidence to the contrary being quite irrelevant). It was a belief shared with Keynes and derived from an important strand in the British economics tradition and more fundamentally in British assumptions about the nature of government, namely that demonstrating the logical errors in the governing elite's conceptions of problems will be sufficient to change the elite's thinking about the nature of those problems and the policies required to solve them.

How much of Joan Robinson's Keynesian economics is attributable to Keynes is in fact extremely difficult to determine. A major reason is a characteristic of Joan Robinson's mind and memory—by no means unique—according to which experience, especially in relation to other people, is interpreted personally in relation to the self, and the self's conception of itself, by a selective process that highlights the features that the self wants to believe or to be believed while supressing or dismissing those that are awkward or inconsistent with the interpretation desired.

---

* One strongly Kaleckian influence, perhaps not obvious to economists unfamiliar with the literature of the 1930s, is the abandonment of much of Joan Robinson's early analytical work on *The Economics of Imperfect Competition* in favour of the assumption that entrepreneurs simply apply a certain exogenously-given profit margin to variable costs, which are assumed constant over the relevant range of variation of production. In Kalecki's early work on income distribution, aimed at explaining the apparent empirical constancy of the share of labour in total income marvelled at by Keynes, the profit mark-up was related to the Lerner 'degree of monopoly', a theoretically indefensible position that was subsequently dropped in favour of the direct assumption of a given profit margin. The early part of Joan Robinson's *The Accumulation of Capital* occasionally (and confusingly for the reader) switches to the possibility that the profit margin or rate of profit required by the capitalists may, in conjunction with the assumed determination of saving by the income shares of capital and labour, be inconsistent with full employment growth. On this last point, see Harry G. Johnson, 'A Simple Joan Robinson Model of Accumulation With One Technique', *Osaka Economic Papers*, Vol. 10 (Spring 1962), pp. 39–46.

As a result, Joan Robinson's own views of what Keynes meant and what the Keynesian revolution was all about, are frequently a much better guide to Joan Robinson's politics than to Keynes's economics—a proposition which can be supported indirectly but reasonably convincingly by the cavalier disregard of fact in the construction of myth that historians of economic thought have documented with regard to her treatment of the writings of Marx.

Leaving such issues aside, the fact was that the 'secret seminar' became more and more an occasion for Joan Robinson to present her new thoughts and writings on her criticisms of 'orthodox' capital and growth theory and the constituents of the analysis that ultimately became *The Accumulation of Capital*—with the adoption of a title borrowed from Rosa Luxembourg and the use of Hebrew letters to stress the departure from traditional analysis and the adventure into new analytical frontiers that the book sought to achieve. The presentation of the work of others became less frequent, and regarded more and more as an interruption of the main task of assisting Joan Robinson to complete her revolutionary work on the theory of capitalist growth. I understand that after I left the seminar deteriorated still more, with increasingly intense arguments between Joan Robinson and Nicholas Kaldor over their rival theories of capitalist growth.

Though Keynes's shadow dominated the Faculty of Economics at Cambridge, it dominated still more King's College where he had been a fellow and bursar, and where I became first a research and then a teaching fellow. In fact, my presence there was, in a sense, due to Keynes, or more specifically, Keynes's incredible success as a bursar in playing the stock and gilt-edged markets. So affluent had it made the College that it was under considerable pressure from the other colleges and the University to share its wealth by expanding. The fellows, who did not relish the contemplation of the changes that the transition from a small to a large undergraduate college would bring, compromised by deciding to leave the college at its customary undergraduate size but to expand greatly the number of fellowships, especially Research Fellowships provided by the College for more senior scholars. (The process of transition incidentally disrupted for a year or two the balance of voting strength between junior and senior members of the fellowship body, requiring among other things, the introduction of a 'middle caucus' between the junior and the senior caucuses). My Berry-Ramsey Research Fellowship, then almost the only one open to competition from the whole university and not merely from the College's own junior members, was one of the results.

In my time at King's the domination of Keynes's memory over the College was immediately evident, physically, to an economist at least, from the geography of the dining arrangements for fellows. The Senior Combination Room was reached through an ante-chamber (and on one side an additional room with pegs for the hanging of gowns, squares and raincoats and other garments). The ante-chamber was dominated by a mounted bronze bust of Keynes, placed to command attention on entering the chamber and to demand it on leaving on the march to the Hall and High Table or merely on departure. The fact that the bust was of Keynes, an economist, is a uniqueness of distinction that only an economist can fully appreciate. The only comparable memorial, and one infinitely more ghoulish to modern sensibility, is the apparelled skeleton of Jeremy Bentham, that sits in a glass-fronted case on the ground floor of University College, London, its skull replaced by a mask but stored in a hat-box between its ankles, and that used to be wheeled out once a year to preside over a formal ceremonial dinner.

Keynes's great contribution to the financial resources of his college permeated the atmosphere of the College in many subtle ways. That contribution can be encapsulated briefly in the fact that Keynes pooled a number of miscellaneous funds secreted by his predecessor, amounting to £20,000 in the 1920s, into an investment fund which he multiplied into £250,000 during his bursarial reign, and which his chosen successor, Kahn, built up to some £1,250,000 by the turn of the 1950s. Affluence was reflected in the fact that the Garden Hostel, a new undergraduate building across the Backs by the Fellows Garden, was paid for from one year's income; in the large number of Research and other non-teaching fellows among the governing body; and in a general sense of comfort and good living day-to-day, and of availability of money for College expenditures deemed to be worthwhile.

But Keynes's shadow was apparent in more obtrusive ways.

The senior fellows who had been his colleagues, both peers and juniors, frequently wondered or inferred 'what Maynard would have said' (or done) in a current controversy or decision problem concerning College business. One evidence of his strong opinions on certain matters was 'conspicuous by its absence'; he had a lifelong contempt and dislike of lawyers, the tangible expression of which was that there was no fellow in law, and the few undergraduates misguided and persistent enough to opt for that subject had to be farmed out to the care of the plethora of legal talent at neighbouring Clare College.

While Keynes's shadow exercised a pervasive influence on King's College life and decision-taking—its presence often apparent only in unexpected asides and explanations or appeals to his authority in the discussion of college business—it was most explicit, naturally enough, in the conduct of the College's investment activities. In this connection, Richard Kahn as bursar (and Angus Macpherson who succeeded Kahn officially but not in reality as bursar when Kahn's election to Professor barred him from official participation on College administration) undoubtedly were following Keynes's style in cultivating and displaying a contempt for the ordinary fellow's capacity to understand, let alone to offer useful advice on College investment policy.

Kahn, indeed, sometimes set the stage for the bursar to inflict a crushing intellectual defeat on the amateur critics of bursarial investment policy, as I found out through being elected a member of the Inspectors of Accounts. The inspectors were three fellows charged with verifying the annual accounts. For this task, which originally involved actually reading the account books, they were recompensed by a crown (five shillings) for 'glove money,' to replace the gloves they had presumably dirtied beyond redemption by leafing through the dusty hand-written volumes in the college office. (In my time the bursar had great difficulty finding crowns for the purpose since they were no longer minted; so he gave us our crowns at the ceremonially appropriate moment on the understanding that we would sell them back to him for a sixpenny premium later.)

In any case, in the last of my three years' term of office, one of my colleagues, by insisting that he knew nothing about accounts, had confined his responsibilities to writing a one-sentence contribution to our report on the condition of the Christmas trees that the College grew for commercial sale on its farm, while the other had somehow persuaded himself that now was the time to sell the college farm and put the proceeds into gilt-edged bonds. Kahn did his best to encourage this fellow to get the inspectors into the position of arguing that the College should 'go liquid' by selling the farm, so that he could ridicule us for overlooking the logical implication that the College should switch its far larger holding of marketable stocks into bonds. Thanks to kindly forewarning by a third party concerned with preserving unity between the bursar and the inspectors, our report limited itself to raising the question of the justifiability of the farm, without committing itself to a definite proposal either for the sale of the farm of for a shift of portfolio towards liquidity. Kahn made an angry speech nevertheless, attributing to us the position that he had wished to discredit and excoriating us for our ignorance of the elements of portfolio management.

The farm was, in fact, Keynes's only specific investment legacy to the College; and it was one which increasingly became a bone of contention between the bursars and the fellowship body. It was the result of Keynes's astute realization in the years of the great depression, when it became impossible to rely on tenants actually paying the contracted rents, that the College would do better to farm the land itself than to look for new tenants. The decision paid off, especially during the war and immediate postwar years of heavy government subsidization of food production; but continued farming became less and less profitable, partly because the College's own land was the less choice part of the total estate acreage (which was presumably why Keynes had been able to take it over from the previous tenants). Meanwhile, the bursars, somewhat in the manner of the stockbroker-gentleman-farmer, had become fondly attached to their role as knowledgeable farm-owner-operators able to discourse as experts on the prospects of the hay, the corn and the potato crops. They thus had two emotional reasons for opposing any rational evaluation of the value of the farm to the College as a whole; the authority of Keynes, and their own psychic income from running a large scale farm. (The latter benefit they tried to generalize by encouraging college fellows and their families to vacation in the appropriately staffed farm manor house free of charge. But the prospect of a holiday in the rustic flatness of Lincolnshire could not have been very attractive to academics who traditionally vacationed in Europe, the Lake District, or Wales). They also had two advantages in quelling dissident opinion: the bursarial style of assuming as unquestionable that amateurs could not possibly understand the subtleties of college farming, and the complexity of the accounting of the farm, which tended characteristically to show a good profit before deductions for special contingencies—such as the collapse of a newly-built silo one year, entailing the death of an employee with a substantial family which had to be provided for—and a negligible profit or actual loss thereafter.

Nevertheless, partly due to the persistence of one of the fellows, there was increasing disquiet among the fellowship body about the farm, and eventually (after my departure) it was decided to have an impartial report on the farm as an investment prepared by a qualified firm of appropriate experts. The result was a defeat for the bursars and condemnation of their past defence-in-depth of the farm. The rate of return on the farm—and this was presumably in nominal terms, uncorrected for inflation—was, so I understand, only about one and a half per cent. It was therefore decided to sell the farm. But a buyer at a face-saving price was hard to find, so much so that when one was finally found the bursars apparently began to take comfort among the fellows in their cleverness at getting a good price for a white elephant. But this joy was short-lived, for the news was published that the buyer had drilled for oil and made a strike!

There was one other aspect of Keynes's career in Cambridge that left a shadow, which I encountered through King's College, and Kahn and other of the fellows—though it was not an official concern of King's College. This was the Cambridge Arts Theatre, which Keynes had financed and built as a gift to Cambridge. It was a magnificent idea, and an imaginative and valuable contribution. But it had been conceived on a scale that, while natural to envisage and probably optimal in terms of British life and labour costs between the wars, was too small for financial comfort in postwar circumstances. Concretely, it was built of odd pieces of property in the centre of a large block of shops close to the market square of Cambridge, and would have been an ideal amenity for a sleepy little town with a stratum of relatively well-off, leisured and cultured people, able and willing to pay for intimate theatre and complementary dining and drinking facilities (provided at reasonable prices by employment of low-wage local labour drawn from a local pool of under-employed, well-educated, limited-aspiration workers). In postwar circumstances it faced the usual problems of having to fill its seats near to capacity at every performance to cover the high wage costs of a performance, and to maximize volume of sale of food and drink. An incidental benefit of this situation was that Kahn, as an executor of Keynes and responsible *inter alia* for the Arts Theatre, would frequently invite a group of economists and their wives to a theatre party involving a dinner and a performance at the Arts Theatre, capped by drinks afterwards in his nearby rooms in King's. Kahn was always a generous and thoughtful host, and the performances always good if rarely memorable, so that his invitations were always an unexpected pleasure. Through them also one acquired indirectly some sense both of the infinitely varied personality, interests and effective contributions of Keynes, and of an ideal academic life that can be described broadly as the last flowering of Victorian England, the possibility of repeating which had already been destroyed for those present by, among other things, the political victory of the Keynesian concept of maintaining full employment.

12

Ruth Cohen:
A Neglected Contributor to
Contemporary Capital Theory*

The central controversy in the theory of capital in recent years, in which Cambridge, England, and Cambridge, Massachusetts, have been the chief protagonists, and value theorists in a variety of other locations and countries have been contributors and partisans, has focused on the so-called 'problem of reverse switching.' Simply stated, the problem is that a reduction in the rate of interest, instead of leading to a more capital-intensive technique becoming the most profitable one, as would be convenient for common-sense description of the relation between capital accumulation, capital-intensity of production, and the rate of interest, may instead produce a reverse switch towards a less-capital-intensive technique as the most profitable. The reverse switching occurs as a result of the influence of the associated change in the real wage rate on the value of capital required for the implementation of a given technique in relation to the surplus of output per man over the real wage producible by that technique. The problem, which incidentally is exactly analogous to the problem of the possibility of more than one solution for the 'internal rate of return' on the time-profile of inputs and outputs specifying an investment opportunity, has led to a hot and continuing controversy. The 'orthodox' or Cambridge, U.S.A., side has been engaged in a fruitless search for plausible conditions that would rule out reverse switching, while the 'radical' or

* A personal tribute and reminiscence (1974).

Cambridge, England, side has delighted in picking holes in any such conditions produced, in the belief that to do so is to destroy the intellectual justification of capitalism. Needless to say, nowhere but in Cambridge, England, would the discovery of the possibility of multiple equilibrium solutions be considered adequate to destroy a whole system of mathematical economic analysis. Indeed, economic theory has absorbed into its formal corpus possible causes of multiple eqilibrium possibilities much more plausible to common sense than anything yet produced by the Cambridge, England side of this particular controversy —such as the Giffen Good, the Sargant man, and the Marshall-Lerner conditions for exchange market instability, to mention only three standbys of the Cambridge Marshallian tradition of partial-equilibrium economics. And nowhere outside the 1920s and early 1930s tradition of what may be called, by contrast with its contemporary counterpart, 'the methodology of negative economics'—the belief that one can refute a theory of how the world works by exposing the unreality of its assumptions rather than the falsity of its conclusions—supplemented by certain ideas about the relation between philosophical disputation and political persuasion derived ultimately from vulgar Marxism, would it be considered an important political strategy for the destruction of capitalism and the triumph of the revolution to insist stridently on an alleged logical flaw in the logic of the competitive system.

Be that as it may, reverse switching has become the focus of contemporary controversy in capital theory, and not a few eminent theoretical economists have made their reputations on the basis of study of the mathematics of it. It would therefore seem appropriate, as an anecdotal footnote to some future history of economic thought, to call attention and give due credit to the economist who was first, at least in terms of the contemporary wave of interest in capital theory, to notice the possibility of reverse switching.* ** The economist in question is Ruth L.

---

* Interest in capital theory among economists tends to peak in thirty-to-forty year waves, the previous one culminating in the 1930s. The reverse switching phenomenon was recognized in the work at least of some contributors to the 1930s wave of interest in capital theory, for example Oskar Lange, 'The Place of Interest in the Theory of Production,' *Review of Economic Studies*, 3, No. 3 (June 1936), 159–92, and 'Correction,' 4, No. 1 (October 1936), 52.

Cohen, of Cambridge University, noted otherwise as a leading British agricultural economist[1] and for a long time as the Mistress of Newnham College, Cambridge.

Ruth Cohen's observation of the possibility of reverse switching occurred towards the end of a session of the so-called 'secret seminar' of Cambridge economics faculty members that met every Tuesday evening during the Michaelmas and Lent Terms from 1949 until sometime in the late fifties or early sixties. The 'secret seminar' was originally inspired and organized by Jan Graaf, the brilliant South African welfare theorist, under the sponsorship of Richard Kahn, who was its host in his rooms in King's College. And, in quintessential Cambridge political style, the whole point of it was that it was not 'secret,' but exclusive, and well-publicized. Its purpose was to discriminate against the right-wing economists and provide choice tid-bits of intellectual cuisine to the left-wingers; and most of the pleasure of discriminating is lost if the person discriminated against does not know that he is being denied access to something desirable on account of a social handicap he can do nothing to correct.

The session of Ruth Cohen's observation occurred sometime between Joan Robinson's early work on the Harrod growth model[2] and the production of her famous article 'The Production Function and the Theory of Capital,'[3] probably early in 1953. The session was one of a number devoted to the explanation of her then unfamiliar diagram graphing techniques (assumed discontinuously variable, to separate the Wicksell and Ricardo effects of a change in the quantity of capital), in ascending order of physical output per head, against the quantity (value) of capital (assumed to consist of a balanced stock of capital per worker) evaluated at a given interest rate and measured in wage units ('real capital'). The basic diagram is shown in Figure I with δ, γ, β,

** A more important task in any future history of English economic theory in the post-World War II period will be to assign appropriate credit to the contribution of Roy Harrod's *Towards a Dynamic Economics* in stimulating English thinking, especially Hick's *A Contribution to the Theory of the Trade Cycle* (Oxford: Oxford University Press, 1950—'it was not until I read Mr. Harrod's book that I realized what it was that I had overlooked . . . I could kick myself for not having seen it before.' —p. 7), and Joan Robinson's work on capital theory, especially the latter part of *The Rate of Interest and Other Essays* (London: Macmillan, 1952) and *The Accumulation of Capital* (London: Macmillan, 1956).

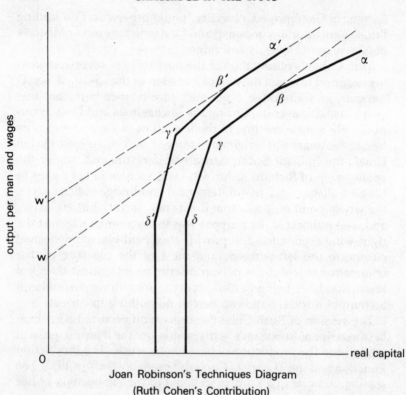

Joan Robinson's Techniques Diagram
(Ruth Cohen's Contribution)

a as successively more productive techniques and real capital evaluated at the interest rate (or corresponding real wage rate w) at which the γ and β techniques are profit-indifferent. The economy can have a larger or smaller stock of capital per head and flow of output per head at this rate of interest, by mixing γ and β techniques in different proportions to arrive at different points on the $\gamma\beta$ segment of the jointed locus δa; but once it reaches β the rate of interest (and the real wage rate) must change, and with it the position of the locus,* with no change in output per man, until the new position $\delta'a'$ is reached. At position $\delta'a'$ techniques β

* It was in connection with her discussion of what happened when point β was reached that Joan Robinson produced one of her famous Joan Robinsonisms. In reply to a comment by Jan Graaf, she said, 'No, the rate of interest is *not* indeterminate; you just don't know what it is.'

and a become profit-indifferent, and the real wage rate and interest rate become again constant, while the economy can have successively larger quantities of real capital per head and of output per head by increasing the ratio of a to β techniques in the mix employed by the economy.

This was the way that Joan Robinson presented the analysis that evening—on the assumption that, despite the shift of the locus, the next stage after the substitution of β for γ techniques would necessarily be the substitution of a for β techniques. It was Ruth Cohen, who had as usual been listening silently to the exposition and discussion, who at almost the end of the evening broke her silence by pointing out that there was no reason in the diagrammatics for assuming that at the higher wage rate it would be a and β rather than γ and δ that would be profit-indifferent.

Joan Robinson considered this remark during the intervening week, and at the next meeting she conceded it as a possibility, christened it 'The Ruth Cohen Case,' and described it as a multiple equilibrium possibility, perhaps 'a mere theoretical rig-marole.'* As such—an interesting curiosum—it remained into and past *The Accumulation of Capital*, probably because Joan Robinson's main concerns in the preparation of that book were a mixture of showing that monopoly could wreck the capitalist system (through the fixing of an arbitrary mark-up on labour cost) and demonstrating the impossibility of the conditions required for capitalist competition to handle the process of capital accumulation. (This last was expressed in her insistence on the concept of 'the golden age,' that is, that it is sensible to think of a capitalist economy's accumulating capital smoothly only on the assumption that it has been growing in exactly the same way since time immemorial). On the technical side, her main object of attack was the general assumption of mathematical production-function-writing that macro-economic problems of income distribution could be handled by treating capital as an original factor of production on the same level as human labour; and the possibi-

---

* See 'The Production Function,' *op. cit.*, p. 106: 'The geometry reveals a curious possibility.[1] [This was pointed out to me by Miss Ruth Cohen.] A good deal of exploration of the possible magnitude and behaviour of the interest effect is needed before we can say whether the above is a mere theoretical rigmarole, or whether there is likely to be anything in reality corresponding to it.'

lity of peculiar anti-orthodox results emerging from the nature of capital goods as produced goods requiring valuation for aggregation purposes was clearly secondary by a long interval to this primary purpose. 'The Ruth Cohen Case' and the possibility of reverse switching only achieved primacy in the capital theory controversy, which it is important to recall has been on the Cambridge, England, side fundamentally political in motivation, after the mathematical economists had shown that their tools were perfectly capable of comprehending the complications of treating capital equipment as a produced means of production.*

And what of the contribution of Ruth Cohen, whose name appears in the literature of contemporary capital theory only in this one isolated context, the broader significance of her observation of the possibility of 'reverse switching' unappreciated at the time and for a long time after? There are those among British theorists—definitely, I should emphasize, *not* including Joan Robinson herself—who hold the view that Ruth Cohen's observation was a flash in the pan, a one-time lucky shot-in-the-dark. As a sometime student and long-time friend of Ruth Cohen's, and a friend and follower of many agricultural economists and applied economists in other fields, I take a different view. I think that Ruth Cohen was and is a really good theorist, good enough to know as a matter of habitual instinct and not merely of lucky guesswork when the logic of the analysis is insufficient to determine the precise new shape resulting from a shift in a relationship plotted on a graph; and I would add that in my own experience elementary teaching in economics, in Cambridge at least, consisted precisely in teaching 'pupils' that kind of theoretical understanding. But, like the vast majority of good applied economists, Ruth Cohen has always been interested in what makes practical sense, and uninterested in intellectual battles over 'orthodoxy' versus 'radicalism' in the global ideology of economics.

* For an account of the failure to realize until later the significance of 'The Ruth Cohen Case,' see G. C. Harcourt, *Some Cambridge Controversies in the Theory of Capital* (Cambridge: Cambridge University Press, 1972), pp. 124–5. Harcourt refers to it as 'the Ruth Cohen curiosum,' an alternative description also used in the 'secret seminar.'

13

Arthur Cecil Pigou, 1877–1959: An Obituary

When I first 'went up' to Cambridge Pigou was already a living legend. The survey lectures on economic principles which he had given for so many years were then being given by his successor in the Chair, D. H. Robertson, and all that remained of his presence was the comment, deeply pencilled into one of the desks at Mill Lane by some departed undergraduate, 'Pigou mumbles.' Because of the post-war influx of students, however, he was for the first time in his life supervising undergraduates for King's College, and sometimes one of them—George Clayton, Frank Davidson, Robin Marris, I. G. Patel, Eric Russell—would repeat some particularly penetrating comment or suggestion he had made on an essay paper. Beyond that, he was a tall, straight figure, eccentrically garbed, glimpsed occasionally walking about the countryside or, when the warm weather returned, reclining in a deck chair on the grass by the porters' lodge inside King's front court.

Later, during my six years as a Fellow of King's College, I naturally saw much more of him; but I never got to know him well. For one thing, he hated to talk shop, an antipathy for which retirement gave an added excuse; I can recall only one such conversation with him, when the *London and Cambridge Economic Service Bulletin* looked like ceasing publication, in which he deplored the loss of the long series which it published. (The only other conversation I recall is one in which we agreed on the demerits of a trashy American 'shocker' which we had both borrowed from the Combination Room.) He disliked above all being asked to meet visiting economists (though he was extremely gracious to Alvin Hansen and his wife); and I soon learnt not to try to introduce strangers, no matter how eminent, to him after Hall dinner. On one such attempt, I remember, he dismissed us with 'I don't know anything any more; I'm gaga.' (This was, of course, a pose; not the least remarkable thing about him was his ability to turn out economic analysis of a respectable quality long after his retirement.) Nor did he attend College meetings, or take an interest in College affairs, with the notable exception of his membership of the Electors to Fellowships (on which he served forty years in all). The full extent of his aversion to ceremonial of all kinds was displayed by his discovery, several months in advance, of a previous engagement which prevented his attending the Service in Commemoration of the Restoration of the Windows of King's College Chapel, an event graced by the presence of the King and Queen and Princess Margaret and preceded by a magnificent luncheon. And he lived up to his reputation for sartorial economy, appearing at the Marshall Library one day in the fifties proudly wearing a suit bought before the First World War.

Nevertheless, he was a familiar and respected figure in the College; and he played an important part in its life, not only as a Fellowship Elector, in which capacity his judgement carried great weight, but much more through his friendships with and interest in the undergraduates, parties of whom he would take to his cottage in the Lake District, and for whom he would organize chess matches. (It was also his doing that the three noisy Chinese geese on the Backs become known to the undergraduates by the names of the three most talkative members of High Table.) It was always interesting to sit near him at dinner—he had the knack of stimulating entertaining conversation. (He always came in late, which had the dual advantage of avoiding grace and enabling him to pick his company.) My last memory of him in the College is of his presiding over the election of a new Provost following the unexpected death of Provost Glanville—a duty which devolved on him as Senior Fellow—and describing the outcomes of successive votes, not altogether to the pleasure of the Fellows, in the horse-racing terms which he sometimes affected.

Arthur Cecil Pigou was born on 18 November 1877, eldest son of an officer in the 15th Regiment. From Harrow, where he was

Head of the School in 1895, he won a Scholarship to King's, where he read for the Historical Tripos, taking a First in 1899. That same year he won the Chancellor's gold medal for English verse, with an ode on Alfred the Great; the last few lines of this ode reflect the idealism which, under the inspiration of Alfred Marshall, led him on to the study of economics:

> Hear ye King Alfred's voice, sons of my blood;
> Not mine to trace the secret of the years;
> I know not what they bring; but this I know;
> I would not that King Mammon held my seat;
> For things there are more worthy praise than gold
> And temples grander than the ordered mart;
> And O! far off, as the long centuries roll,
> I pray to heaven some voice more clear than mine
> May lead this people far from the black slough
> Of soulless greed, into more generous paths
> Onward and upward, following Truth's bright star
> And Reason's light, and that diviner gleam
> That dwells a mystery in the hearts of men.

(It was characteristic of his generosity that the medal was sold after the First World War for the relief of starving Georgians.)

In 1900 he took a First in Part II of the Moral Sciences Tripos, with special distinction in Advanced Political Economy. It was typical of the breadth of his interests that in 1901 he won the Cobden Prize for an essay on 'The causes and effects of changes in the relative values of agricultural produce in the United Kingdom during the last fifty years,' and the Burney Prize of an essay on 'Robert Browning as a religious teacher.' The latter, Pigou's first published work, is characterized by a certain cool contempt for Browning's philosophical inconsistencies, combined with a genuine admiration for his poetry. It failed to win Pigou a Fellowship in 1901, but he was successful in 1902 with the Cobden Essay, and remained a Fellow of King's until his death on 7 March 1959. In 1903 he won the Adam Smith Prize for an essay on 'The Principles and Methods of Industrial Peace,' which became the basis of the Jevons Memorial Lectures he delivered at University College, London, in 1903–04 and of his book of the same title (1905). During this time he was also taking an active speaking and writing interest in the controversy over tariff reform, and produced two short books on the subject of tariffs.

Meanwhile, the Cambridge Economics Tripos had been established in 1903, and Pigou, who had been lecturing on economics for the Moral Sciences Tripos since 1901, was appointed to the Girdlers' Lectureship in 1904. When Marshall retired in 1908 Pigou, who was carrying much of the teaching load, was appointed his successor to the Chair, though he was barely thirty at the time. His Inaugural Lecture, 'Economic Theory in Relation to Practice,' contained a powerful statement of his own version of the Marshallian view of what economics is about—that it is for its fruit-bearing and not for its light-bearing qualities that economic knowledge is worth pursuing. 'If it were not for the hope that a scientific study of man's social actions may lead . . . to practical results in social improvement, I should myself . . . regard the time devoted to that study as misspent. . . . If I desired knowledge of man apart from the fruits of knowledge, I should seek it in the history of religious enthusiasm, of passion, of martyrdom and of love; I should not seek it in the market-place.'

How far Pigou's life-work conformed to the ideals laid down in his Inaugural Lecture, and reiterated on later occasions, is one of those questions which it is unkind to ask and difficult to answer fairly in an obituary. His major work on the economics of welfare undoubtedly carried those ideals into practice, in the sense that it created the apparatus required for, and largely carried out, the exploration of cases in which the operation of the competitive system offered scope for improvement by wisely designed social intervention. But his intellectual bent, and the chronological drift of his work (in method, at least), was towards a mathematical formalism whose justification is easier to make out in terms of light than of fruit. It is somewhat ironical, too, that the reports of two of the three bodies of public inquiry on which he served—the (Cunliffe) Committee on the Foreign Exchanges (1918–19), and the (Chamberlain) Committee on the Currency and Bank of England Note Issues (1924–25), the third being the Royal Commission on the Income Tax (1919–20)—paved the way for the restoration of the gold standard at the pre-war parity, that act of blind traditionalism which did so much to aggravate Britain's economic and social problems in the inter-war period.

Towards the end of his life, indeed, he became disillusioned with his original methodological position. In his presidential address to the Royal Economic Society in 1939, after a scathing description of the abandonment of free trade in 1931, he concluded: 'In view of these things, the hope that an advance in economic knowledge will appreciably affect actual happenings is a slender one. It is not likely that there will be a market for our produce. None the less, by a sort of reflex activity, we cultivate our garden. For we also follow, not thought, but an impulse—the impulse to inquire—which, futile though it may prove, is at least not ignoble.' The fact that protection was the proximate cause of his disillusionment is revealing, both by contrast with the other features of the 1930s which younger economists found much more disturbing, and as an indication of the ardour with which he had defended free trade in writings and speeches thirty years before.

From the problem of industrial peace, Pigou moved on to a study of the cause of unemployment, a study which soon expanded to embrace the whole problem of economic welfare. The result was *Wealth and Welfare* (1912), which contained the essence of his major contribution to economics. In this work, Pigou defined economic welfare as depending on the size, distribution, and variability of the national dividend, and systematically analysed the ways in which the competitive system fell short of the ideal, the methods by which improvement might be achieved, and their economic effects, inventing for the purpose the fruitful concept of divergence of marginal private and marginal social net product, and deploying in the argument a mass of institutional information.

The remainder of Pigou's long working life can be regarded as largely occupied with strengthening the foundations laid in *Wealth and Welfare* and elaborating the superstructure erected on them. As to the foundations, the passage from welfare as states of consciousness to economic welfare to the national dividend is fraught with philosophical difficulties, and the notion of national income itself is beset with conceptual problems, to which the dozen pages devoted to these topics in *Wealth and Welfare* gave scant recognition; in later versions, much more space was taken up with elaboration, though without fundamental concessions.

In addition, the book contained a major theoretical error, the proposition that both increasing and decreasing returns create a divergence between marginal social returns in different industries, requiring bounties in the one case and taxes in the other. The nature of the error—the confusion of rent with real cost—was pointed out by Allyn Young in 1913, but with characteristic stubborness Pigou did not accept the criticism until the second edition of the *Economics of Welfare*. The problem of the laws of return continued to bother him—he returned to it in articles in the late twenties—but he played virtually no part in its solution through the elaboration of the theory of the firm, his own concept of the 'equilibrium firm' being simply an evasion of the issues. (Incidentally, the impression widely held among American economists that Pigou was willing to accept correction only from English, that is, Cambridge or King's College, economists, is erroneous. He was unwilling to accept correction from *anyone*—perhaps because he got his Chair so early—but when finally convinced that his critic was right, as with Young and later with Keynes, he admitted it unreservedly.)

Wealth and Welfare was followed in 1913 by a book on *Unemployment*, the problem from which Pigou had started. Then came the war. For Pigou, as for all that pre-war generation of Cambridge men, the war was a shock, and a source of intense personal strain. He remained at his post in Cambridge, carrying more and more of the lecturing load as well as part-time responsibilities at the Board of Trade, the recipient of offensive letters urging him to join up and let Foxwell (his rival for the Chair in 1908) take over his professional duties while the war was on; but he spent most of his vacations in voluntary ambulance work at the front, first in France and Belgium and then in Italy, and what he saw sickened him. There can be no doubt that this experience was responsible for transforming the gay, joke-loving, sociable, hospitable young bachelor of the Edwardian period into the eccentric recluse of more recent times. In the words of his colleague and life-long friend C. R. Fay, 'World War I was a shock to him, and he was never the same afterwards.' On the professional side, war turned his attention to problems of war economics, and especially war finance.

After the war, Pigou rewrote *Wealth and Welfare* into the first edition of *The Economics of Welfare* (1920), incorporating in it not only a great deal of material and ideas accumulated during the war, but also large selections from his pre-war work on labour problems. The incorporation took the form of the addition of two new parts to the earlier structure, one on 'The National Dividend and Government Finance' and the other on 'The National Dividend and Labour.' The former became *The Political Economy of War* (1921) and later *A Study in Public Finance* (1928), being dropped from the second edition of *The Economics of Welfare* (1924); the part entitled 'The Variability of the National Dividend,' one of the three pillars in the architecture of *Wealth and Welfare*, was also dropped, in anticipation of the completion of *Industrial Fluctuations* (1927). The third (1928) and fourth (1933) editions of *The Economics of Welfare* differed in no important respects from the second.

In the 1930s, Pigou turned his attention once more to the problem of unemployment. His *The Theory of Unemployment* (1933) was one of the main objects of Keynes's derision in *The General Theory*; Pigou was deeply offended by *The General Theory*, more on Marshall's account than on his own, and in his *Economica* review hit back strongly against 'this macédoine of misrepresentations,' at the same time professing to find little positive merit in the book ('We have watched an artist firing arrows at the moon'). But this assessment changed radically with the passage of time, though he continued to deplore the tone of Keynes's criticisms of his predecessors. In the Preface to *Employment and Equilibrium* (1941) he recognized that Keynes had 'rendered a very great service to economics by asking important questions'; in *Keynes's General Theory: A Retrospective View* (1950) he admitted that his original review had failed to grasp the significance of Keynes's conception; and in *Alfred Marshall and Current Thought* (1953) he concluded that Keynes's error lay in attacking the long-run analysis of the *Principles* rather than the short-period analysis of the *Evidence* where Marshall 'would, I like to think, have agreed that Keynes had detected him in a serious mistake.' His own methods of monetary analysis became identifiably Keynesian, except that he continued to use velocity rather than liquidity preference; and his writings, especially *Employment and Equilibrium* and *Lapses from Full Employment* (1945), helped to elucidate the substance and the limitations of the Keynesian Revolution. Indeed, to many young economists, Pigou is famous chiefly for his contribution of 'the Pigou effect' to the counter-revolution.

The foregoing account of Pigou's life and works has perforce concentrated on the main stream, without reference to the many subsidiary inlets and branches along the way. No complete bibliography of his work exists, but the King's College Library catalogue lists nearly thirty books and over a hundred pamphlets and articles. Of these, mention should perhaps be made of the *Memorials of Alfred Marshall* (1925) complied with filial devotion to his master, and of *Socialism versus Capitalism* (1937), which weighed the balance more heavily in favour of the former than he perhaps intended. The very volume of this output, maintaining such a high average standard over such a long period, entitles him to recognition as one of the giants of the Cambridge School and a formative influence on modern economics. Beyond that, *The Economics of Welfare* was an important contribution in its own right; as F. H. Knight remarked in his review of the first edition, it shifted the argument from the choice between conflicting systems of economic organization to the methods of improving on the existing, functioning system. That was at once its originality, in the period when Pigou first developed it, and its obvious limitation during the troubled inter-war period which followed its publication. Now that the Keynesian Revolution has been digested, and the political divisions of the thirties and forties have been reconciled in a system of welfare capitalism, economists are becoming increasingly occupied with policy problems of the kind with which Pigou was concerned, and in whose analysis he was the pioneer.

Part V
Keynesian Economics

14
The Keynesian Revolution and the Monetarist Counter-Revolution

As is well known from the field of economic history, the concept of revolution is difficult to transfer from its origins in politics to other fields of social science. Its essence is unexpected speed of change, and this requires a judgement of speed in the context of a longer perspective of historical change, the choice of which is likely to be debatable in the extreme. Leaving the judgemental issue aside for the moment, one could characterize the history of our subject in terms of a series of 'revolutions,' very broadly defined, as follows. Economics as we know it began with what might be called the 'Smithian Revolution' against the established body of doctrines generically described as 'mercantilism,' a revolution which changed ideas on the nature and sources of the wealth of nations and the policies required to promote the growth of what we now call 'affluence.' The Ricardian revolution turned the attention of economists from concern with national wealth and its growth to the distribution of income among social classes and the interactions of growth and income distribution. The marginalist revolution of the 1870s essentially introduced a new and superior analytical technology for dealing with Ricardo's distribution problem, in the process gradually depriving Ricardian economics of its social content; hence, the results of that revolution have been described as neo-Ricardian or more commonly neo-classical economics.

Contemporary economics is based on this development and on at least four discernible 'revolutions' that occurred in the late 1920s and in the 1930s. One was the imperfect-monopolistic competition revolution, which challenged the validity of the assumption of perfect competition on which value theory had come to be built following the marginalist revolution, and particularly the conclusions about the welfare effects of competition to which that theory led. This revolution has more or less fizzled out, though its fossilized remnants continue to plague both students and their instructors in elementary courses. Another was the empirical or econometric revolution, with its insistence initially on the measurement of economic relationships and, subsequently and more ambitiously, on the testing of economic hypotheses—though the 'testing of hypotheses' is frequently merely a euphemism for obtaining plausible numbers to provide ceremonial adequacy for a theory chosen and defended on *a priori* grounds. The third was the general equilibrium revolution, based on the introduction by Hicks and Allen of the continental Walrasian-Paretoan approach into the Anglo-Saxon tradition in replacement of the then-dominant Marshallian partial-equilibrium approach. Finally, and most sweeping in its effects, there was the Keynesian Revolution in monetary theory.

By contrast with the abundance of revolutions, counter-revolutions are hard to find in the development of economic thought. About the closest one can come to a counter-revolution in the history of economic thought is to interpret the development of the Austrian theory of value as a counter-revolution against the socialist, and especially the Marxist, tradition of economic theorizing; and that aspect of the work of the Austrian school was a side issue in the marginalist revolution. The monetarist counter-revolution of contemporary times is probably the first significant counter-revolution in the development of our subject. In venturing this judgement, however, I should note that the disrepute into which the theories of imperfect and monopolistic competition have fallen, as theories of contemporary industrial competition, in the period since the Second World War could be described as the result of an intellectual counter-revolution, based on a combination of faith in the pre-existing theory of competition and devotion to the empirical revolution; and also that, if one is prepared to disregard the political labels that people choose to attach to themselves, the left-wing student and faculty demand for a politically and socially relevant 'radical' economics and protest against emphasis on mathematical and econometric quantification can be classed as counter-revolutionary, inasmuch as it seeks to revert to the premarginalist-revolution concern with the economic system as a system of relationships among social classes.

As I have already mentioned, the chief problem in identifying revolutions and counter-revolutions and distinguishing them from slower and more comprehensible and rational processes of change in economic thought is to arrive at a judgement of the relative speed of change and the degree to which the speed is justifiable. From this point of view, some of what I have just now described as revolutions were not really revolutionary—notably the Smithian and marginalist revolutions, the imperfect-monopolistic competition revolution, and the general equilibrium and empirical revolutions. The Smithian and marginalist revolutions spread relatively slowly, through the force of their scientific superiority and intellectual appeal and the process of natural wastage of their opponents. The imperfect-monopolistic competition revolution was the end result of puzzling by many minds over a problem that Marshall had stated but had been unable to solve satisfactorily—the existence of downward-sloping cost curves for individual firms. The general equilibrium revolution was a result of the delayed appreciation by economists of the need for a better command of mathematical techniques, the delay being occasioned by the long association of the subject with philosophy in the English academic tradition and its continuing association with law in the continental tradition. And the empirical revolution depended on the development of the techniques of statistical inference—most of the historically great economists were quantitatively oriented, or at least paid lip service to the need for quantitative work, but lacked the requisite tools to carry out such work themselves. For real intellectual revolutions, we are left with three major examples: the Ricardian revolution, the reasons for whose rapid propagation were examined some twenty years ago by S. G. Checkland,[1] the Keynesian revolution, and the monetarist counter-revolution.

My concern, specifically, is with the reasons for the speed of propagation of the monetarist counter-revolution; but I cannot approach this subject without reference to the reasons for the speed of propagation of the Keynesian revolution, since the two are interrelated. Indeed, I find it useful in posing and treating the problem to adopt the 'as if' approach of positive economics, as expounded by the chief protagonist of the monetarist counter-revolution, Milton Friedman, and to ask: suppose I wished to start a counter-revolution against the Keynesian revolution in monetary theory, how would I go about it—and specifically, what could I learn about the technique from the revolution itself? To pose the question in this way is, of course, to fly in the face of currently accepted professional ethics, according to which purely scientific considerations and not political considerations are presumed to motivate scientific work; but I can claim the protection of the 'as if' methodology against any implication of a slur on individual character or a denigration of scientific work.

From this point of view, obviously, the first problem is to identify the elements in the situation at the time of *The General Theory* that accounted for its rapid acceptance and propagation among professional economists. Such elements are of two types, one relating to the objective social situation in which the new theory was produced, the other relating to the scientific characteristics of the new theory itself.

As regards the objective social situation, by far the most helpful circumstance for the rapid propagation of a new and revolutionary theory is the existence of an established orthodoxy which is clearly inconsistent with the most salient facts of reality, and yet is sufficiently confident of its intellectual power to attempt to explain those facts, and in its efforts to do so exposes its incompetence in a ludicrous fashion.[2] Orthodoxy is, of course, always vulnerable to radical challenge: the essence of an orthodoxy of any kind is to reduce the subtle and sophisticated thoughts of great men to a set of simple principles and straightforward slogans that more mediocre brains can think they understand well enough to live by—but for that very reason orthodoxy is most vulnerable to challenge when its principles and slogans are demonstrably in conflict with the facts of everyday experience.

So it was in the 1930s, and particularly in the 1930s in Britain, which had already experienced a decade of mass unemployment associated with industrial senescence and an overvalued exchange rate, mass unemployment which the prevailing orthodoxy could neither explain nor cope with. This, it may be noted, was in large part the fault of the economists themselves. There existed already a body of monetary analysis that was quite capable of explaining both Britain's and the industrial world's unemployment problems as a consequence of monetary mis-management. But, hypnotized by the notion that money is merely a veil cast over real phenomena—the homogeneity post-ulate of contemporary monetary theory—the economists of the time attempted to explain what were essentially monetary phenomena by real causes. Eminent British economists sought to explain mass unemployment as a consequence of the satiation of real human wants, a satiation that should have produced a gen-eral reduction in working hours but unfortunately and inexplic-ably operated instead differentially to reduce the working hours of a substantial part of the population to absolute zero. Other economists viewed the depression as a punishment justly visited upon enterprises and individuals for past sins of speculation and erroneous micro-economic decision-taking. The concern for microeconomic explanations diverted attention from what the available macroeconomic analysis could have said about the problem; it also led to the recommendation of *ad hoc* remedies such as public works that lacked any firm grounding in theory as generally understood.

In this situation of general confusion and obvious irrelevance of orthodox economics to real problems, the way was open for a new theory that offered a convincing explanation of the nature of the problem and a set of policy prescriptions based on that explanation. Such a theory, however, would have to possess certain characteristics if it were to win intellectual acceptance and political success. In particular, it would have to come from within yet offer liberation from the established orthodoxy—for one must remember that orthodoxy includes both an established conserva-tive orthodoxy and an established self-termed 'radical' orthodoxy, and, since each recognizes and accommodates the other's arguments, there is no real hope of progress being achieved by a switch from one position to the other.

To be more specific, a revolutionary theory had to depend for its success on five main characteristics—here I must admit that I am conducting my analysis in the blinding light of hindsight. First, it had to attack the central proposition of conservative orthodoxy—the assumed or inferred tendency of the economy to full employment—with a new but academically acceptable analysis that reversed the proposition. This Keynes did with the help of Kahn's concept of the multiplier and his own invention of the propensity to consume. Second, the theory had to appear to be new, yet absorb as much as possible of the valid or at least not readily disputable components of existing orthodox theory. In this process, it helps greatly to give old concepts new and confusing names, and to emphasize as crucial analytical steps that have previously been taken as platitudinous; hence, in *The General Theory*, the marginal productivity of capital became the marginal efficiency of capital; the desired ratio of money to income, the k of the Cambridge tradition, became a minor constituent of the new theory of 'liquidity preference;' and the *ex post* identity of savings and investment, which previous theorists, including Keynes himself, had rightly recognized as unhelpful to dynamic analysis, became the *sine qua non* of right reasoning.

Third, the new theory had to have the appropriate degree of difficulty to understand. This is a complex problem in the design of new theories. The new theory had to be so difficult to understand that senior academic colleagues would find it neither easy nor worth while to study, so that they would waste their efforts on peripheral theoretical issues, and so offer themselves as easy marks for criticism and dismissal by their younger and hungrier colleagues. At the same time, the new theory had to appear both difficult enough to challenge the intellectual interest of younger colleagues and students, but actually easy enough for them to master adequately with a sufficient investment of intellectual endeavour. These objectives Keynes's *General Theory* managed to achieve: it neatly shelved the old and established scholars, like Pigou and Robertson, enabled the more enterprising middle- and lower-middle-aged like Hansen, Hicks, and Joan Robinson to jump on and drive the bandwagon, and permitted a whole generation of students (as Samuelson has recorded) to escape from the slow and soul-destroying process of acquiring wisdom by osmosis from their elders and the literature into an intellectual realm in which youthful iconoclasm could quickly earn its just reward (in its own eyes at least) by the demolition of the intellectual pretensions of its academic seniors and predecessors. Economics, delightfully, could be reconstructed from scratch on the basis of a little Keynesian understanding and a lofty contempt for the existing literature—and so it was.

Fourth, the new theory had to offer to the more gifted and less opportunistic scholars a new methodology more appealing than those currently available. In this respect, Keynes was lucky both in having a receptive audience available, and to hit somewhere conveniently between the old and the newly emerging styles of economic theorizing. The prevailing methodological orthodoxy was that of Marshall—a partial-equilibrium approach set within a clear appreciation of the two complex problems of general equilibrium and of historical change, and hence both unsatisfactory at the simple level of partial-equilibrium analysis taken by itself, and extremely difficult to apply skillfully in a broader analytical and social context. The new methodological challenge was coming from the explicitly mathematical general-equilibrium approach of Hicks and Allen, an approach whose empirically and historically almost empty generality was of little general appeal. *The General Theory* found a middle ground in an aggregated general-equilibrium system which was not too difficult or complicated to work with—though it demanded a substantial step forward in mathematical competence—and which offered a high degree of apparent empirical relevance to those who took the trouble to understand it.

Finally, *The General Theory* offered an important empirical relationship for the emerging tribe of econometricians to measure—the consumption function, a far more challenging relationship than the demand for sugar, a relationship for which the development of national income statistics provided the raw material needed for estimation, and which could be estimated with surprising success given the limitation of the available data to approximately a single business cycle.

In my judgement, these factors accounted for the success of the Keynesian revolution: on the one hand, the existence of an important social and economic problem with which the prevailing orthodoxy was unable to cope; on the other hand, a variety of characteristics that appealed to the younger generation of that period—notably the claim of the new theory to superior social relevance and intellectual distinction, its incorporation in a novel and confusing fashion of the valid elements of traditional theory, the opportunity it offered to bypass the system of academic seniority by challenging senior colleagues with a new and self-announcedly superior scientific approach, the presentation of a new methodology that made general-equilibrium theory both manageable and socially relevant, and the advancement of a new empirical relationship challenging for econometricians to estimate.

The very success of the Keynesian revolution, however, ensured that it would in its turn become the established orthodoxy, and as such be as vulnerable as the old to revolutionary attack—which would necessarily have to be a counter-revolutionary attack. Keynes himself, as Leijonhufvud's monumental reinterpretation of his thought[3] has reminded us, had a seasoned and subtle mind, conscious both of the flow of economic history and of the role of theory as an adjunct to policy-making in a given set of historical circumstances. His followers—which means the profession at large—elaborated his history-bound analysis into a timeless and spaceless set of universal principles, sacrificing in the process much of his subtlety, and so established Keynesianism as an orthodoxy ripe for counter-attack.

There are several factors in this transmogrification worthy of note. The first, and probably most important, has been the conviction of Keynesians that the mass unemployment of the 1930s represents the normal state of capitalist society—more accurately, of capitalist society unaided by Keynesian management—and that unemployment is always the most urgent social problem. This view was elevated into a dogma in the United States under the leadership of Alvin Hansen.[4] While his theory of secular stagnation has been quietly forgotten, or frugally converted into a theory applicable to the underdeveloped countries, vestiges of it linger on in the thinking of American Keynesians. The view that unemployment is the overriding social problem also lingers on among British Keynesians such as Joan Robinson,

Roy Harrod, and Thomas Balogh, though I should note that Nicholas Kaldor has for many years taken a much more optimistic view of the resilience of capitalism. The corollary of the Keynesian view of the primacy of the unemployment problem has been a pronounced tendency to play down the adverse economic consequences of inflation, and to assume that, if only the unemployment consequences of anti-inflationary policies were properly understood, society would cheerfully agree to adopt and implement an incomes policy instead.

A second factor in the transformation of Keynesianism into an orthodoxy has been that people who made their academic reputations and earned their present status on the basis of an early and enthusiastic conversion to Keynesianism in the late 1930s and early 1940s have continued to trade on their foresight, to the academic detriment of their juniors, who have never had the same chance to jump onto the front—and not the rear—of an academic bandwagon. This factor has been far more effective in paving the way for a monetarist counter-revolution in the United States, where institutional competition prevents centralized control of professional advancement, than in the United Kingdom, where Oxbridge continues to dominate the academic scene.

A third factor has been that, while the Keynesian revolution in its time offered a tremendous liberation to the energies of young economists in the fields of pure theorizing about concepts, the construction of macroeconomic general-equilibrium models, and the estimation of econometric models of the economy, these activities have run into diminishing returns so rapidly that they have ceased to be appealing to young and ambitious economists.

The result has been that—beginning perhaps sometime in the mid-1950s—Keynesianism has become itself an established orthodoxy, ripe for attack in exactly the same way as what Keynes chose to call 'classical economics' and to attack in the 1930s. It has had the same two vulnerable characteristics: inability to prescribe for what has come to be considered a major social problem—inflation, in contrast to the unemployment of Keynes's time—and a dependence on the authority and prestige of senior scholars which is oppressive to the young. Also, ironically enough in view of Keynes's own long concern with the influence of money on the economy, it has suffered from the same major defect as the orthodoxy Keynes attacked—the attempt to explain essentially monetary phenomena in terms of a mixture of real theory and *ad-hoc-*ery, and specifically to explain inflation in terms of real effective demand and the Phillips curve. The fact that Keynesian economics has stumbled into the same pitfall as the 'classical' orthodoxy it succeeded is, perhaps, an indication of the difficulty of monetary theory as contrasted with value theory, as well as of the perils of abandoning monetary theory in favour of what appears seductively to be more reasonable common sense.

If, in accordance with the 'as if' methodology of positive economics that I adopted earlier, one posed the question of how to mount a counter-revolution against Keynesian orthodoxy, and considered the question in the light of the factors that contributed to the success of Keynesian revolution, one would, I think, be driven inescapably to two sets of conclusions.

The first would be the need to find an important social problem that the established orthodoxy is incapable of dealing with, even though it tries its best and claims to be successful. The second would be the need to develop a counter-revolutionary theory that had the requisite characteristics to be academically and professionally successful in replacing the previous revolutionary theory.

The obvious answer to the first problem—finding an important social problem that orthodox theory cannot solve—is to concentrate on the issue of inflation, the issue that Keynesian theory was least well designed to deal with. The trouble with that answer has been that, under the influence of both experienced inflation and Keynesian theory, the public has for the most part not been much concerned about the economic evils of inflation, and so has not regarded inflation as an important test of the intellectual strength of Keynesian orthodoxy. The history of the monetarist counter-revolution has, in fact, been characterized by a series of mostly vain efforts to convince the profession and the public (a) that inflation is an important question and (b) that monetarism can provide an explanation and a policy whereas Keynesianism cannot. Proposition (b) is eminently plausible; but it can only get a hearing if proposition (a) is accepted first; and, aside from a brief interlude in the late 1950s, the public has become convinced of proposition (a) only very recently. It is no accident that the appearance of monetarism as a strong intellectual movement has had to wait until the aftermath of the escalation of the war in Viet Nam in 1965. It is even less of an accident that its current success has depended on a prior Keynesian claim to, and acceptance of, responsibility for efforts to stop inflation by Keynesian fiscal means, under the auspicies of the 'New Economics.' Monetarism has until the past few years been in the position of investing a great deal of intellectual ability in analysing problems and producing solutions that no one else has considered worth the effort involved. It has eventually become a public force less by its own efforts than as a consequence of the 'New Economics' overreaching itself when it was riding high in the formation of national economic policy. The 'New Economics' was favoured by the opportunity to sell Keynesian policies to meet a Keynesian problem; it encountered disaster when it tried to sell reverse Keynesian policies to meet a non-Keynesian problem. And the monetarist counter-revolution has been cashing in on the mistake of intellectual strategy.

Nevertheless, on this score of social relevance, the monetarist counter-revolution has had certain factors working in its favour which have enabled it to survive and prosper despite the absence of an overwhelmingly obvious inadequacy of the established Keynesian orthodoxy, for most of the postwar period. One has been that, with the growing professionalization of economics and the expansion of academic support of interest in it, it has become increasingly possible for an issue to be deemed scientifically interesting and worthy of investigation even if the general public displays no visible interest in it. Another has been the rise of the United States to the position of a world power, which has made the exploration of issues of no direct relevance to the economic interests of the United States nevertheless worth pursuing as potentially matters of the national interest in the world economy. Both the hyper-inflations in Europe and elsewhere that followed the two world wars, and the strong inflations that have characterized Latin American economic history, have lent themselves to investigation with the aid of the quantity theory as matters of potential relevance to U.S. economic policy. But, as already mentioned, while these foreign experiences have provided fodder for monetarism, and in the course of time support for the contention that monetarism rests on a far wider base of empirical investigation than Keynesianism, the real counter-revolutionary thrust of monetarism has only developed since inflation became a major problem for the United States itself. Further, it is only since that event—which, given the world importance of the United States, has meant the emergence of inflation as a worldwide problem—that monetarism has been taken seriously by academic and public opinion in other countries.

Practical social relevance apart, the question of success for a new theory, whether revolutionary or counter-revolutionary, depends on its fitting appropriately into the intellectual climate of its time. Here we may apply what has already been said about the reasons for the successful rapid propagation of the Keynesian revolution to the 'as if' question of how to proceed to mount a quantity-theory counter-revolution. There were, I trust you will remember, five elements in the success of the Keynesian revolution, and I shall take them in turn.

The first was a central attack, on theoretically persuasive grounds, on the central proposition of the orthodoxy of the time. In the case of the Keynesian revolution, that proposition was the automatic tendency of the economy to full employment. In the case of the counter-revolution, the obvious point of attack, in a world characterized by high employment and inflationary tendencies, was the vulgar Keynesian orthodox position that 'money does not matter.' As James Tobin has pointed out, there is a world of difference between two alternatives to this proposition, namely, one, 'money does too matter,' and, two, 'money is all that matters.' But this difference was easily and conveniently blurred, to the benefit of the counter-revolution, by seizing on the extreme Keynesian position that money does not matter at all as the essence of the prevailing orthodoxy.

The second aspect of Keynesian success was the production of an apparently new theory that nevertheless absorbed all that was valid in the existing theory while so far as possible giving these valid concepts confusing new names. This was the technique followed—again I would emphasize the 'as if' character of my interpretation—in Friedman's classic restatement of the quantity theory of money.[5] The restated quantity theory is, as Patinkin has recently pointed out, essentially a generalization of Keynes's theory of liquidity preference on the basis of a more sophisticated analysis of the nature of wealth and the relation of wealth to income. Novelty and the requisite intellectual confusion were provided by the substitution of the concept of 'permanent income' for that of wealth, and the dragging across the trail of the red herring of human capital that was emerging from other work being conducted at Chicago at that time. Nevertheless, the restatement of the quantity theory of money did include one important and genuinely novel element, drawn not from Keynes but from his predecessors in monetary theory, which was highly relevant to the problem of inflation and which continues to distinguish quantity theorists from Keynesians; this consisted in its emphasis on the Fisherian distinction between the real and the money rate of interest and on the expected rate of price inflation or deflation as determining the difference between the two.

For the reasons just given, the restatement of the quantity theory provided a new theory meeting the third criterion for success, a degree of difficulty of understanding just sufficient to deter the old and to challenge and reward the young, and hence to reopen the avenues of professional opportunity for the ambitious.

The fourth criterion for success was a new and appealing methodology. Here the counter-revolutionary theory could appeal against the tendency of Keynesian economics to proliferate into larger and yet larger models of the economic system, a tendency which sacrificed theoretical insights to the cause of descriptive realism and which had the incidental but important detractions of demanding large sums of scarce research money available only to senior economists and of turning young economists into intellectual mechanics whose function was to tighten one bolt only on a vast statistical assembly line, the end product of which would contain nothing that could be visibly identified as their own work. In place of this approach, the counter-revolution set up the methodology of positive economics, the essence of which is not to pursue descriptive realism as represented by the largest possible system of general equilibrium equations, but to select the crucial relationships that permit one to predict something large from something small, regardless of the intervening chain of causation. This methodology obviously offered liberation to the small-scale intellectual, since it freed his mind from dependence on the large-scale research team and the large and expensive computer program.

The fifth criterion for success was the advancement of a new and important empirical relationship, suitable for determined estimation by the budding econometrician. That relationship was found in the demand function for money, the stability of which was claimed to be the essence of the traditional quantity theory of money. Presentation of the stable demand function for money as the essence of the quantity theory offered a close parallel to the Keynesian consumption function of the 1930s—a statistical relationship simple to understand theoretically and not too hard to estimate statistically, which promised, nontheless, to contribute importantly to the resolution of central theoretical issues. Moreover, since intelligent and gifted young men and women will persevere until they succeed in finding statistical validation of an allegedly important theoretical relationship, and will then interpret their results as evidence in favour of the theory that originally suggested the relationship, their efforts will inevitably be extremely favourable to the theory in question. And so it has proved. A stable demand function for money is by no means inconsistent with the Keynesian macroeconomic general equilibrium model, and indeed is presumed to exist in the construction of the standard IS-LM diagram. But the empirical finding of the existence of such a function has been widely adduced in support of the quantity theory as against the rival Keynesian theory, a procedure justified only by the identification of the Keynesian orthodoxy with the proposition that money does not matter and that velocity is either highly unstable or infinitely interest-elastic.

The quantity-theory counter-revolution could therefore make use of the same factors as facilitated the rapid propagation of Keynesian economics—the attack on a central and widely held theoretical proposition, the development of a new theory that absorbed and rechristened the best of the old, the formulation of that theory in terms that challenged the young and enabled them to leapfrog over the old, the presentation of a new methodology that made more immediate sense than the prevailing methodology, especially in terms of accessibility to the young and to those outside the established centers of academic excellence, and a new and presumptively crucial empirical relationship suitable for relatively small-scale econometric testing.

A counter-revolution, however, has to cope somehow with a problem that a revolution by definition can ignore—though it can trade on it in its propaganda—the problem of establishing some sort of continuity with the orthodoxy of the past. Specifically, the monetarist counter-revolutionaries were burdened with the task of somehow escaping from the valid criticisms of the traditional quantity theory, which the Keynesian revolution had elevated into articles of dogma and self-justification. These criticisms were, first, that the quantity theory had assumed an automatic tendency to full employment, which was manifestly in conflict with the facts of experience; and, second, that velocity was a highly unstable variable, useful, if at all, only for the *ex post* description of historical events. The restatement of the quantity theory met these criticisms by two counter-contentions: that the question of whether the economy responds to monetary impulses by price-level or by output changes is an empirical question falling outside the domain of monetary theory properly defined, because the quantity theory is a theory of the demand for money and not a theory of aggregate response to monetary change; and that the essence of the quantity theory as a theory of the demand for money is not presumptive constancy of velocity but the stable functional dependence of velocity on a few major variables. The former counter-contention freed the quantity theory from the charge that it was too silly to be worth considering, and opened the way for fruitful scientific controversy and development in monetary theory—though, as I shall explain later, the abnegation of responsibility for explaining the division of the effects of monetary change between price and quantity movements has subsequently proved a serious short-coming of the counter-revolution, now that the counter-revolution has come to be taken seriously. The latter counter-contention, involving emphasis on the existence of a stable demand function for money, permitted the absorption of the best of Keynesian ideas into the quantity theory cause, without any recognized need for acknowledgement of their source. The problem in the case of both counter-contentions was to establish a plausible linkage with pre-Keynesian orthodoxy.

The solution to this problem was found along two lines. The first was the invention of a University of Chicago oral tradition that was alleged to have preserved understanding of the fundamental truth among a small band of the initiated through the dark years of the Keynesian despotism. The second was a careful combing of the *obiter dicta* of the great neo-classical quantity theorists for any bits of evidence that showed recognition (or could be interpreted to show recognition) of the fact that the decision to hold money involves a choice between holding money and holding wealth in other forms, and is conditioned by the rates of return available on other assets.

Don Patinkin has—over-belatedly, from the standpoint of the history of economic thought—exploded these efforts to provide bridges between the pre-Keynesian orthodoxy and the monetarist counter-revolution.[6] He demonstrates conclusively that in their theorizing the neo-classical theorists did assume a tendency to automatic full employment, and that in their analyses of practical policy problems they regarded the inherent instability of velocity as a major disturbing element and made no use whatever of the functional relationship between velocity and other aggregate variables implied by their own *obiter dicta*. And he shows specifically that the Chicago quantity theorists—Simons and Mints—were no different from their quantity theory colleagues elsewhere in these respects. There was no lonely light constantly burning in a secret shrine on the Midway, encouraging the faithful to assemble in waiting for the day when the truth could safely be revealed to the masses; that candle was made, and not merely lit, only when its light had a chance of penetrating far and wide and attracting new converts to the old-time religion.

Nevertheless, one should not be too fastidious in condemnation of the techniques of scholarly chicanery used to promote a revolution or a counter-revolution in economic theory. The Keynesian revolution derived a large part of its intellectual appeal from the deliberate caricaturing and denigration of honest and humble scholars, whose only real crime was that they happened to exist and stand in the way of the success of the revolution. The counter-revolution had to endow these scholars, or at least their intellectual successors, with a wisdom vastly superior to what their opponents had credited them with. *Obiter dicta* and an oral tradition are at least semilegimate scholarly means to this polemical end. Moreover, as time has passed and the counter-revolution has acquired increasing academic respectability, it has become increasingly possible to admit, and even to brag, that the useful ideas have been drawn from the revolution and not from the preexisting orthodoxy. Indeed, this is a necessary element in a sucsessful counter-revolution, an element for which a previously successful revolution inevitably provides the foundations— because it ultimately becomes possible to draw an intellectually acceptable distinction between the sophisticated ideas of the revolutionary leader and the unsophisticated ideas of the revolutionary followers and executors, and to absorb the former into the counter-revolutionary ideology while discarding the latter as beneath intellectual contempt. The service of drawing this distinction in intellectually acceptable terms has been performed for the monetarist counter-revolution with great scholarly distinction by Axel Leijonhufvud's book on Keynesian economics and the economics of Keynes.

I have been concerned primarily with the intellectual and social factors that make it possible to launch a successful revolution or counter-revolution in economic theory. However, I would judge that the key determinant of success or failure lies, not in the academic sphere, but in the realm of policy. New ideas win a public and a professional hearing, not on their scientific merits, but on whether or not they promise a solution to important problems that the established orthodoxy has proved itself incapable of solving. Keynes, and many other economists in Britain and elsewhere, spent much time in the 1920s and 1930s advocating public works as a cure for umemployment—a cure that, because it conflicted with prevailing orthodoxy, was unacceptable. *The General Theory* was successful, precisely because, by providing an alternative theory to the prevailing orthodoxy, it rationalized a sensible policy that had hitherto been resisted on purely dogmatic grounds. Similarly, the monetarist counter-revolution has ultimately been successful because it has encountered a policy problem—inflation—for which the prevailing Keynesian orthodoxy has been able to prescribe only policies of proven or presumptive incompetence, in the form of incomes or guidelines policy, but for which the monetarist counter-revolution has both a theory and a policy solution.

No particular point would be served here by recounting the stages of accomplishment in the monetarist counter-revolution.[7] The advance from strength to strength can be summarized in a few key phrases: the restatement of the quantity theory, a statistical illusion in the judging of Keynesian models, velocity versus the multipler in U.S. monetary history, monetarism versus fiscalism, and 'the new new economics.' The question of interest is whether the monetarist counter-revolution will sweep the board and become the orthodoxy of the future, itself ripe for attack by a new revolution, or whether it will gradually peter out.

Personally, I expect it to peter out, for two reasons. The first, and most important, is that I believe the Keynesians are right in their view that inflation is a far less serious social problem than mass unemployment. Either we will vanquish inflation at relatively little cost, or we will get use to it. The odds are that we will accept it as a necessary price of solving other pressing domestic issues—and in that case monetarism will again be reduced to attempting to convince the public of the importance of the problem it is equipped to solve before it can start arguing about the scientific superiority of its proposed solution to the problem. The second reason is that monetarism is seriously inadequate as an approach to monetary theory, judged by prevailing standards of academic economics, and in the course of repairing its intellectual fences and achieving full scientific respectability it will have to compromise irretrievably with its Keynesian opposition.

The most serious defects of the monetarist counter-revolution from the academic point of view are, on the one hand, the abnegation of the restated quantity theory of money from the responsibility of providing a theory of the determination of prices and of output, and, on the other hand, its continuing reliance on the methodology of positive economics. Abnegation of responsibility for analysing the supply response of the economy to monetary impulses, and particularly the disclaiming of the need for an analysis of whether monetary changes affected prices or quantities, was, as I have explained earlier, necessary to the restoration of the quantity theory to a position of academic respectability. But this need was transitory: once the quantity theory regained academic respectability, it was obliged to resume responsibility for the short-run forecasting of aggregate movements of prices and quantities.[8] This it has begun to do, most importantly through the research work of the Federal Reserve Bank of St. Louis, and with appreciable success; but it has been lured into playing in a new ball-park and playing according to a different set of rules than it initially established for itself.

In similar fashion, the methodology of positive economics was an idea methodology for justifying work that produced apparently surprising results without feeling obliged to explain just why they occurred, and in so doing mystifying and exciting the interest of noncommitted economists and wavering Keynesians. But the general equilibrium and empirical revolutions of the recent past have taught economists to ask for explicit specification of the full general equilibrium system with which the theorist or empiricist is working, and to distrust results that appear like rabbits out of a conjurer's hat—and an old-fashioned top hat at that. The demand for clarification of the mechanism by which results can be explained is contrary to the methodology of positive economics, with its reliance on the 'as if' approach. But it will have to be answered satisfactorily if the monetarist counter-revolution is to win general acceptance among the profession; and the attempt to answer it will necessarily involve the counter-revolutionaries in the opposing methodology of general-equilibrium systems and multi-equation econometric models. The quantity theorists have already begun to extend their efforts into simultaneous-equation formulations and estimations of economic relationships. In so doing, they have been making important methodological compromises with the Keynesian opposition—or, to put it another way, reaching out for a synthesis between the revolution and the counter-revolution.

In summary, it seems to me that the monetarist counter-revolution has served a useful scientific purpose, in challenging and disposing of a great deal of the intellectual nonsense that accumulates after a succesful ideological revolution. But its own success is likely to be transitory, precisely because it has relied on the same mechanisms of intellectual conquest as the revolution itself, but has been forced by the nature of the case to choose a less important political issue—inflation—to stand on than the unemployment that provided the Keynesian revolution with its political talking point, and has also espoused a methodology that has put it in conflict with long-run trends in the development of the subject. If we are lucky, we shall be forced as a result of the counter-revolution to be both more conscious of monetary influences on the economy and more careful in our assessment of their importance. If we are unlucky (those of us who are not good at jumping on bandwagons) we shall have to go through a post-counter-revolution revolution as the price of further progress on the monetary side of our science.

15

Keynes and British Economics

Much of what I have to say is not about Keynes himself so much as about the younger generation of Keynesians, who constitute the older generation of economists to the younger generation to which I belong. And since much of what I shall say on both counts is unflattering, I should emphasize, first, that these are personal views, though derived from considerable thought about the evolution of economics since the First World War; and second, that to trace the subsequent impact of a man's ideas on his subject and his society is not to hold him responsible for the consequences of his thoughts—by the opposite assumption, all the great thinkers who have influenced human history (including most notably Jesus Christ) would be guilty of crimes against mankind.

Keynes's Contribution to Economics—A Reassessment

According to an admittedly drastically over-simplified but widely-propagated view of Keynes's professional contribution, the orthodox economic theory in which Keynes was trained held that the 'invisible hand' tended to produce automatically a state of full employment in the economy, unless prevented by worker insistence on too high a level of money wages. This was contrary to the facts of years of British experience of mass unemployment. Keynes produced an alternative theory that explained the facts, to the effect that the level of production and employment depends on the level of aggregate demand. Aggregate demand is the sum of aggregate consumption—determined largely by aggregate demand itself in its alternative identity of aggregate income according to the 'fundamental psychological law' that when income rises consumption also rises but not by as much—and of aggregate investment—influenced by business expectations and the rate of interest—with investment determining aggregate demand through its 'multiplier effect' on consumption; that the level of aggregate demand is normally not such as to produce full employment; and that money wage reductions can influence employment only indirectly, through their very uncertain effects on investment through the quantity of money in real terms and the equilibrium rate of interest, and through business expectations. Thus unbridled capitalism meant chronic unemployment, and the maintenance of satisfactory employment required policy management of the level of aggregate demand; and while Keynes himself was always confident of the powers of monetary policy to control the level of aggregate demand, both certain aspects of his theory and the apparent failure of 'easy money' to achieve economic recovery in the 1930s made it easy for his followers to read into the theory the need for control of aggregate demand by budgetary policy (setting the levels of taxes and government expenditure—'fiscal policy,' in American terminology).

In the light of historical hindsight and retrospect, the place of Keynes and of *The General Theory* in the evolution of economics appears very different and the interpretation of it outlined above appears strongly circumscribed and biased by the peculiar economic and political situation of the early 1930s against the background of which *The General Theory* was written. To appreciate this point, it is necessary to refer to British economic and monetary history, the state of British academic economics at this time, and the character of Keynes himself. The first reference is relevant to an explanation of why no 'Keynesian Revolution' was really necessary (what was necessary, however, was for economists to apply the economics they had). The second two references are relevant to why a 'Keynesian Revolution' nevertheless occurred (and may indeed have been necessary after all, given the inability or refusal of economists to apply the tools of their trade to their society's most pressing social and economic problem).

To recapitulate the history briefly, the mass unemployment in

Britain in the 1920s—which, far more than the additional mass unemployment in Britain and the novelty of mass unemployment in other countries created by the great depression after 1929, was the focus of Keynes's prolonged professional concern—was the result of two interacting forces, one inevitable but the other the result of a perverse act of policy decision by the British government. The inevitable force was Britain's gradual loss of her early nineteenth-century industrial supremacy, which some economic historians trace back to the 1890s and others to the 1870s. (Certainly Keynes's great teacher Alfred Marshall was aware of Britain's relative decline in his time and anxious about its implications). The perverse decision was the return to the gold standard at the prewar parity for sterling. This made British goods uncompetitive in money terms and necessitated a restrictive monetary policy to retain foreign capital and maintain foreign confidence in the pound, both of which necessitated mass unemployment which in turn aggravated the problems of industrial obsolescence. Somewhat paradoxically, however, the overvaluation of the pound meant a higher standard of living for the upper class of civil servants and professional people (including academics), for rentiers and owners of established businesses and large estates, and the majority of workers who managed to obtain full-time employment, than they would probably have enjoyed with an appropriate lower exchange rate. The result was to preserve an increasingly tenuous myth of Britain as a wealthy and powerful country—with obvious implications both for foreign policy and for potential domestic social welfare policy— while widening the gap between the status of the unemployed and the employed and the social and political tensions associated with it. (There is, incidentally, an interesting parallel in economic policy views between that period of overvaluation with mass unemployment and precarious balance-of-payments equilibrium and Britain's chronic post-World War II situation of overvaluation with full employment and a balance of payments deficit; in both cases a way out of the dilemma was sought in 'the rationalization of industry' and in lower wages, though in the 1920s the argument was for reduction of money wages and in the 1950s–1970s for achievement of essentially the same result through increasing productivity to reconcile rising money wages with lower money prices and more recently through 'incomes policy.')

Had the exchange value of the pound been fixed realistically in the 1920s—a prescription fully in accord with orthodox economic theory—there would have been no need for mass unemployment, hence no need for a revolutionary new theory to explain it, and no triggering force for much subsequent British political and economic history. The country would have been worse off than it remembered being before the First World War, due to the inevitable pressures of industrial obsolescence, and the large majority of the assuredly employed or otherwise provided with money income would have been worse off than they actually were, but this would have been more than offset by the gains those of who would have been employed instead of unemployed. With reasonably full employment in the 1920s, moreover, the economic adjustment to industrial obsolescence would probably have been both easier and more effective (involving less concentration on promoting the survival of traditional industries and the preservation of traditional markets for their products—including the Empire) and the political adjustment to Britain's declining importance in the world less crisis-torn and traumatic (for example, Britain might have joined the Common Market at the beginning, or else remained determinedly aloof from it).

The universal mass unemployment that struck the capitalist world after 1929, and enabled a theory developed for the special circumstances of Britain in the 1920s to become accepted as a universally applicable theory of the failure of unmanaged capitalism, can also be attributed to the perversity of monetary management, national and international. What began in 1929 as the depression phase of a normal short trade cycle was converted by the Federal Reserve's failure to prevent a collapse of the American money supply into an unprecedentedly deep and prolonged depression; and the American monetary collapse precipitated the collapse of the international gold exchange standard, including the adoption of a floating pound in 1931 under political crisis conditions that have inhibited rational discussion of exchange rate policy for sterling ever since. Keynes's *General Theory* distracted attention from all this background—which fits without trouble into the orthodox tradition of economic theory, unless one rejects a great deal of work on the trade cycle as not belonging to that theory—by focusing on a closed economy and on mass unemployment as an equilibrium situation instead of a long-lagged adjustment to a severe monetary disturbance. Keynes's followers did extend his theory to an open economy, but regarded exchange rate adjustments—in the light of their 1930s experience of them—as of very doubtful efficacy in affecting employment and the trade balance. In this, they failed to distinguish between a devaluation by one country required to align its domestic price level with world market prices—the British problem of the 1920s—and a devaluation of all currencies against gold as one means (not necessarily the most efficient and least painful) of increasing world liquidity. (The same problem has recurred in recent years in the international monetary system, with respect to inflation, and equally eluded the understanding of many international monetary experts.) In justice to Keynes, it must be recalled that when later confronted directly with the problem of international monetary reform, in the course of preparations for the Bretton Woods negotiations of 1944 that established the International Monetary Fund, he pioneered the intellectual foundations of a system vastly superior to the previous gold exchange standard. (One cannot really blame him for the fact that the IMF system eventually developed internal strains very similar to those that destroyed the gold standard, with the result that it has recently been temporarily dropped in favour of a floating rate system and if reconstituted, as is probable, will incorporate arrangements for much greater exchange rate flexibility.)

Had the policy-makers of the 1930s really understood what was occurring in the international monetary system and their own part in it, or had the economists of the time understood it (as they could have done by developing available monetary theory) and explained it effectively, the great depression of the 1930s would have been nipped in the bud and *The General Theory* either not written, or received as one eccentric English economist's rationalization of his local problems. Had Keynes been a different type of personality, he might have produced and in the 1930s published the international monetary reform plan he pioneered in the 1940s, together with an explicit rationale for the plan more firmly based in monetary theory than the IMF Articles of Agreement (and still more, subsequent plans for international monetary reform) have ever been. As it occurred, however, the great depression and international monetary collapse set the stage for a view of capitalism and of appropriate government policy to manage it oriented towards the problems of Britain in the 1920s to become the majority view of economists in the Anglo-Saxon countries ever since.

I have argued that the sources of the problem of mass unemployment with which *The General Theory* was concerned lay in severe monetary disturbance created by perverse monetary policies, thoroughly reconcilable with the orthodox neo-classical tradition of monetary theory, and not in any inherent deficiency of capitalism requiring a new causal theory and a new set of policy prescriptions and governmental responsibilities. Clearly what is so obvious to economists now, two generations later, was not at all obvious to economists (or the accepted leaders among them) then. For this there are several reasons, applying either to economics in general or to British economics in particular.

We may begin with the quantity theory of money. In its simplest and broadest form, this theory asserts that in a closed economy the level of money prices will tend to proportion itself to the quantity of money in relation to the volume of transactions to be effected in a given period and the speed with which money turns over in transactions (this last factor can be formulated alternatively and more fruitfully in terms of the ratio the public wishes to hold between its money stock and the money value of its transactions per period). What makes the theory a theory and not a mere tautology is the assumption that the latter two factors are determined by other forces than the quantity of money itself; but this assumption makes the theory true only in a long enough time perspective for the assumption to be approximately valid. The classical and neoclassical economists, living in a world of normally slow economic change, could safely rely on the assumption and the theory, since in the long run the volume of transactions would be governed by the stock of productive resources accumulated from the past because competition would tend to ensure full employment of those stocks and money-holding habits would be stable. Moreover, for various reasons those economists were primarily concerned with the allocative functions of relative prices and wages, and their main interest in monetary theory was to establish that in the long run money was 'neutral,' merely casting a 'veil' over the results of the interaction of real wants and productive possibilities without affecting the 'real' equilibrium of prices and quantities towards which the operation of these forces tended; and in the circumstances of before the First World War, this concentration was natural and reasonable.

For the few specialists in monetary theory, however, the quantity theory as expressed in the quantity equation described above was only a starting point. Their interest shifted increasingly towards 'the conditions of monetary equilibrium,' i.e., the conditions under which money would have to behave or should be made to behave in order to perform merely as a veil and so as not to impede or distort the operation of the underlying 'real forces.' Work on this problem reached its full flower in the 1920s and early 1930s, with the work (in English) of Robertson, Keynes in the *Treatise on Money*, and Hayek, (in Dutch) of J. J. Koopmans, and beginning earlier (in Swedish) of Wicksell and later Myrdal and others. This was a much shorter-perspective problem than that with which the earlier quantity theory was concerned, yet the theory continued to be built on the assumption of full employment as the condition to which the economy would approximate, though the shorter perspective made this assumption questionable, particularly in the case of severe monetary disturbances. In an important sense, *The General Theory* can be considered as a successful (and theoretically useful) challenging of the relevance of the full employment approximation to the problem under analysis. In terms of the framework of present-day monetary-theoretic controversy, Keynes can be interpreted as insisting that both output and prices are variable in the short run relevant to monetary changes, and dramatizing the need for analysis of the division of response to aggregate demand changes between prices and output by assuming, in opposition to classical and neoclassical theory, that quantities and not prices (except indirectly) respond to short-run changes in aggregate demand. In short, contemporary monetary theory was guilty of sticking to traditional assumptions in the face of the evidence that these were empirically invalid for the problem under examination; and it compounded this stupidity, when questioned, by seeking for reasons why mass unemployment constituted a real equilibrium (witness Robertson's attempt to convince the Macmillan Committee that mass unemployment was attributable to the satiation of human wants). In so doing, it paved the way for a revolution in monetary theory when what was called for was a drastic effort at application.

In similar but less obvious fashion, when international trade and investment are extensive the world as a whole becomes the closed economy of monetary theory, and the relevant related variables are the world stock of money and the world price level. Recognition of this is implicit in Hume's price-specie-flow mechanism, and explicit in important neoclassical studies of such phenomena as the effects of the inflow of precious metals to Europe after the Spanish conquests in Latin America. But monetary theorists faced with the collapse of the 1930s were unable to make this intellectual leap, and instead tended to stop short at the limitations imposed on national stabilization policy by adherence to the gold standard. As mentioned, Keynes's assumption of a closed national economy ruled international monetary phenomena out of the theoretical purview of *The General Theory*, and his followers naturally saw no reason to disturb their logically self-contained view of macroeconomics by introducing consideration of them in more than a peripheral way.

The failure of economists generally to understand the nature and sources of the great depression of the 1930s as a matter of international monetary collapse is probably considerably more excusable than the general failure of British economists to relate the mass unemployment of the 1920s to the maintenance of an overvalued exchange rate. For this latter failure there are many explanatory factors, such as the fact that Marshall never managed to write the intended monetary companion volume to his *Principles of Economics*, while Pigou, his successor to the Cambridge Chair, was neither interested nor competent in the field, and the British tradition in monetary economics, which untill very recent years was concerned with history and institutions rather than with theory, and with theory only as a part of historical and current policy debates. Something is attributable to the prestige of the Bank of England and its commanding social dominance at the time over politicians, civil servants, and academics, a dominance that it has begun to lose only recently, long since its nominal nationalization. Probably a considerable amount is attributable to the effects of the First World War both in slaughtering a significant proportion of the country's best young brains or making them, as erstwhile conscientious objectors, outcasts from their decision-taking class—alternative fates that Keynes's invaluability enabled him to escape gracefully, despite his early Apostolic beliefs—and in creating something of a national 'backs-to-the-wall' attitude which made loyalty to national policy decisions, right or wrong, a virtue, and outspoken and sustained fundamental criticism of policies unpopular, a ticket of assignment to the political wilderness. Such criticism in any case consorted ill with the symbiotic, to some extent parasitic, relationship between the ancient universities and Whitehall and Westminster. (Both elements, national loyalty and symbiosis, have, if anything, strengthened since the Second World War, and have helped to squelch any fundamental debate over crucial policy decisions such as the failures to float the pound in 1951 and to devalue the pound in 1964, and the decision to enter the Common Market in 1971.) To be blunt, whatever the balance of the reasons, British economics lacked the confident grasp of applied monetary theory and the intellectual courage to insist that the exchange rate was crucial to Britain's problems and that continued overvaluation would make a solution impossible; instead, it joined the government in the hunt for ways around the impasse.

This brings us to the character of Keynes. Keynes was—without any intention of slurring him—an opportunist and an operator, the glowing exception being his expression of moral outrage in *The Economic Consequences of the Peace*—and even that redounded to his personal and professional benefit. He was also—and this helped—a brilliant applied theorist; but the theory was applied when it was useful in supporting a proposal that might win current political acceptance, and dropped along with the proposal when the immediate purpose had been served or had failed. Thus Keynes realized fully, and exposed brilliantly in *The Economic Consequences of Mr. Churchill*, the adverse consequences for Britain of the return to the gold standard. But once that decision had become a part of the order of things, he absorbed it and turned to advocating public works as a way of increasing employment; and in 1931 he came out in favour of protection. These gyrations, which frequently made him seem inconsistent to his contemporaries, actually can be easily reconciled by reference to the modern theory of second-best, but Keynes never spelled out such a theory. *The General Theory* represents the apotheosis of opportunism in this sense, in two ways. Mass unemployment had lasted so long that it appeared to the average man to be the natural state of affairs, which economics was powerless to explain and political processes powerless to alter; a new theory of its causes that promised an easy cure was thus virtually certain to sell, provided its author had impeccable professional credentials. But to be a new theory it had to set up and then knock down an orthodox theory, not merely explain what traditional theory really was and develop its application to the problem in hand—a procedure Keynes had applied frequently in his younger days but which in this case would have required a major effort of theory construction and probably made the product unsaleable to the relevant public anyway. It was far easier to set up the dry aridity of Pigovian reasoning and the labrynthic alien Austrian logic of Hayekian capital theory as the targets, and to sacrifice the subtle and sensitive, intellectually more menacing but emotionally more vulnerable, personality of his former student Robertson to his coterie of young lions in the bitter in-fighting that followed the Revolution.

To make these points is not to dispute that *The General Theory* is nevertheless one of the few classics in the history of economics. But its importance from the long-range point of view of the development of economics, as distinct from the contemporary and subsequent politics of economic policy in Britain and the United States lies not in its refutation of a classical 'orthodoxy' but in its application of capital theory to the theory of demand for money and the stimulus it provided to study of the dynamics of price and quantity adjustments to changes in aggregate demand.

Keynesianism and British Economics

There can be no doubt that, at least in the historical short run, the publication and reception of *The General Theory* gave British economics a prestige in the outside world that it had possessed up to and including the heyday of Marshall but which had been waning ever since, the publication of Joan Robinson's *Economics of Imperfect Competition* constituting the major exception to this generalization. As time has passed, however, it has become increasingly apparent that Keynes's work in a sense marked the end of an era in British predominance in economics, an era which may be termed the Marshallian era and includes both Pigou's contributions to welfare economics and Cambridge work in the 1920s on the problem of reconciling the theory of the individual firm with the assumption of perfect competition. It has also become apparent that other important British work in the inter-war period, notably that of Hicks and Allen on general equilibrium systems and of Hicks on demand theory and welfare economics, work of at least comparable importance to Keynes's in monetary economics to the development of modern economics, was overshadowed by Keynes and unjustly denigrated by Keynes's Oxbridge followers—a misjudgement later underlined by the award of the Nobel Prize in economics to Hicks. Finally, it is a fair generalization not only that leadership in economics has decisively passed from Britain to the United States in the postwar period, but that Britain has contributed very little in the way of new ideas and directions to the process of scientific development of economics. The only exceptions that spring to mind, by this extremely stringent standard, are Harrod's extension of Keynesian economics to the context of economic growth, and, of relatively greater fundamental significance, Meade's monumental though tedious-to-read works on the theory of international economic policy.

For this there is a variety of general reasons, including the vastly superior numbers and resources of the American economists and the economies of specialization and division of labour that size and wealth make possible, the exhaustion of the intellectual curiosity and energy of many of the active contributors of the 1930s in the service of the government during the war, the closing of ranks in loyalty to the national society in a country that felt itself far more beleaguered by uncontrollable internal and external economic forces in the post-World War II peace than it had after the first world war, and the excessive preoccupation with current politics and policy problems generated thereby. But the nature of the Keynesian revolution and of Keynesian economics in its British version have played an important part. Two specific aspects have been especially influential: a view of the nature of scientific work and the character of progress in economics derived from the intellectual success of *The General Theory*, and the identification of Keynesian economics with left-wing politics. Both aspects, it should be emphasized, are the creation of the Keynesians, and quite contrary to the life-work of Keynes the economic scientist and the political stance of Keynes the political economist.

The view of economic science in question consists of positing an orthodoxy which is committed to defense of every aspect of the existing system and denies that any improvement on its performance is possible, and identifying as a contribution the use of clever reasoning to dispute this posited orthodoxy at some point. Thus economics becomes a crooked game the winning of which by the 'good guys' requires intelligence but not sustained hard work. For most of his long professional career, before *The General Theory* (he was in his fifties by the time it was published), Keynes put in the hard intellectual labour of learning monetary theory by study and application; and the book was presented as a challenge to orthodoxy, not merely for the strategic reasons discussed above, but because he honestly believed that he had found a crucial flaw in what his contemporaries regarded as orthodox economics. He was fortunate to be right, at least superficially—and superficiality represented as deeply as a very busy man could go into the foundations of monetary theory as then commonly understood. This made him an easy act to imitate but a very hard act indeed to follow. Unfortunately his followers have tried only too often to imitate the act without putting in the long hours of preliminary practice. Even where they have put in the practice, as is true of the most eminent of his Cambridge followers, the usefulness of their work to scientific progress has been largely vitiated by Procrustean forcing of it into the framework of capitalist orthodoxy, to be knocked down by the force of superior intellect. Thus Joan Robinson writes the most arid of technical capital theory in the belief that, contrary to all the empirical evidence, capitalism cannot possibly work, because she can to her own satisfaction make a nonsense of the concept of the production function and of distribution by marginal productivity; and Nicholas Kaldor goes her one better by admitting that capitalism does work, but maintaining that it cannot possibly work according to orthodox theories of how it works, proper understanding of it requiring acceptance of revolutionary, new, but unverified theories of his own devising. Each derives support and satisfaction from the knowledge that there are eminent professional economists in the United States who are prepared to take their arguments seriously, little realizing that if they did not exist it would be necessary for American economics to invent them to meet its own need for an orthodoxy against which to demonstrate its own scientific superiority.

The damage done to professional work by a methodology requiring an orthodoxy to assault unfortunately does not end with its stultifying effect on the work of those who espouse that methodology. The myth of a mindless but majority orthodoxy has to be given some degree of verisimilitude by the existence of a few professionally reputable specimens at whom the finger of scorn may be plausibly pointed. Since no young scholar can afford the professional risk and no senior mature scholar fancies the role, volunteers are not forthcoming and hapless innocents have to be pressed into service, willy-nilly. The results are personal and professional destruction or at least serious damage for the thinner-skinned scholars such as Robertson, and the suppression of the free spirit of scientific enquiry by the use or threat of the witch-hunt. An economics profession in which people have to think 'before I dare to say what I think, I have to be sure that what I say will not damn me as hopelessly orthodox' is not one likely to discover new and important scientific truths.

This baneful influence of concern about orthodoxy or heterodoxy as the hallmark of 'bad' or 'good' economics is vastly reinforced by the identification of Keynesian economics in Britain with left-wing or at least Labour Party politics, and the politicization of economics that it has entailed. (Keynes is well known to have had strong Liberal sympathies, but he carefully kept out of party politics to protect his professional reputation, and while he consistently sought for solutions to current problems that might be acceptable politically there is no reason, so far as I know, to suspect him of ever having produced or endorsed a solution because it conformed to the credo of a party he favoured.) The evidence of politicization ranges all the way from the scandal attending certain recent appointments to Chairs at Cambridge, through the consensus version of accepted economic principles expressed by economic and financial commentators and journalists and the significant failure of leading economists known to be Labour Party sympathizers to speak out in public against the decisions not to devalue in 1964 and 1966 and to seek entry to the Common Market in 1966, to the report by Samuel Brittan in his recent *Is There An Economic Consensus?* that an unexpectedly large number of academic economists gave the scientifically wrong answer to a question involving comparison of provision of below-cost public housing and direct social security payments to poor people and his suggested explanation that 'when they came to as politically charged a subject as homes for the poor, they dug in their heels and were determined to provide no comfort to the opponents of subsidized council building.' The adverse effects of political self-censorship on both the progress and propagation of scientific understanding and the professional reliability of economic advice on policy questions are too obvious to require further comment.

Keynesian Economics and British Economic Policy

The success of the Keynesian revolution and its defeat of orthodoxy and the subsequent adoption of Keynesian policies of demand management, is widely credited with responsibility for the fact that the post-World War II period has been characterized by the disappearance for some thirty years of the mass unemployment that characterized the British economy in the interwar period. The critics of Keynesian economics implicitly concur by blaming the chronic inflation that has characterized the same period on the same adoption of Keynesian policies. The validity of the attribution in both cases is extremely doubtful. Other countries have had at least as good luck without following Keynesian policies or even knowing what they are—the 'new economics' won acceptance in the United States only as recently as the tax cut of 1964, and Japan's economic policy seems to have been orthodox in the extreme—and one can with fair plausibility attribute Britain's success to prosperity in the rest of the world coupled with the good fortune of a forced devaluation of the pound in 1949. Economic growth is a different story, but even there Britain has done far better than she did for many decades before stretching back into the nineteenth century; and some would argue that she would have done still better by far had it not been for the crippling load of the mixture of protectionist policies for industry and the regions and of Keynesian policies for employment inherited from her interwar time of torment. (In any case, the promotion of economic growth was no part of Keynes's thinking, or indeed of Keynesian economics until sometime in the later 1950s.) About the most one can say is that Keynes's demonstration of mass unemployment as an avoidable evil has been popularly accepted to the extent that the government could no longer get away with the egregiously deflationary errors of policy it committed in the interwar period; and even this is not necessarily a plus point, since under postwar conditions the temptations have generally been to aim in the inflationary direction, and in a generally inflationary world environment the social costs of inadvertent errors in the deflationary direction have generally been low as compared with those of errors in the inflationary direction.

Leaving those issues aside, it is worthwhile to call attention to the naïveté of the concept of full employment as a policy goal, which has been one of the main legacies of Keynes and Keynesianism to economic policy-making in Britain and elsewhere. That goal is very intimately related to Keynes's essentially aristocratic Victorian view of the economic requirements of a happy society. In that view, social happiness consisted of a job for everyone in his appointed place in life—Keynes was little concerned about providing more equal opportunities for advancement within the ordered hierarchy of employment. Social misery of a severe and completely avoidable kind resulted from the failure of society to keep demand high enough to provide the expected and deserved jobs. (This simple view, incidentally, is consistent with and indeed necessary to another of Keynes's beliefs, one which demarcates him sharply from postwar Keynesianism with its emphasis on the necessity of economic growth to the good society: this was his confidence that it would take no more than a generation or so of capital accumulation at the normal rate to satiate society's demands for goods and services and free man for the cultivation of the finer things of civilized life. There is in fact an obvious disagreement between first-generation and second-generation Keynesians on the issue of the importance of economic growth, reflecting a basic difference between aristocratic and democratic attitudes to the desire of the lower order for improvement in their material standard of life.)

The identification of social welfare with full employment not only represents an extremely narrow aristocratic and paternalistic attitude towards the working class, but also leads to serious biases in attitude on policy issues, evident particularly in the pronouncements and writings of some of the leading British Keynesians. Their view neglects the role of voluntary unemployment in providing flexibility, a capacity for adjustment to economic change, opportunities for seeking better jobs, and in permitting individuals to escape from the boredom of working the same number of hours doing the same thing week after week into the freedom of disposal of their own idle time. It leads to a serious exaggeration of the social loss from unemployment and the social benefit of full employment. If unemployment actually means both total waste of the lost labour time of the unemployed and the psychological and social demoralization of the individuals concerned, then virtually no amount of inflation is too high a price to pay for full employment (and if inflation is bad for the balance of payments, no amount of interference with international transactions to control the balance of payments is too costly either). But, as a logical corollary, if full employment is such a great boon to the workers, they ought to show their gratitude for the full employment conferred on them by Keynesian policies by not making inflationary wage demands in the first place; and if, nevertheless, they irresponsibly persist in doing so, as some of them do, it is not only socially fair but in their own long-run interests, as they ought to see, to force an incomes policy on them.

Identification of social welfare with the single, simple index of the unemployment percentage, and disregard or denial of the manifold elements of voluntary choice that enter into the determination of the unemployment rate, lead to disregard of another important fact. The unemployment percentage that corresponds in principle to what Keynes can be deemed to have had in mind in the concept of full employment is not a social constant determinable by technical calculations based on aggregate labour market statistics; it is, rather, a variable changing in response to other kinds of change. Specifically, there are two major kinds of relevant changes which will tend to raise this unemployment rate. One is the provision of more generous social security benefits. The other is the general progress of affluence and increase in educational levels, which makes it easier for individuals to finance voluntary unemployment out of past savings or the current earnings of other members of the family, and to be more conscious of the possible gains to be obtained by devoting time to the search for a better job. Improved social security is especially important, as an alternative and in many ways more sensible method of presenting the socially evil consequences of unemployment than the Keynesian panacea of maintaining a high pressure of aggregate demand. One of the areas in which the naïveté of the Keynesian concentration on employment is most evident, incidentally, is that of regional variations in unemployment rates. It is extremely difficult to believe, after even the most cursory thought on the matter, that an abnormally high unemployment rate that has persisted in a region for several generations represents a failure of the competitive system to provide job opportunities rather than some sort of social choice in favour of a lower probability of employment at high wages and a higher probability of leisure time in a broad sense, over a greater certainty of employment and less individual free time.

All in all, it is difficult to avoid the conclusion that Britain has paid a heavy long-run price for the transient glory of the Keynesian revolution, in terms both of the corruption of standards of scientific work in economics and encouragement to the indulgence of the belief of the political process that economic policy can transcend the laws of economics with the aid of sufficient economic cleverness, in the sense of being able to satisfy all demands for security of economic tenure without inflation or balance-of-payments problems, or less obvious sacrifice of efficiency and economic growth potentialities. A good case could even be made to the effect that Keynes was too expensive a luxury for a country that was inexorably declining in world economic and political importance and obliged to scramble for dignified survival.

16

What Passes for Economics in the English Establishment

A generation ago, England and English economists dominated the English-language economics profession and represented the Anglo-Saxon tradition to the respect of economists of other languages. Marshall's *Principles* was the textbook *par excellence* for micro-economics, complemented for normative purposes by Pigou's *Economics of Welfare*; and Keynes's *General Theory* had stolen the limelight from the Swedish School and become the foundation of a revolutionary new approach to monetary economics and macro-economics. The world of professional academic economics looked to England for new ideas, and graduate students with ambition flocked to Cambridge, Oxford, and the London School of Economics to sit at the feet of the acknowledged masters of the subject.

In the period of one generation, all that has changed. England has become the sick man of Europe, and English economic policy the object lesson of how not to run an economy—or how to run an economy into the ground. Good graduate students and eminent professional economists from overseas no longer come, at least for professional training or refreshment at the top level. Those who do come, come either to relax in the atmosphere of civilized incompetence—much as the Romans used to visit Greece—or to find a ready audience for superficial critiques of the contemporary economic system delivered from a loftily patrician point of view. English economics has become a synonym for amateur incompetence, invincible ignorance of the rudiments of economic logic, and wilful disregard of the work of competent economists pursuing their subject in other countries—not to mention continual reassertion of non-facts about the British economy and economic behaviour itself.

This description, of course, pertains to the vocal and visible top layer of the English economic establishment. Exception must be made on the one hand for the mathematical economists, whose work is so irrelevant to economic and social reality that it has to be performed according to the world rules of the genre, and the econometricians, who are safely preoccupied and non-competitive for professional leadership; and on the other hand for the competent economists at the provincial universities, though these are rapidly emigrating out from under the professional and financial discrimination against them imposed by governmental policies recommended and endorsed by the establishment's economic ideas men. What is under discussion here, however, is the general flavour of English 'economics' (the quotation marks are used intentionally) as it is expressed particularly in the policy pronouncements of its most prestigious practitioners.

The flavour of a national academic culture is of course notoriously difficult to summarize and encapsulate, especially as economics tends to appear before the public in the form of controversy between individuals, each seeking to differentiate his product in order to establish a potential market for it—and for himself as an intellectual salesman. This is particularly true of the United Kingdom, where knighthoods and peerages for academics are awarded with little regard for scientific and academic standards of accomplishment, and much regard for political visibility and service. Nevertheless, British establishment economics can be summarized in five main interrelated propositions, all of them connected with the career and the writings of John Maynard Keynes—by which is meant, not what Keynes actually wrote and thought, but what Keynes is believed or construed to have thought (or would have thought, if he had understood his own theory) by his modern-day successors, who do not feel it necessary to read him to understand and propound him.

The first, and most fundamental and pervasive, proposition is that all economics in the main tradition of scientific economics is mere 'orthodoxy', and as such to be despised and turned on its head by the clever economists. One implication of this proposition is the assumption that the more startlingly 'unorthodox' a new proposition is, the more true it must be. Examples abound in both macro-economics and micro-economics: in the former context, one may cite the view that demand inflation is a sure-fire recipe for promoting economic growth and improving the balance of payments; in the latter, there is the view that profits and high entrepreneurial salaries are completely unnecessary to stimulate entrepreneurial risk-taking and innovation, that entrepreneurs are condemned by nature to take pleasure in their repulsively grubby little activities and can safely be taxed, or subject to a maximum limit on net earnings, down to the level of real income of a middle-rank civil servant. A second implication is that any evidence, no matter how well scientifically validated, to the effect that economically two plus two makes four and neither five nor three, either does not exist—except in the prejudiced imaginations of 'orthodox' contemptibles—or is wrong because a clever armchair critic can think of some reason why, if someone else did a few years' work reinvestigating the evidence, he might possibly be able to validate an alternative 'unorthodox' interpretation. Both aspects of English economics make it either puzzling or contemptible to economists elsewhere, whose motivation is to understand their economic world rather than baffle their audience with intellectual legerdemain, and who know that bright ideas are cheap to come by but new knowledge intellectually expensive to acquire.

A second proposition is that money cannot possibly matter—because Keynes triumphantly established this point against the barbarous forces of orthodoxy, and demolished the quantity theory once and for all. If the evidence seems to suggest that money *does* matter after all (no sensible economist ever claimed, in his scientific writings, that money is *all* that matters), then the evidence needs reinterpretation to reveal to the uninitiated orthodox that money is merely a veil over the all-powerful force of fiscal policy (the budget). Economists elsewhere find this orientation of theory puzzling to the point of incomprehensibility. Anyone competent to think clearly knows that Keynes was a quantity theorist, as all monetary theorists must be, in the sense that his theory gave a crucial role to monetary policy and changes in the quantity of money. His novel contributions were to shift the focus of analysis from changes in prices (with 'full employ-ment' output) to changes in output and employment (with 'sticky wages'), a shift that was more appropriate to the interwar British economy than it has been to the post-war second world; and, in monetary theory proper, to shift the analysis from the mechanical frame of velocity of circulation to the role of money as an asset alternative to other assets, and the influence of expectations on money-holding. The issue still in controversy is how loose or tight the connection between money and monetary policy and the operation of the economy is, as compared with that of fiscal policy (or possible other policy instruments, e.g., incomes policy). And in debating and analysing that issue, theoretically and empirically, the question of who is to be called 'Keynesian' and who 'orthodox', and on what grounds, is an anti-scientific Eng-lish eccentricity.

The third proposition is that 'full employment' is an exclusive definition of social well-being, and as such to be pursued at virtually any cost. Economists elsewhere take the view—to the extent that the brow-beating of English and English-trained economists will let them—that the workers, and especially their trade unions, are not a species of animal to be husbanded by a beneficent live-stock-breeder state, but people with the same cantankerous desire as other people for more than they can pay for, and the same propensity to establish monopolies in order to have it anyway. Such economists also recognize that social sec-urity is an alternative to full employment as a means of shielding people against economic distresses and disasters, and that abso-lute primacy of the objective of full employment at all times has lost whatever rationale it had in interwar Britain or the 1930s elsewhere, and become a dangerously inflationary and growth-inhibiting misdirection of policy in the context of the contem-porary welfare state.

The fourth proposition, briefly put, is that the workers ought to be so grateful for the efforts of their intellectual and political superiors to give them the benefits of full employment that they will refrain from any embarrassingly inflationary wage demands. If they are ungrateful and irresponsible enough to behave in an inflationary manner, they must be conned or coerced out of their selfishness by one or another kind of incomes policy. So axiomatic has this proposition become, in the thinking of the Oxford followers of Keynes, that, in the last British election, belief in the need for an incomes policy became a distinguishing characteristic of 'Keynesian' as opposed to 'orthodox' economists—to the complete astonishment of Keynesians elsewhere, who typically regard incomes policy as an anti-inflationary governmental ploy that might conceivably work, but only if its intention was to save the public the discomfort of learning the hard way that the government is absolutely serious in its determination to stop inflation by the use of whatever degree of restrictive monetary and fiscal policy is required (and who know, though English establishment economists have conveniently forgotten, that incomes policy has been tried five times already in Britain and failed miserably each time).

The final proposition, mentioned in passing above, is that faster economic growth is the panacea for all England's economic (and for that matter political) problems and that faster growth can be easily achieved by a combination of generally inflationary demand-management policies and politically appealing fiscal gimmickry, notably by subsidies to fixed capital investment. Usually, this proposition is not even accompanied by recognition that, for the investment to occur or to result in higher English resident income, saving must be increased as well as investment. Nor is it usually recognized that investible resources poured into the salvaging of moribund industries in order to preserve employment of workers and executives in those industries do not generate growth. More fundamentally, there is little if any recognition of the fact, well established by the empirical research of Edward F. Denison and others, that the pursuit of efficiency in the use of all resources, including human as well as material capital, and the quantitatively far more important stock of existing resources as well as the margin of newly-accumulating resources, is more important than the indiscriminate accumulation of material fixed capital.

These five propositions contain, in outline, the unique flavour of English 'economics', and the reason why the word 'economics' has to be put in quotation marks to describe the phenomenon accurately. As mentioned, all the propositions can be traced back in one way or another to the writings and ideas of John Maynard

Keynes. To do so in detail, however, is beyond the scope of this short essay. Suffice it to say that Keynes was an exceptional economist when he lived, but has become a malevolent myth since he died.

17

Keynes and Development

Keynes's only major work in what would now be called 'development economics' was *Indian Currency and Finance*, based on a plan worked out at the India Office and researched from there. His only major policy contribution as a British official involved a clear case of imperial-colonial exploitation: arranging to buy for British consumers in the First World War a surplus of Indian wheat available at a price below the world market price because the India Office had held the price down with the aid of an export embargo to prevent the Indian peasant from becoming unwarrantedly affluent. It is true that towards the end of his career he publicly favoured international commodity agreements, a fact now being used to give intellectual support to the demands for 'a new international economic order'; but that is a culturally insignificant part of his literary legacy to modern economic culture.

If 'development' is defined in a broad economic rather than political, sense, as economic growth, its sources, and policies for promoting it, Keynes certainly had ideas on it that were influential. But those ideas were social, a-scientific, and distracting in the worst sense of the term. They derived from, and were conditioned by, the opulent euphoria of deeply class-organized late 19th century Britain, compounded less or more by the contempt of the educated in careers of responsible social management—the don and the civil servant—for the intellectually inferior who live by working and by making money from organizing the work of others. In economic theory they were shaped and sharpened by the principle of Occam's Razor, on which the lazy theorist frequently cuts his own scientific throat—in economics, the principle that everything else can be related to one key macro-economic variable; this principle unites (at least in their worst moments or in their vulgar followers) Marx (the rate of profit), Keynes (fixed capital investment), and Milton Friedman (the quantity of money).

These ideas led Keynes to three views: that, if the British economy were properly managed, it could accumulate all the capital it could use in a generation or so; that entrepreneurs would happily perform their entrepreneurial functions for modest after-tax incomes; and that policy directed at fixed capital investment was the key to full employment and social bliss. The first view has been decently forgotten by active economists in this more democratic age of 'rising aspirations,' but its simple substitute has been the view that subsidization of fixed investment is the key to the promotion of growth, with the only room for debate being between emphasizing the subsidies themselves, or providing them indirectly via demand pressure, and if the latter whether via domestic inflation or via currency under-valuation. (The recent book by Robert Bacon and Walter Eltis, *Britain's Economic Problem: Too Few Producers*,[1] typifies the Keynesian 'fixed investment' tradition; Lord Kaldor has long been an advocate of the policy of deliberate undervaluation of the pound, the centre-piece of much past British Socialist policy.) This emphasis on fixed industrial investment, and on demand policies and subsidies to encourage it, has implied the exclusion from Keynesian thinking of both the old English classical and neo-classical emphasis on human motivations which encourage or discourage investment and innovation, and the modern American emphasis on a completely different concept of 'capital,' a concept which includes 'human capital' or ability, training, and self-improvement as a major form of capital and assigns to the accumulation of education and knowledge a major role in economic growth.

With regard to the narrower concept of 'development,' the economic growth (especially in per capita terms) of the poor regions of the world, Keynes's intellectual influence was to be exercised through his disciples. But the influence has been great—and, distracting, in the pejorative sense. That influence can be associated with two theoretical concepts, each identifiable with a still-living first-generation disciple of the master; and, understandably, both ideas have been especially influential in the formerly-British colonial region of the Indian sub-continent.

The first, and simpler, idea is that of 'disguised unemployment,' attributable to Joan Robinson. The concept, in its original context and formulation, was indisputably relevant and useful: it is simply the idea that in times of mass unemployment many of the formerly appropriately employed turn, not to the dole (or unemployment assurance and assistance), but to lesser types and degrees of economic activity that fail to use, or to compensate appropriately, the productive abilities they possess, but which do keep them out of the official measurements of the total of unemployed. (In fact, an American economist, Arthur Okun, gained international fame for a more sophisticated and quantified version of the same idea, elevated to the status of 'Okun's Law'.) Where it proved superficially plausible, but fundamentally misleading, was in its transmogrification into a description, analysis, and policy principle for the poor countries, with their characteristic preponderance of people in rural districts who seem to do little or nothing to contribute to agricultural output. The notion that there exist masses of 'disguised unemployed' people leads easily into the idea that 'development' involves merely the mobilization and transfer of these presumably costless productive resources into economic activities, primarily investment or industrial production, at an obvious and virtually costless social economic gain. What is required to realize this gain, gratifyingly enough, is merely cleverness on the part of the economist in outwitting the stupidity of the competitive system, and determination by the political leaders in generating the social will needed to implement the appropriate economic policies.

Tremendous efforts have been made, notably in India, to define operationally and to measure the amount of 'disguished unemployment,' and to develop and incorporate into policy and into cost-benefit analysis of policy proposals and projects the implicit difference between the money and the social (alternative opportunity) cost of labour. Attempts have also been made to discredit the 'neo-classical' alternative approach, represented particularly by T. W. Schultz's *Transforming Traditional Agricul-*

ture. Schultz argued that farmers are efficient in exploiting the technology available to them, and that the phenomena of 'disguised unemployment' are symptoms of a low-productivity technology. The conversion to a superior technology, he said, required a complex of changes involving not merely the technology itself but also the supply of appropriate inputs (fertilizer, water, seeds, pesticides) and the education of the farmer as well. Schultz was clearly right, as centuries of agricultural economic history have shown; but the city man's contempt for the farmer, and the Keynesian belief that there is something wrong with the economy that is attributable to the competitive system and that could be understood and set right by a feat of economic brilliance, have remained in control of the theory and policy of economic development.

The second extremely influential Keynesian idea was the so-called Harrod-Domar equation, the centre-piece of R. F. Harrod's extension of the Keynesian model for the explanation of short-run unemployment in a capitalist system into a model of self-sustaining economic growth in such a system. The equation states, briefly, that the growth of fixed capital will generate just sufficient increased sales and profits to justify the investment involved in increasing the capital stock if g, the growth rate is equal to s, the proportion of full-employment-of-capital output saved, divided by k, the normal ratio of capital stock to output. Harrod's own interest lay in the question of whether this growth rate, which he assumed would satisfy entrepreneurs and keep them investing for further growth, would be lower or higher than the 'natural' rate of growth made possible by the natural growth of population and the rate of technical advance. If lower, there would be a growing reserve army of the unemployed, if higher, the economy would encounter bottle-necks of labour supply that would throw it back into recession. But the equation provided a framework for planned economic growth, since the attainable growth rate would depend on the proportion of total production that the planners could extract from the economy as saving, and the amount of additional output that could be obtained per unit of investment by the planners' choice of projects (the capital-output ratio).

The Harrod-Domar equation had the important advantage of

concentrating on the central structure of the development-planning problem, and emphasizing the requirement of overall consistency in the planning process. But it automatically involved the same error as the 'disguised unemployment' concept, through its emphasis on physical investment and implicit disregard of the availability of labour, especially skilled and technical and scientific labour, to work with the material capital created by investment. (Underlying the process of growth through investment, of course, is a complex of other requirements, reaching into such areas as political stability, the rule of law in contractual arrangements, and social approval or toleration of the receipt of profits from successful investment).

The role of labour supply as a constraint on production similar to the constraint imposed by the stock of capital was only gradually recognized. Initially, recognition took the form of distinguishing between average and marginal or 'incremental' capital-output ratios ('ICOR's'), on the grounds that the average capital-output ratio includes the productive contributions of the other productive resources used as well as capital. Subsequently, it took the form of large-scale exercises in 'manpower planning,' i.e., forecasting the additional supplies of skilled labour of various types that would be required by the planned growth of industry and its material capital equipment in the economy, and planning the expansion of educational facilities and the growth of their intakes of students to produce skilled labour in the numbers that would be needed to fit the planned growth of capital. This effort was, however, as poorly grounded in economics as previous planning exercises in terms of physical capital only had been. The fundamental error was in assuming both that there is a fixed ratio between total output and the labour of each specification required to co-operate with material capital in producing the output, and that labour skills are a form of highly specific capital equipment that can be produced only by a formal educational process applied to the human raw material at a particular age of presumably transient malleability. In fact, people are quite capable of devising informal techniques for acquiring particular productive skills if there are strong enough economic incentives for doing so. On the other hand, as the evident failure of post-Sputnik education to produce a new type of technologically-oriented Englishman has shown, people are not stupid enough to embark on forms of industrial and technological training which the government claims will be required in future, if the evidence of their own eyes is that the arts man has a more rewarding career than the scientist, and the lawyer enjoys a higher standard of living than the sanitary engineer.

Both of the concepts just discussed—disguised unemployment, and the Harrod-Domar equation—while not of Keynes's own coining, are essentially Keynesian both by direct discipleship and by intellectual affinity with the concentration on fixed capital investment as the prime economic mover in *The General Theory*. They are related to significant strands in his earlier work, including at some stretch of the imagination his conviction that Germany could not possibly pay the reparations demanded of her after the First World War—European and especially German experience after the Second World War showed conclusively that, provided its stock of human capital and the mechanisms for generating it remained basically intact, a country could recover fairly quickly from large-scale destruction of its material capital stock).

No mention has been made thus far of the second of Keynes's leading ideas mentioned above, that entrepreneurs will (should? should be expected to?) perform their mundane tasks of business management, innovation, and risk-taking for relatively small rewards. It is, in fact, extremely difficult to separate the influence of the urbane, civilized, and patrician view of Keynes on this score from, on the one hand, that of the welfare economics tradition set by his teacher A. C. Pigou and his mentor Alfred Marshall, and on the other hand, that of the mixture of attribution of entrepreneurial decisions to unexplained but vaguely contemptible 'animal spirits' and denial of any economic justification to profits, spiced with Marxist class hatred of the capitalists as a class, that has come to characterize 'Keynesian economics' as taught by Keynes's disciples at Oxford and Cambridge. Keynes himself is probably blameless, in the sense that anyone confronted directly with Keynes's own statement of his views would recognize and discard them for what they are, a Victorian *fin-de-siècle* intellectual period piece. But 'Keynesian economics' has had a great deal to do with the emergence of development economics, beginning as it did with the faith that capital accumulation in the form of planned industrialization would quickly result in the closing of the gap between the poor or less developed countries and the rich or 'advanced developed' countries, becoming disillusioned with the social results of this kind of development, particularly with its failure to reduce economic inequalities *within* the developing countries, and culminating in some vocal advocacy of abandoning the goal of 'development' in favour of a more just and equitable society. That evolution itself is easily understood. It is a consequence of exaggerated expectations generated by the Keynesian concentration on fixed capital investment, the predictable effects in increasing the more blatant appearances of inequality of methods of capital accumulation that were bound to concentrate its ownership in the hands of the few possessing scarce managerial skills or the political skill to cajole monopoly privileges and subsidies out of the machinery of centralized government, and the Keynesian failure to appreciate the effects of rapid population growth in soaking up the gains from capital accumulation and technological improvement that would otherwise accrue to labour in the form of increasing real wages and real income per capita.

In summary, Keynes himself was little concerned with the problem of economic development; and to the extent that he was so concerned, his embeddedness in the English class society led him to regard it as a problem readily and quickly solveable by a modicum of additional capital accumulation. His disciples, however, provided extensions of his ideas that seemed readily applicable to the by-then-more-serious problem of promoting economic development in the poorer parts of the world. But the apparent advance of knowledge was illusory. Their failure lay in turning simplifications of reality that were appropriate to the problem of mass unemployment with which Keynes was concerned (notably, the crucial importance of the level of fixed capital investment, given the implicit assumption that savings behaviour had become habitual, and the availability of labour in the right quantity and right 'skill-mix' to man the capital equipment) into unverified assumptions about the facts of a different reality; with respect to which a quite different question was being asked and was demanding a scientific answer.

18

Keynes's *General Theory*: Revolution or War of Independence?

There are two alternative views that one may take—in each case with considerable supporting evidence—of both the intentions and the results of political revolutions. One view is that the intent and the result is to change the political and social leadership of society—to change the names and the origins of the personnel in charge—on the assumption that immeasurable social improvement will follow automatically from the elevation to control of people with ethically impeccable motivations and intentions. The other view is that the intent and result is to rid the society of control by outmoded forms of organization and ways of doing and deciding things, in order to free it to cope more realistically, rationally and effectively with its problems. The two views are exemplified by two phrases used to describe the events leading up to 1776 in the United States, namely 'Revolution' (as Canadians and Englishmen think of it) and 'War of Independence' (as Americans think of it). It is a theme which I hope my greatest teacher in economics, Harold Innis, would have liked, or at least considered tolerantly, provided my approach to it is sufficiently sceptical about big ideas, in the spirit on one of his favourite quotations of my student days: 'Above all, no zeal!' Innisian scepticism obliges me to observe that man as a political animal has a carnivorous preference for significant social change to be seasoned liberally with shed blood—a preference that serves the immediately useful revolutionary purpose of vacating property that can then be redistributed among the successful revolutionary survivors, but in the longer run may have the counter-

independent as well as counter-revolutionary effect of merely substituting a new cast of characters in a re-enactment of the same old play.

My theme, then, or more accurately my question, is how far *The General Theory* produced a revolution, in the sense of a circulation of leadership in a basically unchanged system of economic ideas, and how far it represented a war of independence, leading to clearer understanding of the economic system and the possibility (and actuality) of more rational economic policy-making.

Keynes himself, in the book and in comments on it, fairly evidently thought of his contribution as belonging to the 'war of independence' rather than the 'revolutionary' *genre*—a fact which his more ardent still-surviving disciples find it difficult to reconcile with their revolutionary fervour, though the indefatigable revolutionaries have as usual proved equal to the task and have been able to ignore with equanimity Keynes's political position as a lifelong liberal. There is, of course, the famous letter to George Bernard Shaw to the contrary, written in 1935: 'To understand my state of mind, however, you have to know that I believe myself to be writing a book on economic theory which will largely revolutionize—not, I suppose, at once, but in the course of the next 10 years—the way the world thinks about economic problems.'[1] But the Preface to *The General Theory*, read seriously, as an author's own view of what he has been doing in his book, is I think conclusive: 'The composition of this book has been for the author a long struggle of escape, and so must the reading of it be for most readers if the author's assault upon them is to be successful—a struggle of escape from habitual modes of thought and expression. The ideas which are here expressed so laboriously are extremely simple and should be obvious. The difficulty lies, not in the new ideas, but in escaping from the old ones, which ramify, for those of us brought up as most of us have been, into every corner of our minds'.

The essential, simple idea was that aggregate output is variable and not fixed; that it changes under the influence of changing views and ideas about the future, as expressed through a monetary (as contrasted with a barter) economy; and that its determinants can be expressed in terms of (a variant of) ordinary demand-and-supply analysis, monetary technicalities being suppressible into the analytical background. But to arrive at it, as he explained in a well-known letter to Harrod in the summer of 1936,[2] Keynes had first to appreciate the significance of his 'psychological law of consumption' and to elaborate its extension into the principle of effective demand, then to fit the monetary technicalities into the picture by means of the concept of liquidity preference, and finally to tie the package together by means of a satisfactory definition of the marginal efficiency of capital. And each element of the essential simple idea was certain to come into head-on opposition from 'habitual modes of thought and expression'; the assemblage of elements from traditional theory under new names and unfamiliar descriptions was certain to be confusing and controversy about them more productive of heat than of light; and the production of a well-heralded 'revolutionary' theory whose genesis lay in Britain's problems of the 1920s, near the end of a deep world depression accompanied by and expressed in sharp political controversy over capitalism against socialism, communism, and fascism, was certain to convert the theory into an instrument of politicization of economics in a sense that its author clearly never intended. Add to these influences the unhappy fact that the year after publication the author suffered a severe heart attack from which he returned to active professional duty only on the outbreak of the Second World War, with the result that a work in pure theory intended as a stage in the continuing revision of the *Treatise on Money* fell to interpretation by a generation that had lost faith in the importance of money and monetary policy, and replaced faith with science in the form of general-equilibrium mathematics and primitive econometrics. One can easily understand why the forty-odd years since display certain obvious similarities to the biblical forty years in the wilderness that had to be passed before the promised land hove into sight.

To provide perspective on *The General Theory* viewed as war of independence rather than revolution it is necessary to place it in the long perspective of the development of monetary theory. From that point of view, the so-called Keynesian Revolution has to be viewed as the third stage of evolution of the theory of a monetary (and capitalist) economy. The first stage was that of classical economics, in which the intellectual or scientific problem was to elucidate the nature of the economic system as a coherent, interdependent system that tended towards an equilibrium solution in the price and quantity variables, a solution determined by the given data of tastes, productive resources and their ownership, and technology. Understanding of the role of prices in the equilibrating process was difficult enough, and was made still more difficult by the close correspondence in the classical period between type of factor ownership and social class (which made factor pricing equivalent to the distribution of income among social classes), together with the inherent difficulties of understanding interest as the intertemporal price ratio of resources in general. It was natural enough, therefore, for monetary theory to concentrate on the proposition that money made only a difference of monetary scale or numéraire value, but no real difference to the real equilibrium towards which the system would converge. In other words, the chief purpose of monetary theory was to demonstrate the neutrality of money; and this was the purpose of the quantity theory as expressed in the quantity equation.

As time and understanding of both theory and the world of reality progressed, however, the interest of monetary theorists shifted from demonstrating the neutrality of money to investigating the conditions under which money would in fact be 'neutral'—put differently, the conditions of monetary equilibrium and the sources of monetary disequilibrium. And the appropriate tool of analysis was not the quantity equation, but a dynamic equation of a type described in economics as period analysis and in mathematics as a first- (or sometimes higher-) order difference equation. Much of the 1920s and 1930s work on this problem, incidentally, was of first-class quality, but was suppressed by the success of the Keynesians and had to be reinvented in the 1960s by writers on monetary growth models and the (misnamed) 'optimum quantity of money.' However, ingenious as they were in developing a different type of model for a different kind of analytical problem, the writers in question (including the Keynes of the *Treatise*) retained the classical monetary-theoretic assumption of a system in real full-employment equilibrium, and hence were constrained to treating business cycles and similar fluctuations either in terms of changes in the composition of a given (full-employment) total of output, or in terms of unemployment and idle capacity that was either unexplained, or explained in terms of the classical (actually, neoclassical) real-theory mechanism of an excessively high level of real wages. It was Keynes's deliberate jettisoning of this analytically and empirically stultifying assumption, and his replacement of it by the assumption, as a first approximation, of rigid money wages, that introduced the third stage of evolution of monetary theory. That assumption—which following Leijonhufvud can be described as the replacement of a price-adjustment by a quantity-adjustment system of general economic equilibration—was in its turn a source of considerable difficulty in understanding what the new theory was all about, for two reasons.

First, Keynes accepted the marginal productivity theory of distribution (which a group of his followers led by Joan Robinson and Nicholas Kaldor have since come vociferously to reject) and hence had to reconcile the agreed conclusion that increased employment had to be accompanied by reduced real wages with the rejected inference of real theory that employment could be increased by reducing wages. (In this connection, one should note the source of the basic confusion in Marshallian partial-equilibrium analysis, which managed, by sophisticated legerdemain with the assumption of a constant marginal utility of money, further complicated by confusion between the marginal utility of *money* and the marginal utility of *income*, to theorize about real relative prices as if they were identical with money prices.)

Second, the assumption of wage rigidity was in fact deeply grounded in Keynes's conceptions of the meaning of a monetary economy; but it lent itself easily to the interpretation that Keynes's theory rested on choice of an arbitrary and irrational pattern of behaviour on the part of wage-earners. Further, it could be shown fairly easily that the reduced output and unemployment Keynes associated with a monetary economy could equally readily be generated by a pure barter production and exchange economy.

As mentioned, Keynes was removed from professional action by a heart attack the year after *The General Theory* was published; and this left the way clear for the emergence and elaboration of

'Keynesian economics' as something quite different from 'the economics of Keynes'—to use Leijonhufvud's (1968) extremely convenient distinction[3]—and the burgeoning of *The General Theory* into 'the Keynesian Revolution,' with all that that implies in terms of the obliteration of the alternative of a war of independence, which was, in my view, Keynes's own constructive objective. The 'revolution' is best discussed in terms of two separate aspects, the political and economic policy aspect and the scientific economic and specifically monetary theory aspect, the political-policy aspect being especially necessary to discuss separately because its manifestation and its importance have diverged sharply on the two English-speaking sides of the Atlantic.

To take the political aspect first, the Keynesian revolution had an over-whelming appeal to two different groups of would-be revolutionaries: the politically motivated, anti-capitalist radicals, and what might be termed the Fabians or technocrats, convinced of their capacity to manage the system more efficiently and rationally than could the 'blooming, buzzing confusion' of free competition. But circumstances differed significantly between the United Kingdom, with its Labour Party destroyed by adhesion to the gold standard, its National (Conservative) Government firmly committed to masterly inactivity of government as used-to-be-usual, and its Treasury-view orthodoxy of economic policy, which could stretch only to cheap money within orthodox limits on interest rate reductions; and the United States, with its New Deal and Brains Trust days behind it, the Democrats in the saddle, its pragmatism on economic policy reflected in professional concern with the possibilities of fiscal policy as developed by Hansenian Keynesianism at Harvard, and the economist rapidly replacing the lawyer as the professional expert from outside government who could rise rapidly to a high place within it. To put the matter briefly, the American radical had only foreign roots or a very brief experience of unsuccessful American capitalism to draw on for sustenance, and the American intellectual-cum-technocrat was not confined to outside criticism of an inner governing establishment, whereas the British radical had over a century of documented grievances and class conflict to draw on, and the British technocrat was naturally excluded from the inside workings of government.

As a result, Keynesianism as a political force or major intellectual movement became and remained much stronger in Britain
than in the United States. Further, and more important in recent
years, radical and technocratic Keynesianism in Britain has come
to incorporate various aspects of the syndrome of behaviour of
the elite of a former imperial power that has lost its empire, has
failed to find a substitute or a tolerable modus vivendi, and has
perforce fallen back on its one claim to contemporarily relevant
greatness: that it produced Keynes, and therefore automatically
understands the true inwardness of his theory better than any
upstart nouveau-riche world power can possibly hope to do.
Hence on the one hand the flowering of a hagiographic 'Keynes
industry,' devoted to producing publications in commemoration
of the master, and on the other hand the axiomatic assumption
that if British Keynesianism has failed as a policy guide, it is not
British Keynesians, or Keynesian policy theory, that has failed,
but the whole of economic science root and branch. Hence also
the strong impression that the point of Keynes's work was to
prove that the American economic system is a pernicious system
and the theory of it a hopeless nonsense.

This impression, I am sorry to say, seems to attract a number of
Canadian intellectuals, who seem unable to appreciate the extent
to which they are being seduced into colonial service to a
moribund cultural imperialism. It is in a sense our Canadian
national fate to refuse to recognize the winner in the War of
Independence and to continue to try to persuade ourselves that it
was a Revolution, and as such a nasty and ghastly mistake that
might still be rectified. It may be true, to paraphrase a remark of
Innis's, that Canada has evolved historically in record time from
colony to empire to colony; even so, there seems little to be said in
favour of switching our colonial attachment back to dependence
on a manifestly non-viable imperial centre.

Be that as it may, Keynesianism in the United States, in contrast to that in Britain, has never become a governmental and elite
orthodoxy. The closest it came was in the heyday of the Kennedy
Administration and the New Economics of Walter Heller. It
remains alive as a radical political movement only among a small
group of followers of Joan Robinson, and as a popular political
force only among a somewhat fragmented subgroup of Demo-

crats; but it is not a powerful force in American government and economic policy, let alone an official orthodoxy.

This has been a fortunate fact for the United States—though not as fortunate as it might have been, to the extent that the Keynesian policy objective of 'full employment' has become an objective and touchstone of American economic policy, and by the same token more fortunate for the United States than for Canada, which tends in this as in other things to demonstrate its national independence to its own satisfaction by espousing the British extreme of American popular ideas. For Keynesian ideas on economic policy appear increasingly with the passage of history to be severely and dangerously limited in relevance by the presuppositions about the economic and social world implicit in Keynes's position as a successful member of the Cambridge academic community and the British establishment. Keynes's theory of liquidity preference was as 'a College Bursar's theory of interest'; more broadly, it was a stock-market speculator's theory of asset prices and price movements. But, in addition, Keynes's theory of wages and employment was a college resident's theory of labour and industrial work, summarizable in the view that to keep the porters happy one should not pay them more than the competitive wage, but should provide playing fields, pensions, and security of employment. And his theory of entrepreneurship was that of an English academic, used to seeing the worthy, games-loving souls but inferior minds among his pupils going off year by year to staff British industry, where their success would depend on 'animal spirits' or British grit but in any case deserved only a modest recompense in hard cash and social prestige. This *gestalt* of social presuppositions and attitudes involves two crucial oversights. First, the workers, the future businessmen, and the investments with which a College Fellow deals are a biased and largely self-selected sample of the many varieties necessary for the functioning of a successful capitalist system (or indeed any other populous self-sustaining social system); and the majority are not likely to be satisfied with social and economic policies aimed at the partial sample. Second, full employment is only one of two alternative ways of providing economic and social security on a mass basis, the other being social insurance and assistance and the public provision of satisfaction for common human needs; and as social provision is expanded, as it has been on a large scale since the 1930s and earlier, which constituted Keynes's socioeconomic environment, the Keynesian emphasis on full employment as a policy objective becomes increasingly both misdirected and misleading.

To return to the 'Keynesian Revolution,' and to turn to the scientific economic and monetary theory aspect of it, a major development was the conversion of a theory designed to illuminate the role of money and monetary policy in a monetary economy into the dogmatic contention that money does not matter. This conversion was partly the result of the circumstances of the Depression, the current reality which was all that most Keynesians were aware of—in contrast to Keynes himself, whose adult professional life stretched back into the heyday of the nineteenth-century 'golden age' of Victorian and Edwardian peace and prosperity—and a reality which quite understandably made any sensible economist extremely sceptical about the efficacy of monetary policy. Partly, also, it was an incidental result of the concern of 1930s Oxford with empirical economic research and testing, which included the finding that business investment behaviour was apparently insensitive to interest rates, in contrast to the central thrust of Keynes's monetary theory. One must be careful to note that English Keynesianism, at the popular and policy level, is a creation of Oxford and not of Cambridge, and moreover owes a great deal to the concentration of militarily unusable refugee economic talent (none of it, incidentally, well trained in classical monetary theory) at the Oxford Institute of Statistics during the Second World War.

Of much more fundamental importance, however, was the crystallization of the rather loose Keynesian 'model' of a monetary economy, in the hands of a new younger generation of mathematically-trained economists, into the familiar Hicksian (and Hansenian) IS-LM geometrical macroeconomic model of general equilibrium, and with it the emergence of 'Keynesian economics' as a corpus of theoretical analysis, in contrast to 'the economics of Keynes.' The IS-LM formulation, intentionally or not, focused attention on the question of whether or not Keynes's 'general theory' was a special case dependent on the assumption of rigid wages. This was a question of counter-revolutionary import, set in the framework of revolutionary claim and counter-revolutionary response, to which the initial answer was 'yes—except in the cases of a liquidity trap or completely interest-inelastic savings and investment schedules'; and the final agreed answer removed the exceptions by bringing in the 'Pigou effect.' (The 'Pigou effect,' incidentally, gave Pigou a claim to end-of-scientific-life scholarly contribution otherwise unequalled in the history of our profession, at the expense of throwing monetary theory backward by at least half a century into an assumed institutional setting characterized by 'outside' commodity money rather than 'inside' credit money created against other debts. A great deal of effort has been used up in the meantime, in working monetary theory's way back into the context of a modern system of financial organization.)

What may be described as the 'Keynesian Revolution's' third stage in the historical evolution of monetary theory, a stage lasting for something like fifteen years after the publication of *The General Theory*, culminated in the rather unsatisfactory synthesis of acceptance of the 'full employment' policy objective and the Keynesian analytical model, together with the admission that 'underemployment equilibrium' was an abstract theoretical special case dependent on either a short-run approximation of wage rigidity or some very peculiar and not seriously empirically defensible behavioural assumptions. This phase was followed by a fourth phase, which may be characterized as consolidation and extension of the new theoretical approaches and insights provided by Keynes the monetary theorist. Three major lines of development can be distinguished.

The first was the elaboration, under the leadership of James Tobin at Yale,[4] of the 'assets approach' or 'portfolio-balance approach' to the demand for and the relative interest yields on money and other assets suggested in rudimentary form by Keynes's theory of liquidity preference. This approach has followed Keynes in simplifying the problem by assuming (initially at least) a constant price level—which has the great advantages of making money the only completely riskless asset and identifying changes in money magnitudes with changes in real quantities—and separating the analysis of the monetary and financial sector of the economy from the influence of monetary changes on the real economy, the linkage between monetary and real being concentrated, following Keynes, on the valuation of real assets relative to their cost of production.

The second, largely the work of Don Patinkin,[5] was the integration of monetary and value theory in a formal and self-consistent model of a monetary economy, both the integration and the preservation of the classical property of neutrality of money being provided by the 'real balance effect.' This work built on the earlier work of Hicks, on general equilibrium systems, and more directly on Oskar Lange's effort to recast the Keynesian model in terms of a dynamic microeconomic general equilibrium model. Unfortunately, as Clower and Leijonhufvud[6] have emphasized, the formulation of monetary theory in this framework results in losing the essential characteristic of a monetary economy, which is that money exchanges for goods and goods for money but not goods for goods, and the resultant necessity to hold money as an intermediate stage in the transaction process introduces all the problems of expectations and uncertainty that distinguish a monetary from a barter economy (or, perhaps more accurately, an economy characterized by specialization and division of labour but not centrally controlled, since the fundamental source of uncertainty is the process of production of goods for exchange with other producers). But, equally unfortunately, it is virtually impossible to find a simple and comprehensive mathematical device for converting a general equilibrium system of mathematically formulated relationships into a fruitful technique for the study of persistent 'disequilibrium' and 'market failure.'*

The third development was the resurgence of the quantity theory of money, primarily the work of Milton Friedman.[8] On this large subject only three remarks are relevant to the present context. First, the restatement of the quantity theory involved absorbing and improving on all of Keynes's insights into the nature of money as an asset and the demand for money as a

---

* The essential problem is that it is virtually impossible to invent a plausible mechanism that leaves the economy in disequilibrium with unexploited possibilities for profits or increased labour incomes, and at the same time specifies exactly how the economy will respond to a *change* in profit or labour income opportunities. On this point see Lucas.[7] See also Clower and Leijonhufvud.

demand for one among a number of alternative assets. Second, it involved in an important sense a step backward, from the interwar concern with the dynamics of monetary disturbance and the associated assumption of instability of velocity, towards the first phase of concern with the neutrality of money, a step in the course of which the stability of velocity was shifted from being a very long-run assumption to being a relatively short-run assumption, albeit one whose understanding required mastery of the distinction between 'transient' and 'permanent' values of variables, and, in general, an appreciation that in the short run 'things are not what they seem.' Third, there remains a crucial distinction between the neo-quantity theory approach and the 'Keynesian' approach (including here the approach of J. M. Keynes himself). That distinction lies in the explicit recognition, derived from the monetary theorizing of Irving Fisher, of the influence of expected changes in the price level on the cost of holding real balances and assets dominated in money terms, and the associated distinction between real and nominal rates of interest or yields.

The fourth phase of evolution of monetary theory, the phase of consolidation and extension of Keynes's insights into monetary theory and synthesis of these insights with the insights of previous monetary theorists, and most notably with those of Irving Fisher—it is, incidentally, an interesting question what has become of the work of Keynes's other approximate contemporaries, Wicksell, Robertson, and especially Hayek, who still lives—has been succeeded by a fifth, and contemporary, phase. This has been, and is, a phase of questioning of both Keynesian theory and monetary theory in general, amounting in some cases to almost hopeless despair about the relevance and usefulness of economics to society, allied with heartfelt prayer to the sociologist to get economics off the hook. Witness especially an *Economic Journal* article entitled 'Is Progress in Economic Science Possible?' by the archbishop of the British Keynesian establishment, more mundanely the director of the National Institute of Economic and Social Research, G.D.N. Worswick.[9] (The National Institute, it should perhaps be explained to those who are (quite justifiably) unknowing or uncaring, is a nominally independent economic forecasting and policy advisory agency distinguished by an unshakable belief in the desirability and feasibility of achieving full employment and growth through expansionary demand management, and an equally unshakable belief that if the workers are not sufficiently grateful for the demand-inflationary efforts made by their governmental masters on their behalf to refrain voluntarily from selfishly inflationary wage-push behaviour, the proper remedy is an incomes policy imposed by government for their own good—and if that remedy does not work as it should, the only course left is to abandon economics and call in the sociologists.)

In other quarters, notably among the 'radical Keynesians' or, as Schumpeter used to call them, the 'Marxo-Keynesians,' the solution to present disorders is to be found in the eschewing of what this group refers to as 'Bastard Keynesianism' and a return to the pristine purity of the true intellectual Keynesian lineage.* This group has something to be said for it—like the Mona Lisa, its smile is intriguing even though one has good reason to think that the piquancy of the smile results from concealing an extreme case of dental decay. The question is, where does it take us? The message that men cannot foresee the future, but have to rely on rules of thumb, advises us to be careful in applying our formal theory, but does not provide a convincing case for social change or revolution, since all organized life operates largely by rules of thumb. The message that if unemployment is necessary to secure labour discipline and you promise not to use that disciplinary weapon you have to resort instead to some kind of political force or agreement is logical simplicity made blatantly obvious—though not necessarily very obviously helpful, as either a description of or a prescription for the current problems of the full-employment policy object. Equally obvious logically, but doubtfully useful economically, is the attachment of criticisms of 'Bastard Keynesianism' ('Keynesian economics' in Leijonhufvud's less emotionally contemptuous terminology) to the resusci-

---

* See Joan Robinson, 'What Has Become of the Keynesian Revolution?' in Milo Keynes (ed.), *Essays* on John Maynard Keynes, (Cambridge: Cambridge University Press, 1975). This paper is notable for its introduction of the term 'bastard Keynesians,' though this term is not explicitly defined. The main emphasis is on the problem of decision-making in the face of (historical not mathematical) uncertainty. A similar theme is developed in Shackle.[10]

tation of Keynes's mentioned but undeveloped concept of 'the aggregate supply curve.'[11] As is well known—and in this respect the construction of Keynes's theory follows the procedure common to all theory, of depending on a starting point whose characteristics cannot be explained in terms of the theory itself—the Keynesian model leaves unexplained the determination of the level of money wages itself. Consequently, any theorist is free to extend or modify the theory—without inconsistency with the master's own construct—by adding in any theory or hypothesis about money wages he finds convenient or congenial. And, in the context of current practical concerns, one obvious way of proceeding is to formulate one's own version of Keynesian theory and one's criticisms of other avowed Keynesians in terms of their neglect and one's own understanding of the crucial role of the aggregate supply curve.

Both the establishment appeal to sociology and the radical appeal to 'non-bastard' Keynesianism embody, in their separate ways, the 'revolutionary' interpretation of Keynes's contribution to economic theory. Either revolution is not powerful enough to subordinate the Old Adam in human nature, or the spirit of revolution has been suborned by the adventurers and profiteers among the revolting masses and needs to be revived by a denunciation of the bastards and a return to the pure principles and noble spirit of the original revolution (as remembered, reconstructed, or invented by the saved survivors and elect descendants of the disciples).

On the alternative interpretation, Keynes in *The General Theory* was concerned to break loose from a tradition of monetary theory that for purposes of analysing the central theoretical problem it was concerned with—monetary neutrality, and perhaps subsequently a type of business fluctuation that affected primarily trade and commerce rather than production and employment—formulated its problems in terms of a real economic system characterized by full employment. This framework became increasingly difficult and uncongenial for him to work with, primarily as a result of its inconsistency with the realities of British economic experience and policy problems in the 1920s and secondarily as a consequence of more general world experience in the Depression of the 1930s. Modernization of the framework required on the one hand sharp (and sometimes quite unfair) doctrinal conflict with contemporaries wedded to the old framework of assumptions. On the other hand it required the construction of a theoretically satisfactory model of a system characterized by quantity rather than price adjustments, the prevalence of quantity adjustments being necessitated in turn by the existence of a monetary economy and its two salient characteristics. One of these is confidence in the stability of the value of money (necessary to its use as a numéraire and intermediary in the production of goods and their exchange for other goods and factor services in the market). The other is the existence of markets for assets, in which expected flows of revenues and costs and changes in them are capitalized immediately into asset values.

From this perspective, *The General Theory* provided no less and no more than what some contemporary critics attributed to it, namely, a theory of deep depression or, in another terminology, of capitalist crisis. Of greater fundamental significance, it involved a process of looking past the models and problems of pure theory to the real world to which theory claimed to be a scientific guide, recognizing a glaring gap between the assumptions and hypothetical economy of the models and the actual behaviour of the real world, and attempting to remedy the deficiency by redesigning the machinery of theory while thriftily cannibalizing those component parts that remained useful.

The relevance of this interpretation to the current situation in monetary and macroeconomic theory requires some brief elaboration. Very broadly, from the end of the 1930s until the early 1970s, the capitalist or competitive enterprise system functioned fairly smoothly and normally, without experiencing the economic trauma of the Depression, and in Britain's case the economic disaster of the whole interwar period. As a result, economic theory was once again privileged to retreat, by and large, into the scholarly disputation supported by an invalidated confidence in ultimate empirical relevance that characterized interwar monetary theory up to *The General Theory*. The experience of 'stagflation'—unusually deep recession in terms of unemployment, accompanied by continued rapid inflation—has produced the same sort of trauma as the Depression, and similar social phenomena, including the politicization of economists and of economic debate and appeals for help from outside the discipline of economics itself—including occasionally forlorn hope for the second coming of Keynes the saviour of economic man. *The General Theory*, as I have interpreted it, points in a quite different direction—towards the use of trained common sense, supported by but not subordinated to mastery of the tools of the economist's trade, to define the problems as they really are and to set about solving them, and if necessary along the way to revolutionize traditional ways of professional economic thinking about the economic system. The revolution, be it noted in contrast to much current writing about Keynes, is an incidental instrument (and a potentially dangerous one) for the advancement of scientific knowledge, not an objective in and of itself. When it comes, however—and I am confident that it will—it is very unlikely to bear the name of any individual economist: for economics has broadened and deepened itself well beyond the stage of being describable as what (a relatively small number of) economists do, and become a large and truly international community of co-operating, competing, and complementary scholars.

References

Chapter 1.
1. R. F. Harrod, *The Life of John Maynard Keynes* (London: Macmillan, and New York: Harcourt, Brace, 1951).

Chapter 2.
1. 'The Dilemma of Modern Socialism', *Political Quarterly*, 3 (April–June 1932), pp. 155–61.
2. 'Liberalism and Industry', H. L. Nathan and H. Heathcote Williams (eds.), *Liberal Points of View* (London: Benn, 1927).
3. 'Democracy and Efficiency' (interview with Kingsley Martin), *New Statesman and Nation*, 28 January 1939, p. 122.
4. 'The World Economic Conference, 1933', *New Statesman and Nation*, 24 December 1932, p. 826.
5. 'National Self-Sufficiency' (part 5), *New Statesman and Nation*, 15 July 1933.
6. 'The Problem of Unemployment' (broadcast talk), *Listener*, 14 January 1931, p. 46.
7. 'Sir Oswald Mosley's Manifesto', *Nation and Athenaeum*, 13 December 1930, p. 367.
8. 'After the Suspension of Gold' (letter), *The Times*, 29 September 1931; reprinted in *Essays in Persuasion*, *The Collected Writings of John Maynard Keynes*, Vol. IX (London: Macmillan St. Martin's Press for the Royal Economic Society, 1972), pp. 243–4.
9. 'Economic Notes on Free Trade II. A Revenue Tariff and the Cost of Living', *New Statesman and Nation*, 4 April 1931.
10 'The Question of High Wages', *Political Quarterly*, 1 (January 1930), pp. 110–24.
11. 'Mr. Keynes's Plan. Control of Boom and Slump' (letter), *The Times*, 10 April 1940.

Chapter 4.
1. Clive Bell. *Old Friends* (London: Chatto and Windus, 1956).
2. R. F. Harrod, 'Clive Bell on Keynes', *Economic Journal*, Vol. LXVII, No. 268, (December 1957), pp. 692–9, and 'A Comment', *Economic Journal*, Vol. LXX, No. 277, (March 1960), pp. 166–7.

Chapter 5.

1. This and following quotations, except those from the letters of Keynes and Melchior, are from the memoir 'Dr. Melchior: A Defeated Enemy', first published posthumously in *Two Memoirs* (London: Rupert Hart-Davis, 1949); reprinted in *Essays in Biography, Collected Writings*, Vol. X (1972).
2. Keynes's letters to his mother appear in *The Treasury and Versailles, Collected Writings*, Vol. XVI (1971).
3. *Carl Melchior: Ein Buch des Gedenkens und der Freundschaft* (Tübungen: J. C. B. Mohr (Paul Siebeck), 1967).
4. For the correspondence of Keynes and Melchior see *Treaty Revision and Reconstruction, Collected Writings*, Vol. XVII (1977), and *The End of Reparations, Collected Writings*, Vol. XVIII (1978).
5. Keith Middlemas and John Barnes, *Baldwin: A Biography* (London: Weidenfeld and Nicolson, 1969, and New York: Macmillan, 1970), pp. 180–1.
6. Unpublished letter to Mme. Marie Melchior de Molènes, 9 February 1946, Keynes Papers, Marshall Library, Cambridge University.

Chapter 6.

1. J. Ronnie Davis, *The New Economics and the Old Economists* (Ames, Iowa: Iowa State University Press, 1971).
2. F. A. Hayek, *A Tiger by the Tail* (London: Hobart Paperback, 1972).

Chapter 7.

1. For a modern version of this point of view, see Robin L. Marris, *The Economic Theory of Managerial Capitalism* (New York: Free Press of Glencoe, 1964).

Chapter 11.

1. Joan Robinson, 'The Rate of Interest', *Econometrica*, Vol. 19, No. 2 (April 1951), pp. 92–111.
2. Harry G. Johnson, 'Some Cambridge Controversies in Monetary Theory', *Review of Economic Studies*, Vol. XIX, No. 2, (February 1952), pp. 90–104, especially 97–8.
3. R. F. Harrod, *Towards a Dynamic Economics* (London: Macmillan, 1948).
4. John Hicks, *A Contribution to the Theory of the Trade Cycle* (London: Oxford University Press, 1950).
5. Piero Sraffa, 'The Laws of Returns under Competitive Conditions', Economic Journal, Vol XXXVI (December 1926), pp. 535–50.
6. John Hicks, *The Theory of Wages* (London: Macmillan, 1932; new edition, 1963).
7. Gerald Shove, 'Review of J. R. Hicks, *The Theory of Wages*', *Economic Journal*, Vol. XLIII (September 1933), pp. 460–72.

Chapter 12.

1. R. L. Cohen, *The Economics of Agriculture* (London: Nisbet, 1940).
2. Joan Robinson, *The Rate of Interest and Other Essays* (London: Macmillan, 1952).

3. Joan Robinson, 'The Production Function and the Theory of Capital', *Review of Economic Studies*, Vol. XXI, No. 2 (1954), pp. 81–106.

Chapter 14.
1. S. G. Checkland, 'The Propogation of Ricardian Economics in England', *Economica*, New Series, Vol. 16, No. 61 (February 1949), pp. 40–52.
2. Harry G. Johnson, 'Monetary Theory and Monetary Policy', *Euromoney*, December 1970, 2, pp. 16–20.
3. Axel Leijonhufvud, *On Keynesian Economics and the Economics of Keynes* (London and New York: Oxford University Press, 1968).
4. Alvin Hansen, 'Economic Progress and Declining Population Growth', *American Economic Review* (March 1939), 29, pp. 1–15.
5. Milton Friedman, 'The Quantity Theory of Money—A Restatement', in Milton Friedman (ed.) *Studies in the Quantity Theory of Money* (Chicago: University of Chicago Press, 1956).
6. Don Patinkin, 'The Chicago Tradition, The Quantity Theory, and Friedman', *Journal of Money, Credit and Banking* (February 1969), 1, pp. 46–70.
7. Harry G. Johnson, 'Recent Developments in Monetary Theory—A Commentary', in David R. Croome and Harry G. Johnson (eds.), *Money in Britain, 1959—1969* (Oxford: Oxford University Press, 1970), pp. 83–114.
8. Milton Friedman, 'A Theoretical Framework for Monetary Analysis', *Journal of Political Economy*, 78, No. 2 (March–April 1970), pp. 193–238.

Chapter 17.
1. Robert Bacon and Walter Eltis, *Britain's Economic Problem: Too Few Producers* (London: Macmillan, 1976).

Chapter 18.
1. *The General Theory and After, Part I, Collected Writings*, Vol. XIII (1973), p. 492.
2. *The General Theory and After, Part II, Collected Writings*, Vol. XIV (1973), p. 85.
3. Axel Leijonhufvud, *On Keynesian Economics and the Economics of Keynes* (London and New York: Oxford University Press, 1968).
4. Donald D. Hester and James Tobin, *Risk Aversion and Portfolio Choice*. Cowles Foundation Monograph No. 19; *Studies of Portfolio Behaviour*. Cowles Foundation Monograph No. 20; *Financial Markets and Economic Activity*. Cowles Foundation Monograph No. 21 (New York: John Wiley and Sons, 1967).
5. Don Patinkin, *Money, Interest, and Prices: An Integration of Monetary and Value Theory* (New York: Harper and Row, 1967).
6. Robert Clower and Axel Leijonhufvud, 'The Co-ordination of Economic Activities: a Keynesian Perspective', *American Economic Review*, Vol. 65, No. 2 (May 1975), pp. 182–8.
7. Robert E. Lucas, jr., 'Econometric Policy Evaluation: A Critique', in K. Brunner and A. Meltzer (eds.), *The Phillips Curve and Labor Markets*, Carnegie–Rochester Conference Series, *Journal of Monetary Economics* (Amsterdam: North Holland, 1975); 'Understanding Business Cycles', in K. Brunner and A. Meltzer (eds.), *Stabilization of the Domestic and International Economy*, Carnegie-Rochester Conference Series, *Journal of Monetary Economics* (Amsterdam: North Holland, 1977).

8. Milton Friedman, 'The Quantity Theory of Money—a Restatement , in Milton Friedman (ed.), *Studies in the Quantity Theory of Money* (Chicago: University of Chicago Press, 1956).

9. G. D. N. Worswick, 'Is Progress in Economic Science Possible?' *Economic Journal*, Vol. LXXXII, No. 325 (March 1972), pp. 73–86.

10. G. L. S. Shackle, *Keynesian Kaleidics* (Edinburgh: Edinburgh University Press, 1974).

11. Sidney Weintraub, *Keynes and the Monetarists* (New Brunswick, N.J.: Rutgers University Press, 1973). See also Paul Davidson, *Money and the Real World* (London: Macmillan, 1972), and Hyman P. Minsky, *John Maynard Keynes* (New York: Columbia University Press, 1975).